DATE DUE

MY 29 '97		
NO 18 '97		
OC 19 '98		
NV 31 '00		
NO 16 01		
MY 28 '02		
DE 11 '02		
JE 1 '04		
JE 9 '04		

THE ANDEAN COCAINE INDUSTRY

PATRICK L. CLAWSON
AND
RENSSELAER W. LEE III

St. Martin's Press

New York

ISBN 0-312-12400-7

Library of Congress Cataloging-in-Publication Data

Clawson, Patrick, 1951-
    The Andean cocaine industry / Patrick Clawson and Rensselaer W.
Lee III.
        p.   cm.
    Includes bibliographical references and index.
    ISBN 0-312-12400-7 (cloth)
    1. Cocaine industry—Andes Region. 2. Medellin Cartel.
3. Narcotics, Control of—Andes Region. 4. Narcotics, Control of–
–Colombia. 5. Narcotics, Control of—United States. 6. Drug
traffic—Andes Region.   I. Lee, Rensselaer W., 1937-
II. Title.
HV5840.A5C58 1996
363.4'5'098—dc20   95-52824
                                                         CIP

First Edition: August 1996
10 9 8 7 6 5 4 3 2 1

Contents

Abbreviations

ACDEGAM	Asociación Campesina de Agricultores y Ganaderos del Magdalena Medio (Colombia)
CEDRO	Centro de Informacíon y Educación para la Prevención del Abuso de Drogas (Peru)
CIA	Central Intelligence Agency
CORAH	Control y Reducción de la Coca en el Alta Huallaga (Peru)
CORDEP	Cochabamba Regional Development Project (Bolivia)
CRDP	Chapare Regional Development Project (Bolivia)
DANTI	Antinarcotics Directorate, Colombian National Police
DAS	Department of Administration Security (Colombia)
DEA	Drug Enforcement Agency
DINANDRO	Dirección Nacional de Drogas (Peru)
DIRECO	Dirección Nacional de Reconversión Agrícola (Bolivia)
ELN	Ejército de Liberación Nacional (Colombia)
EPL	Ejército Popular de Liberación (Colombia)
ESF	Economic Support Funds
FARC	Fuerzas Armadas Revolucionarias de Colombia (Colombia)
FBI	Federal Bureau of Investigation
FELCN	Fuerzas Especiales de La Lucha Contra Narcoticos (Bolivia)
FETCTC	Federación Especial de Trabajadores Campesinos del Trópico de Cochabamba (Bolivia)
GDP	Gross Domestic Product
GNP	Gross National Product
IDB	Interamerican Development Bank
INCSR	International Control Strategy Report
INL	Bureau for International Narcotics and Law Enforcement Affairs
MORENA	Movimiento de Restoración Nacional (Colombia)
MRTA	Movimiento Revolucionario Tupac Amaru (Peru)

NNICC	National Narcotics Intelligence Consumers Committee
ONDCP	White House Office of National Drug Control Policy
PEAH	Proyecto Especial Alto Huallaga (Peru)
PEPES	People Persecuted by Pablo Escobar (Colombia)
PRI	Partido Revolucionario Institucional (Mexico)
SAS	Special Air Services (U.K.)
SCU	Sacra Corona Unita (Italy)
TDB	Trade Development Bank (Switzerland)
UMOPAR	Unidad Mobilaria de Patrullaje Rural (Bolivia)
UN	United Nations
UNDCP	United Nations Drug Control Program
UNDP	United Nations Development Program
UP	Union Patriótica (Colombia)
USAID	United States Agency for International Development
YPFB	Yacimientos Petrolíferos Fiscales Bolivianos (Bolivian State Petroleum Company)

Acknowledgements

This volume presents an overview and analysis of the South American cocaine industry as it has developed in the 1990's. Our focus is on the Andean side of the cocaine problem, rather than the North American side. That said, our aim is, at the end of the day, to set forth what U.S. policies towards the Andes offer the best hope of reducing the drug scourge in our country.

Policy advice on the drug war is tough in part because the problem is many-sided. We collaborated in part because our interests and backgrounds complement each other to cover a wide range of issues: Rensselaer Lee is by profession a political analyst more involved in studying Colombia, and Patrick Clawson is an economist more focused on Peru and Bolivia. Dr. Lee is an established expert on the drug problem, while Dr. Clawson's work is more on political economy and development issues. Furthermore, we think our work benefits from our broad international experience, which helps us understand which problems are uniquely Andean and which are more general to developing countries. Neither of us began life studying Latin America; Dr. Lee's first love (on which he continues to do much work) was Russia and China, while Dr. Clawson writes primarily about the Middle East and worked on Africa for years at both the World Bank and the International Monetary Fund.

In putting together such a volume, one incurs many debts. We owe thanks to all those cited in the endnotes and others who directly or indirectly contributed to the production of this book. We are grateful for the invaluable assistance we received from agencies of the U.S. government and their staff, including the Office of National Drug Control policy; the U.S. Agency for International Development (USAID); the State Department Bureau of International Narcotics and Law Enforcement Affairs; the U.S. Information Agency; the Drug Enforcement Administration (DEA); the DEA Library; the U.S. embassies in Bolivia,

Colombia, and Peru; and the USAID missions in Bolivia and Peru. We hesitate to single out the dedicated public servants who have, over the years, encouraged our research on the Andean drug wars, but we hope they know how much we appreciate their support.

This volume would not have been possible without the insights and information from Andean researchers and officials who were unfailingly generous with their time. At every level, from the cabinet minister to the farmer in his coca field, Andeans went out of their way to provide us with as much information as they could. We are also grateful for the generous cooperation from the Andean offices of the United Nations Drug Control Program (UNDCP) and the United Nations Development Program (UNDP). We would like to particularly thank four people who have an extraordinary grasp of the impact of the cocaine industry on their countries: Oscar Antezana, USAID-La Paz; Tito Hernández, UNDP-Lima; and Sergio Uribe and Francisco Thoumi of the University of Los Andes in Bogotá. In addition, we would like to acknowledge the assistance of the Center for International Studies at the University of Los Andes, which proved to be a valuable resource for this project.

We also owe much to three U.S. researchers on crime who have been kind enough to advise us, namely: Peter Lupsha, University of New Mexico; Peter Reuter, University of Maryland; and Sid Zabludoff, formerly of the Community Coordinating Group of the Counter Narcotics Center at the CIA. Also, this project could not have reached fruition without Yvette A. Young, who typed the different iterations of this manuscript.

We are sure that each of those we have acknowledged would disagree with a number of the points we have made. The opinions expressed here are ours and ours alone. In particular, they do not represent the viewpoints of the U.S. government or any of its agencies. While Patrick Clawson is employed at the National Defense University, his work on this volume was done on his own time.

Washington, D.C.
March 1996

Introduction

Over the years the United States has spent a great deal of money on the war on drugs, but the problem remains. In the fifteen years from 1981 through 1995, the federal government alone spent $125 billion (at 1994 prices) on drug control.[1] States and cities have to devote a large portion of their criminal justice resources to fighting drug dealing and the crimes drug users commit. Private business and individuals spend vast sums on the detection of drug use, protection against drug-induced crime, and treatment of addicts.

Cocaine, in particular, remains frustratingly resistant to all the efforts to control it. It is humbling that a superpower such as the United States cannot exorcise a curse that has been laid on millions of its citizens. The temptation is great to say that Americans should go to the source and rip cocaine out at its roots in the three Andean nations—Colombia, Peru, and Bolivia—where 99 percent of the world's supply comes from.

One of the two major themes of this book is that the United States cannot stop the Andean cocaine trade. In part, this is because the United States is not prepared to commit much in the way of resources to any such effort. For example, between 1981 and 1995, the United States spent only $5.3 billion (again at 1994 prices) on all international drug control programs, including those in Asia, the Middle East (controlling Turkey's opium poppies), the Caribbean (Jamaican marijuana control), and South America. When programs to interdict drugs en route to the United States are factored in, the total spent on drug control outside this country was 21 percent of the federal

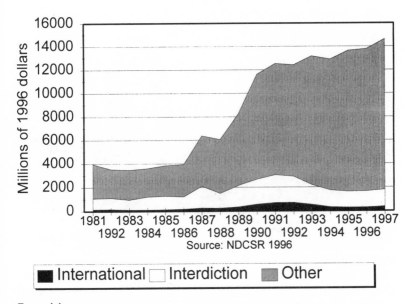

FIGURE I.1
NATIONAL DRUG CONTROL BUDGET
Source: Office of National Drug Control Policy, *National Drug Control Strategy Budget Summary.*
Washington DC: The White House, 1996.

government's drug control budget in the years under discussion. The other 79 percent was spent on demand reduction and domestic law enforcement.

International programs consumed only 4 percent of the federal government's drug control budget during the period. As indicated in figure I.1, the share spent on international programs has been low every year. Irrespective of rhetoric, the programs have never commanded much financial support. Nor is it realistic to expect any large increases in such international programs. Quite the contrary; recently their share of the U.S. drug control budget has been slipping. Under the Clinton administration, in 1995 a mere 1.2 percent of the federal drug control budget was spent on international programs. As figure I.2 shows, international drug control was slashed not just relative to the total drug control budget but in actual dollars. Spending on international drug control fell 57 percent under the Clinton administration: from $707 million in 1992 to $300 million in 1995. (The 1996 request is $371 million.)

At $300 million, the 1995 Clinton international drug control program is six-tenths of 1 percent of the value of all illegal drugs sold in

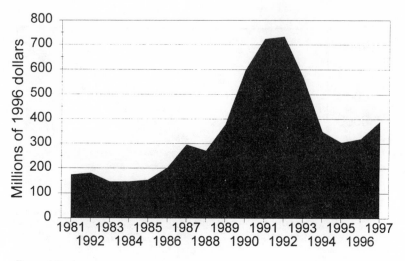

FIGURE I.2
FUNDS FOR ALL U.S. INTERNATIONAL DRUG CONTROL (USAID, DEA, INL, ETC.)
Source: Office of National Drug Control Policy, *National Drug Control Strategy Budget Summary.*
Washington DC: The White House, 1996.

the United States in 1993, according to data in the White House Office of National Drug Control Policy's *National Drug Control Strategy 1995.* In other words, 60 cents are spent on international drug control for every $100 of drugs sold.

These budget levels sound shocking. However, there is no particularly compelling argument for the United States to spend more on international drug control programs. The nation has neither the power nor the obligation to assume responsibility for combatting all the evil in the world. The programs that the United States has supported have not been great successes, nor have most been total failures; instead, the record is one of mixed success. In light of this fact, a case can be made for continuing with the programs, but expectations should be kept realistic.

The second major theme of this book is that what happens in the Andean countries depends much more on the locals than on the Americans. And while the United States can influence what the locals do, the basic factor determining their actions is and will remain local conditions. The adage that all politics is local applies in the Andes as well as in the United States. Andean politicians may listen carefully to what U.S. envoys say, but the politicians will decide what to do based on the sociology, economics, and politics of their own countries, not primarily because of U.S. pressure.

Consistent with this theme, much of this book is spent examining the local conditions that set the framework within which Andean politicians act. We ask just how much money the locals make from the cocaine industry; the answer turns out to depend on which part of the business they are in. We also look at the alternatives for those in the cocaine business: Are there opportunities in the legal economy? Are those in the cocaine industry now hardened to a life of crime, such that if they left the business, they would go into another criminal venture? And perhaps as important as any other factor: How much of a threat is the cocaine industry to the state? Can it coexist with the government, if the latter turns a blind eye, or does cocaine undermine the very foundations of the state (by providing funds for guerrillas, for example)? Can governments negotiate successfully with cocaine lords? The future of the war against drugs in the Andes hangs on these sorts of issues much more than on the level of U.S. interest and financing.

Recent developments give some grounds for optimism. Almost all of the founding fathers of the Colombian cocaine industry are dead or in jail. As of this writing, the Cali cartel hierarchy is under relentless attack by Colombian police and prosecutors. Cocaine represents a small and declining portion of the national economy in Peru and Bolivia. Also, perceptions of the industry have changed: Largely gone is the 1980s mystique that cocaine can be a vehicle for the economic salvation of Andean nations. However, the cocaine portion of the economy in Colombia remains considerable; cocaine trafficking organizations have shown a remarkable capacity to adapt, to innovate, and to develop new markets for their products; and the cocaine industry, which has struck deep roots in Andean societies, has demonstrated considerable staying power. In Colombia, the egregious flow of drug money to the top most governing echelons threatens the stability and integrity of the socio-political system.

The analysis in this book is fine-tuned to local conditions, which differ considerably from country to country. As a rule of thumb, Peru and Bolivia are relatively similar to each other while Colombia is different. The cocaine business in Peru and Bolivia consists mostly of small farmers growing coca plants for the leaves, which have long been cultivated for the local chewing market; Colombia, however, is the center of drug processing and smuggling to foreign countries. To be sure, the distinction is not iron-clad. Some drug trafficking occurs in Peru and Bolivia, and Colombia has some small traditional farmers growing coca. And there are some points on which the basic distinction in the Andes is not Colombia versus Peru and Bolivia—for instance, Peru and Colombia have both had guerrilla problems, while Bolivia has not. But it is true on more points than not.

Our concern here is the cocaine business. While much of what we have to say also applies to the production of other illegal drugs in the Andes—heroin in Colombia and to a lesser extent Peru, and some marijuana in Colombia—we do not pretend to offer a complete analysis of those problems.

This book is divided into four parts. Chapter 1 presents the basics about cocaine use: how many people use the drug, how much income it generates, and the importance of the industry to the Andean economies.

The next part, chapters 2 through 4, is about cocaine trafficking, that is, the highly profitable business of buying coca paste in the coca-growing regions, smuggling it to advanced industrial countries, and selling it there. Chapter 2 analyzes the history and structure of the Medellín and Cali cocaine "cartels," which are certainly not cartels in the dictionary sense of a business association that fixes prices. Chapter 3 details the international links of the cocaine cartels, focusing on their relations with Italian organized crime. Chapter 4 analyzes Bogotá's negotiations with drug lords to get them to surrender and cooperate with justice in return for lenient terms.

The third part, chapters 5 through 8, looks at the effects of the cocaine industry on Andean societies, economies, and politics. Chapter 5 looks at the situation of the farmers who provide the coca leaves from which cocaine is made and considers alternatives they have to raising coca bushes. The chapter concentrates on Peru and Bolivia, where the indigenous peoples have grown coca for centuries to provide leaves that are chewed. Chapter 6 examines the economic, political, and social effects of the cocaine industry in Colombia, which has little tradition of coca chewing and where the drug trafficking is concentrated. Chapter 7 examines the relationship between the drug trade and guerrilla movements in Colombia and Peru, while chapter 8 brings together the evidence about the problems that the cocaine industry causes Andean society.

The fourth part, chapters 9 and 10, asks what can be done to shrink the Andean cocaine industry. Chapter 9 examines the effects the existing Latin American counternarcotics efforts have had on U.S. cocaine use. Chapter 10 asks where to go from here: What are realistic goals? What are the most important policies? From whom is leadership required?

Part I

The Basics About Cocaine

1

Cocaine and the Andes

INTRODUCTION

Cocaine is a big business and the Andean countries have small economies. These facts lead to the obvious conclusion that cocaine is an important, or even vital, part of the Andean economy. That view is widely accepted among politicians, commentators, and ordinary people in the United States and, to a lesser extent, in the Andean countries themselves.

Yet this conclusion is not entirely valid. In both Peru and Bolivia, the cocaine industry's revenues today do not exceed 4 to 5 percent of gross domestic product (GDP). In Colombia—the source of most refined cocaine entering world markets—total trafficking earnings are larger relative to the economy, but only a portion of narcodollar proceeds return to the country each year. While cocaine is an important industry overall—one that is well entrenched in individual producing states—it does not dominate the Andean economy the way oil dominates the Persian Gulf countries where oil provides, on average, half of national income. In other words, cocaine is not a decisive force propelling national economic development in the Andes. Coca has been a mixed blessing to Andean nations: It has brought much income, but it also has introduced significant distortions into national economies, and it has corrupted political life. Furthermore, while the legal economies of the Andean countries are poised to take off, cocaine offers poor growth prospects. The future does not lie with cocaine.

HOW MUCH COCAINE?

It is difficult to estimate the cocaine industry's dimensions and impact. Since it is illegal, traffickers do not volunteer information about the size of their activities. Analysts are unable to agree on the most basic numbers about the industry—such as the amount of coca leaf (the raw material for cocaine) cultivated and produced each year in the Andean region. Estimates of cocaine production in Latin America are difficult to reconcile with estimates of cocaine consumption in the United States. In addition, the industry itself is in constant flux: Traffickers' innovations, such as the development of crack, have greatly enhanced their sales volumes and their overall cash-flow picture, thus greatly complicating the estimation process.

The global volume of cocaine and cocaine income is a subject of considerable speculation. For years, the principal U.S. government report on illegal drugs in source countries has been the State Department's *International Control Strategy Report* (INCSR, pronounced "ink-sir"). It has published figures for potential cocaine production in the Andes: In 1994 it estimated 840 tons (all tons in text are metric tons), and in 1995 the figure cited was 780 tons. Such numbers are astonishingly large. Seven hundred eighty tons of cocaine sold at the average U.S. retail price of $80 per gram in 1995 would earn $62 billion, equivalent to 8 percent of total U.S. imports in 1995 ($765 billion). In fact, though, the INCSR includes careful caveats—its estimate of world cocaine supply is meant to be an unrealistic upper bound, not a statement of actual availability. Consider, for example, the following disclaimer:

> In 1995, taking into account estimates of local consumption and local seizures, the USG calculates that if virtually every coca leaf were converted in cocaine [hydrochloride], and there were no losses because of inefficiencies, bad weather, disease, or the deterrent effects of law enforcement, 780 tons of cocaine theoretically could have been available from Colombia, Bolivia, and Peru for worldwide export [of which, 460 was from Peru, 240 from Bolivia, and 80 from Colombia]. . . .
> In publishing these numbers, we repeat our caveat that these are theoretical numbers, useful for examining trends.[1]

Of course, in the real world there are inefficiencies, bad weather, disease, and deterrent effects of law enforcement. The INCSR notes elsewhere that its "estimates do not allow for losses, which could represent up to a third or more of a crop in source areas for some harvests."[2] Furthermore, factors such as unfavorable coca prices, labor shortages, and local violence may diminish the amount of leaf actually harvested.[3] In addition, the efficiency of the labor that processes coca into cocaine represents an important constraint on production. In 1993 the Drug Enforcement Agency (DEA) sent a team of experts, including agronomists from the U.S. Agriculture Department, into Bolivia's coca fields to interview coca processors and to process coca themselves using typical techniques.[4] They found that the so-called labs— really, simple farmyard affairs without any sophisticated equipment—were not as efficient as had been assumed. In light of this information, the 1995 INCSR includes a footnote showing that the DEA thinks that the actual 1994 output from Bolivia was 211 tons, not 270. Using similar assumptions about processing efficiency, the U.S. Agency for International Development (USAID)'s office in La Paz estimated that output was even lower—194 tons.[5] Thus the actual amount of cocaine packed for shipment from South America in 1994 could have been well below the 840 tons shown in the INCSR.

An additional issue concerns the amount of South American cocaine that actually enters the U.S. marketplace. Constructing a profile of the illicit drug business in the United States requires assumptions about consumption patterns and trends. Perhaps the most complete studies of national consumption have been performed by the Boston-based consulting firm Abt Associates, working under contract to the White House Office of National Drug Control Policy (ONDCP). The studies, entitled *What America's Users Spend on Illegal Drugs,* draw together information from many different sources. They compare what the State Department, DEA, and intelligence community say about supply with what the National Institute on Drug Abuse, the law enforcement community, and treatment specialists report about consumption. Abt Associates examined the consistency of information from various sources and has found that the discrepancies usually can be explained by methodological differences. For instance, the widely cited National Household Survey on Drug Abuse is a survey of households, which means that it misses the heaviest consumers of drugs, who are homeless or in institutions (jails). Indeed, virtually no heroin addicts answer the survey. In the end, Abt Associates has been able to fit together into an apparently consistent story the information from all these different sources. Of course, the numbers are still approximations, and it is more appropriate to cite broad ranges rather than precise numbers.

The 1995 Abt Associates report, which also was used in ONDCP's *National Drug Control Strategy 1995,* shows that a lot less cocaine was available for consumption than the INCSR production figure that is so often miscited. (See table 1.1.) It estimates that in 1993, the cocaine available for export from Latin America was between 583 and 711 tons.[6] About 145 to 178 tons of that was shipped to Europe or other parts of the world besides the United States. Some was seized or lost en route. The report cites seizures of 82 tons, which puts too much faith in the honesty of underpaid police in the source or transit countries: Some analysts suggest that up to 30 percent of the seized amount is resold. (But then Abt Associates does not include losses in transit, while smugglers do in fact lose shipments to plane crashes by dumping when the police approach.)

TABLE 1.1
COCAINE SUPPLY, 1993
(IN TONS OF COCAINE EQUIVALENT)

Available for export	581-711
Shipped to non-U.S. destinations	145-178
Seized abroad en route to U.S.	82
Arrived in U.S.	353-450
Federal seizures	110
Available for U.S. consumption	243-340

Source: Abt Associates, *What America's Users Spend on Illegal Drugs, 1988-1993* (Washington D.C.: ONDCP, 1995), p. 6.

Furthermore, federal authorities seize a significant portion of the cocaine that is counted as the United States' share. Indeed, the 110 tons seized in the United States was roughly one-quarter (24 to 31 percent) of the total amount shipped to the country, according to the report. Such a seizure rate—which is much higher than the 4 to 15 percent rate sometimes cited in official U.S. estimates—obviously would be a significant cost of doing business for cocaine traffickers. (The Cali cartel's reliance on containerized transport to smuggle cocaine suggests that the rate may be much lower, a point to be discussed later.) According to the Abt study, in 1993, between 243 and 340 tons were available for consumption in the United States after seizures, some 30 to 44 percent of the potential cocaine production for that year cited in the INCSR. Multiplying the U.S. volume by the retail prices of $120 to $151 per gram (the 1993 range cited by ONDCP's 1995 Strategy Report) produces a U.S. sales figure of $29 billion to $51 billion. Adding European sales, say 100 tons at a price 50 percent above the U.S. level, results in a range of $47 billion to $74 billion, a reasonable if conservative estimate of the size of the global retail cocaine market.

To understand how much is spent on cocaine, we must recognize that not all of the drug is sold for the reported average price: Some is consumed by the dealers, some is provided for sex or services, and some is lost in the selling process. Factoring in these and other elements, Abt Associates estimates that $30.8 billion was spent on cocaine in the United States in 1993.

One way to cross-check this figure is to multiply the number of users by the amount each used. The division of users into hardcore and occasional users makes good sense, because their patterns of drug use are so different. Abt Associates estimates that in 1993 there were 2.1 million hardcore users of cocaine (including cocaine hydrochloride and crack) in the United States. If they used cocaine two days out of three, they would each spend $200 a week, which means their total annual spending would be $22.2 billion. If the 4 million occasional users spent $40 a week each, annually they would spend $8.3 billion. The total amount spent is $30.5 billion, close to Abt's figure of $30.8 billion.

Because hardcore users buy the most cocaine, the amount of cocaine sold depends much more on the number of hardcore users than on the total number of users. This fact explains what might otherwise seem to be a paradox: The number of cocaine users has been declining rapidly, while the amount spent on cocaine has been declining only slowly. (See figures 1.1 and 1.2.)

The declining number of users and the declining expenditures suggest that the demand for cocaine in the United States has been falling, which would account for its decline in price. (See figure 1.3.)

However, there is a another possible reason for the price decline: a supply increase. Economic theory provides three reasons for price declines: reduction in demand, increase in supply, or both.[7] In fact, as shown in figure 1.4, the best evidence is that the supply of cocaine available in the United States appears to be staying constant or declining. Notice that when the price declines, less can be spent on cocaine while the volume consumed stays roughly flat. And because most consumption is by hardcore users, many fewer people can be using cocaine while the volume used does

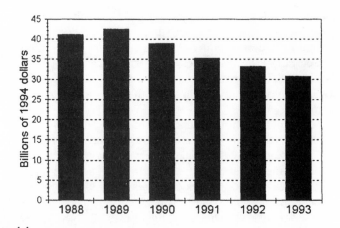

FIGURE 1.1

EXPENDITURES ON COCAINE IN THE U.S.
Source: Abt Associates (William Rhodes, team leader). *What America's Users Spend on Illegal Drugs, 1988-1993.* Washington, DC: Office of National Drug Control Policy, 1995.

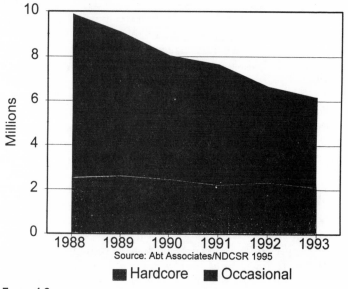

FIGURE 1.2

COCAINE USERS IN THE U.S.
Note: Casual is defined as less often that weekly; heavy is defined as at least weekly.
Source: Office of National Drug Control Policy, *National Drug Control Strategy Budget Summary.* Washington DC: The White House, 1995, p. 139.

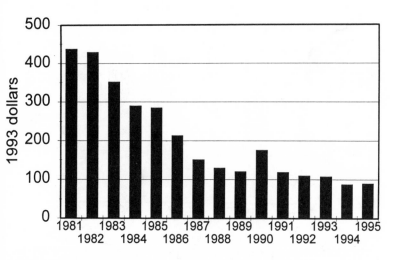

FIGURE 1.3

COCAINE PRICE IN THE U.S. (PER OUNCE PURE COCAINE, 5 OZ. BUYS)
Source: Office of National Drug Control Policy, *National Drug Control Strategy, 1996.*

not change: A slight increase in the average consumption per hardcore user makes up for a large drop in the number of casual users.

The figures paint quite an optimistic picture: Supply is flat, the number of users is down, as is the amount Americans are spending on cocaine. And indeed, there have been some notable achievements in the war on cocaine, for all the breast-beating that goes on about the failures. We do not know what has caused the reduction in casual use, but it is particularly encouraging. With fewer occasional users today, perhaps in a few years there will be fewer addicts. Indeed, the average age of the hardcore user has been increasing. Already the cocaine problem appears to be concentrated largely in a hard core of substance abusers who have a host of problems, of which cocaine use is only one.

Still, although trends suggest increasing saturation of the U.S. domestic market for cocaine, major uncertainties continue to plague estimates of the size of the industry. We simply do not know for certain how much cocaine is produced in South America and how much is smuggled successfully to the United States and other countries. A worrying possibility is that the INCSR's estimates of potential production are understated, perhaps significantly so. For example, Peruvian studies cite substantially higher coca cultivation and production

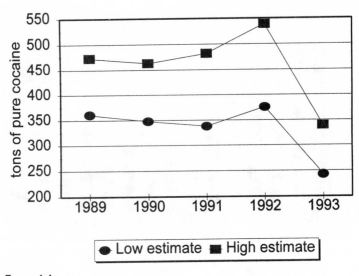

FIGURE 1.4
COCAINE AVAILABLE IN THE U.S.
Source: Abt Associates/NDCSR 1995

figures than those recorded in the INCSR. The Peruvian consulting firm Cuánto S.A., working under contract to USAID, estimated that Peru's coca leaf production in 1992 was 400,000 to 450,000 tons, compared to the INCSR's estimate of 224,000 tons in that year. A University of Los Andes researcher, Sergio Uribe, who conducted extensive field surveys in illicit crop areas during 1994 and 1995, calculates that average coca leaf yields per hectare in Colombia are almost 4 tons compared to an INCSR estimate of 0.8 tons. Uribe also believes that 65,000 to 85,000 hectares are planted with coca in Colombia, compared to the U.S. satellite-based estimate of 50,900 hectares (after eradication).[8] If this amount of coca were produced, potential cocaine production in South America would soar to 1,200 to 1,400 tons. Obviously, such numbers are difficult to square with U.S. consumption estimates of 250 to 350 tons, even taking losses and seizures into consideration. Thus it is impossible to make any categorical statements about the size or earnings of the cocaine industry.

ADAPTATION AND INNOVATION

Despite the fact that, in the United States, prices and consumption of cocaine are declining and large seizure rates are cutting into traffickers' profit margins, the organized sector of the business is not withering away—indeed, trafficking organizations have sought in various ways to compensate for these "unfavorable" circumstances. One way to do so is to increase production efficiency. For example, today some Colombian and Bolivian laboratories are equipped with chemical recycling and recovery plants as well as with vacuum-packing facilities and microwave drying ovens. (Removing moisture lengthens cocaine's shelf life.) Also, in the face of government efforts to limit traffickers' access to common, essential chemicals used in cocaine processing, they have shown considerable ingenuity in finding alternatives; for example, in Colombia, chemists have increased extraction rates for cocaine base by 10 to 15 percent by substituting alcohol for gasoline or kerosene in the initial processing phase. Also in Colombia, farmers and traffickers reportedly are pulverizing coca leaves prior to macerating them (the first step in extracting cocaine alkaloids) in an effort to increase base yields.

A second way to increase profit margins is to improve and diversify smuggling methods. For example, the Cali cartel relies on cargo containers, which can carry multiton loads of cocaine to major markets and limit theft. The Medellín cartel, by contrast, relied principally on light aircraft with a transport capacity of 400 to 1,000 kilograms. The shift to containerized transport may reduce the chance of interdiction—according to U.S. Customs estimates, only 3 percent of the 9 million containers that enter the United States each year are seized during inspections. (Abt Associates cited an interdiction rate of 25 percent.) Furthermore, the sheer variety of vehicles that modern smugglers use to move bulk cocaine shipments—cargo jets, merchant shipping, tractor trailers, camouflaged small boats, and even (in Colombia) specially produced semisubmersible vessels—represents a daunting challenge to law enforcement officials. Also, traffickers' reliance on state-of-the-art communications methods—encryption devices, faxes, express courier mail, and the like—tends to defeat traditional surveillance tactics.

A third response of traffickers to shrinking profits has been to increase downstream penetration of U.S. markets. Instead of merely selling cocaine to a U.S. importer-wholesaler, Colombian traffickers (especially the Cali-based organizations) have set up distribution offices, or "cells," in a number of U.S. cities. By incorporating distribution, which is farther along in the chain that starts on the farm and ends with the retail sale, into their activities, the exporting organization has maintained profits in the face of declining prices.

Finally, trafficking organizations are attempting to maximize earnings through product and market diversification. They encouraged

U.S. drug retailers to develop crack, which increased cocaine sales in inner cities. The Cali cartel especially has made a significant effort to penetrate the lucrative European market, where wholesale prices for cocaine can be two to three times the prices in the United States. Colombian exporters have established strategic alliances with European organizations to expand sales opportunities and to reduce operating risks. Moreover, in recognition of the fact that the U.S. cocaine market is approaching its saturation point, Colombian traffickers developed an alternative source of income—heroin production. At least four Cali organizations currently refine or distribute heroin. The traffickers finance the cultivation of the opium poppy, disseminate the technology for producing morphine base to the farm level, refine the base into heroin, and distribute the drug through their cocaine sales networks in the United States.

PERU AND BOLIVIA:
COCAINE INCOME AND EMPLOYMENT

Just as estimates about worldwide cocaine use vary enormously, so too do estimates of how much the Andean countries earn from the drug. The obvious reason for this is that the industry is illegal, so there is a strong incentive to hide the income. We can only give the most approximate estimates of cocaine income.

One point on which all observers agree is that coca farmers, like farmers of legal products around the world, make little from the drug. The U.S. Department of Agriculture calculates that U.S. farmers earn only 10 percent of the retail price of white bread.[9] Overall, farmers earn 24 percent of the price of foods grown in the United States, and that is for legal crops that do not incur all the costs and risks of smuggling and evading police required for cocaine. Most of the revenue from the cocaine business comes from the stages of smuggling, wholesale distribution, and retail sale. Since Peru and Bolivia are involved primarily in growing coca and doing the basic processing (also a low-income part of the cocaine business), their income from cocaine is not as high as might appear from the large volumes of coca leaf they grow.

Neither Peruvian nor Bolivian traffickers maintain sophisticated transport or marketing networks outside their respective countries. Traditionally, cocaine products have been exported mostly in Colombian aircraft flown by Colombian pilots. Some Peruvian trafficking organizations are in fact joint Peruvian-Colombian ventures—a situation that further underscores Colombia's international dominance of the cocaine trade. Peru sells nearly all of its cocaine hydrochloride output to Colombian buyers. A group of traffickers operating near the northern Peru city of Trujillo was able to ship cocaine directly to Mexico for a time, but a Peruvian police raid shut down this operation in early 1995. An increasing percentage of the Bolivian production is sold to Brazilian and Mexican traffickers. A rise in yearly Brazilian cocaine seizures from an average of 2.3 tons for 1988 to 1992 to an average of 8.4 tons for 1993 to 1995 provides evidence of this trend.

For Peru, the private economic firm Cuánto estimates that cocaine industry income was $1.5 billion in 1992, equivalent to 3.4 percent of Peru's gross domestic product. (See figure 1.5.) By comparison, that is about the size of the U.S. utility industry (electricity, gas, water, and sewer) relative to the U.S. GDP. In other words, the industry is sizable but not the motor force of the economy. Furthermore, cocaine's share in the GDP has been declining more or less steadily since its peak in the early and middle 1980s. And the Cuánto estimate may be high: USAID estimates the Peruvian cocaine industry added $640 million to GDP in 1993, of which $482 million stayed in the country while $158 million was held abroad.[10]

The picture in Bolivia is much the same. (See figure 1.6.) The size of the cocaine industry was estimated in 1991 and 1994 by the private consulting firm Müller y Asociados, by the World Bank in 1992, and by USAID in La Paz in 1995. Their estimates differ somewhat, but they are in the same ballpark. In fact, all three organizations agree that by the mid-1990s cocaine income was well under 5 percent of GDP. The USAID data show a decline of cocaine's share of GDP from 8 to 9 percent in 1988 to 4 percent in 1994, a trend reflecting both declining prices for coca products and significant positive growth in Bolivia's legal economy.

The share of the cocaine industry in GDP may increase in Bolivia and Peru in the future because the industry is modernizing. Locals are making more cocaine hydrochloride, rather than leaving the final processing to Colombians. USAID estimates that, in 1994, half of the cocaine made from Bolivian leaves was produced within that country. And Peruvians and Bolivians are becoming more involved in trafficking, which is the high-profit part of the business. Still, these developments, which are factored into the estimates just cited, have not been sufficient to prevent coca's share in GDP from declining as the legal economy grows and coca prices and volume stagnate.

The cocaine industry's share in export receipts is, of course, higher than its share in GDP, because the cocaine industry produces primarily for export. According to the Cuánto study, the cocaine

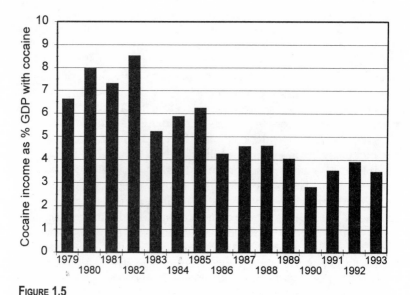

FIGURE 1.5

PERU: COCAINE RELATIVE TO GDP

Source: Richard Webb and Graciela Fernández Baca de Valdez, *Peru en Números*. Lima: Cuánto S.A., 1994, p. 507.

industry made up 53 percent of Peru's exports in 1992. Yet this high share was partly a legacy of Peru's past antiexport policies, wherein a succession of leftist governments believed that the government was better served by producing for local consumption rather than for export. The current Fujimori government favors export growth; indeed, legal exports increased significantly between 1992 and 1994, from $3.7 billion to an estimated $4.5 billion. In Bolivia, USAID estimates that cocaine amounted to 23 percent of the nation's exports in 1994, compared to almost 90 percent in 1988; this reduced share reflects the improved health of legal export industries.

While the cocaine industry provides an important source of employment, estimates of the numbers employed vary widely. Two carefully researched studies about Peru, both using 1992 data, are representative of this pattern.[11] The first, by State University of New York at Albany economist Elena Alvarez, calculated that the cocaine industry employed 175,000 people, including 145,500 growing coca and 29,500 engaged in processing the leaf. Using this estimate, the industry accounted for approximately 6 percent of the agricultural labor force and 2 percent of the national labor force. The second estimate, by the Peruvian consulting firm Cuánto under contract to

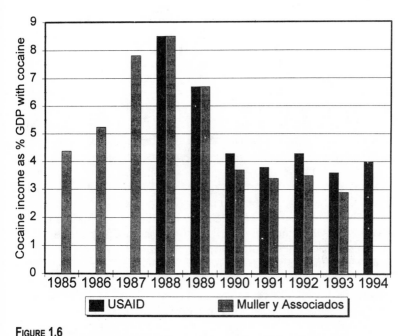

FIGURE 1.6

BOLIVIA: COCAINE RELATIVE TO GDP

Sources: USAID La Paz, *Bolivia's Coca Sub-economy in 1994: A Computer Model.* La Paz: USAID La Paz, 1995; Müller y Asociados, *Estadísticas Socio-economicas,* 1994. La Paz: Müller y Asociados, 1995; and Müller y Asociados, *Estadísticas Economicas 1991.* La Paz: Müller y Asociados, 1992.

USAID, calculated that the cocaine sector produced almost 300,000 jobs, including 290,000 in farming and 5,000 in manufacturing cocaine base. Such figures suggest that 10 percent of the agricultural workforce and 4 percent of the total labor force worked in cocaine-related activities. And just to add to the confusion, the 1995 estimate by USAID was that 120,000 farmers engage in coca cultivation while "some estimates show as many as 110,000 more persons involved in related processing, trafficking, and financial operations."[12]

A similar disparity in estimates of cocaine-related employment is apparent with respect to Bolivia. A 1995 USAID study calculated that approximately 74,000 persons—3 percent of the workforce—were employed in the industry, full- or part-time, while a 1992 USAID study by the same team had estimated that 104,600 people worked in the cocaine industry.[13] The change was due to new assumptions used in the estimates, not to some dramatic change in the coca fields. Private estimates were even higher than the 1992 USAID figure. A 1991 study by Müller y Asociados found cocaine employment to be 207,225, or nearly twice the highest USAID figure.

The employment numbers cited here do not include cocaine's indirect employment effects in the Andes. According to Victor Hugo Canelas, Bolivia's secretary of social defense, the population of the Chapare includes some 16,000 to 18,000 people—prostitutes, bartenders, restauranteers, and the like—who make a living by providing goods and services to the industry.[14] To this number could be added the legions of corrupt officials who collect bribes for allowing tons of chemicals used in processing cocaine to pass into the region and for turning a blind eye to exports of cocaine base. Recent construction booms—hence new construction jobs—in La Paz, Cochabamba, and Santa Cruz have been financed partly with proceeds of cocaine sales. In a 1992 interview the late Medellín kingpin Pablo Escobar Gaviria rhapsodized that "the entire economy benefits from drug money, those who traffic and those who do not. For example, if a drug trafficker builds a home, the peasant who cuts the wood for it benefits from that."[15] Obviously, the industry supports Andean constituencies that extend far beyond the relatively small populations employed in growing, processing, and trafficking in coca and its derivatives.

Structurally, the cocaine economy in Peru and Bolivia is fairly "democratic." The industry not only benefits large populations (mainly rural dwellers), but the distribution of cocaine income seems to favor farmers and small-scale processors. According to Cuánto S.A., almost two-thirds of the $1.48 billion earned by the industry in 1992 accrued to leaf and paste producers—that is, to farmers. In Bolivia, the above-cited 1995 USAID study supports the belief that producers of leaf and base (in Bolivia, the paste stage is bypassed in the conversion of coca leaf to cocaine hydrochloride) could receive half or more of the total export revenues. Colombia presents a contrasting picture. There the benefits of the trade accrue disproportionately to wealthy trafficker-entrepreneurs: Producers of leaf, base, and cocaine hydrochloride receive only 10 percent or less of export earnings. Most of the value added in the Colombian phase of the industry results from smuggling between Colombia and the U.S. or European markets.

COLOMBIA'S ILLICIT DRUG INDUSTRY

Drug Cultivation

Colombia is a source country for several illicit drugs—cocaine, opium, heroin (which is produced from opium), and marijuana. Marijuana, which covers an estimated 5,000 hectares, represents a relatively minor portion of Colombia's total narcotics exports—5 to 10 percent, according to most estimates. While the revenues from the marijuana trade are generally considered minuscule compared to those from cocaine, revenues of the heroin industry are significant—at least $1 billion or more annually, according to unofficial U.S. estimates.

Colombia's opium fields, some 6,500 hectares in 1995, according to a State Department estimate, are the fifth largest in the world, and Colombia already is a significant supplier of heroin to the United States. According to the Drug Enforcement Agency's heroin analysis program, 32 percent of the heroin seized in the United States in 1994 originated in Colombia. Colombian heroin is distinguished by exceptionally high purity, 80 to 99 percent, according to the DEA. While the INCSR estimates that Colombian coca cultivation was 55,900 hectares in 1995—less than Peru's though more than Bolivia's—Colombia generally is acknowledged as the world's foremost cocaine hydrochloride producer, accounting for 70 to 80 percent or more of the drug sold in international markets.

Drug crop cultivation is widespread in Colombia. Quantities of coca, opium, or marijuana have been found in 27 of Colombia's 32 departments and in 212 of the country's 1,060 municipalities. Coca alone is cultivated in at least 19 departments and 117 municipalities.[16] Most coca is grown on low-lying plains or jungle areas whereas opium is grown at higher altitudes and cooler temperatures. Approximately 75 to 80 percent of opium is cultivated in three departments—Tolima, Huila, and Cauca—that lie astride the main north-to-south Andean ridge; 75 to 80 percent of coca is found in the lower-altitude southeastern departments of Meta, Guaviare, and Caquetá. Opium cultivation has boomed in recent years (from being negligible in 1990) in response to apparently increasing demand for heroin in the United States. Opium appears to be the more profitable crop. Net income from coca, which is converted to cocaine base at the farm level, is approximately $4,000 per hectare per year, while equivalent annual income for opium may reach $13,000 to $14,000. The reason for the price differential is that many farmers have learned how to process poppy latex into vastly more valuable morphine base, which is convertible to heroin at a 1:1 weight ratio.[17] Drug crops appear to be a mainstay of the economy in many rural areas of Colombia. Up to 500,000 people—farmers, transporters, shopkeepers, small businessmen, Marxist guerrillas, prostitutes, and the like—depend directly or indirectly on production of coca, opium, and marijuana. In some areas, dependence on coca is almost total. The Bogotá newspaper *El Tiempo* notes that the mayor's office of La Hormiga, a town in lower Putumayo department, finances public works with the proceeds of illegal crops.[18]

Evidence points to an important recent shift in the configuration of the cocaine industry in Colombia and in the Andean region generally. Apparently, Colombia's cocaine syndicates made a strategic decision in the early- or mid-1990s to shorten their supply lines and to increase in-country procurement of intermediate cocaine products. The decision is not difficult to understand. The installation of U.S.-built radar systems at Leticia and Araracuara (Colombia), Lago (Ecuador), and Yurimaguas (Peru) and an aggressive air interdiction effort by the Peruvian air force raised the risks and costs of transporting cocaine between Peru and Colombia. The destruction of tens of thousands of hectares of coca bushes by the fusarium fungus was another factor affecting traffickers' calculations. These factors apparently precipitated a substantial increase in coca cultivation and production in Colombia, an increase reflected in official U.S. data: According to the INCSR, gross (pre-eradication) Colombian cultivation rose 57 percent from 1992 to 1995, from 38,050 hectares to 59,650 hectares. Sergio Uribe's numbers, if taken at face value, imply a leaf output of 260,000 to 330,000 tons, yielding 450 to 650 tons of cocaine per year. If we consider the fact that, according to U.S. State Department data, Colombian cocaine hydrochloride laboratories have an estimated production capacity of 600 to 720 tons per year, it is clear that Colombia might be almost self-sufficient in the raw material for cocaine. That would explain the apparent reduction in demand for Peruvian and Bolivian coca leaf in 1995.

To be sure, the extent of Colombian coca self-sufficiency can be debated. Uribe's figures may be exaggerated; his research methodology depends on information furnished by local residents of coca zones, including farmers themselves, who may overstate production in order to raise the costs to governments of crop substitution and alternative development schemes. At the same time, the State Department's INCSR data probably understate production. Although the U.S. government has been wedded to the same Colombian yield figure—0.8 tons—for more than a decade, entrepreneurial Colombian farmers cultivating large coca plantations of up to 30 hectares reportedly have been able to obtain much higher yields using intensive applications of fertilizer and better farming techniques. Clearly, more on-site research and more sophisticated sampling techniques will be needed to resolve such disparities.

Structure of the Industry

In Colombia, the cocaine industry is organized in a roughly hierarchial though nonbureaucratic pattern. Coordination of different functions and different levels of responsibility occurs through a complicated system of contracts and subcontracts. According to a pioneering work by a former

Central Intelligence Agency (CIA) analyst, Sidney Zabludoff, a small elite of approximately 500 entrepreneurs dominates the cocaine business in Colombia.[19] (Zabludoff based his research at the Agency on extensive interviews with U.S. law enforcement officials, intelligence experts, and other knowledgeable observers.) This elite supervises every aspect of the cocaine business, including movement of cocaine from source countries to consumer markets, overseas distribution, and recycling of narcotics proceeds. Below the top elite, according to Zabludoff, are echelons of 8,000 specialized operators—pilots, chemists, shippers, overseas distributors—who handle day-to-day cocaine operations. Additionally, according to this scheme, some 10,000 semi-professional and unskilled workers—laborers, guards, couriers, money launderers—perform a variety of menial tasks for the industry. (See figure 1.7.)

In Zabludoff's model, the 500 industry leaders are distributed among ten distinct "core" organizations, or exporting groups. Such groups typically comprise the principal kingpins, their close associates, functional vice-presidents, and representatives stationed abroad. (See figure 1.8.) Core boundaries, however, are fluid: Larger organizations, for example, might maintain their own aircraft and pilots instead of relying on outsider-owned airline companies. Zabludoff notes that core organizations collaborate to improve smuggling logistics or to thwart government counternarcotics efforts. (Specific examples of such joint initiatives are detailed in later chapters.) So-called cocaine cartels based in Valle de Cauca, Antioquia, the North Coast, and elsewhere in Colombia are, in effect, regionally based patterns of cooperation among major exporting organizations.

Of course, this construct is merely an approximation of reality—it is not meant to be accurate in every detail. Certain specifics can be challenged—for example, Colombian economist Francisco Thoumi, author of a recent book, *Economía, Política y Narcotráfico,* estimates that as many as fourteen important exporting groups operate in Colombia.[20] Nevertheless, Zabludoff's work is the most detailed portrait of the cocaine industry appearing to date; it deserves careful scrutiny by students of Andean drug issues.

At the bottom of the pyramid are the growers and processors of coca leaves. Narcotics agriculture in Colombia is a poorly studied subject; the remoteness of and lack of security in the growing areas is a major deterrent to research. Estimates of employment in the coca sector therefore must be considered extremely tentative. According to Sergio Uribe, the harvesting of 65,000 hectares and conversion of the leaf to cocaine base would require 40,000 to 45,000 full-time workers. Assuming that each person devoted one-third of his or her time to

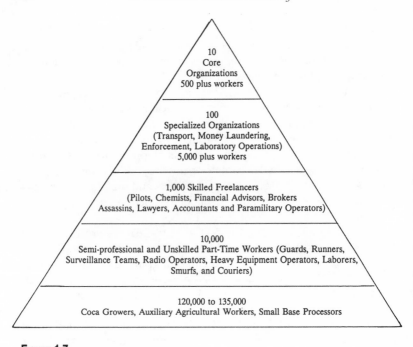

FIGURE 1.7

COLOMBIAN COCAINE TRAFFICKING INDUSTRY

Source: Adapted from Sidney Zabludoff, "Colombian Narcotics Organizations as Business Enterprises." In U.S. Department of State, Bureau of Research and Intelligence and the Central Intelligence Agency, *Economics of the Narcotics Industry Conference Report.* Washington DC: State Department and CIA, 1994.

coca-related activities, the number of persons engaged at least part time in cultivation and processing could be 120,000 to 135,000.

Zabludoff estimates that the core organizations handle 60 percent or more of the cocaine reaching U.S. and European markets. This would translate to a 75 percent or more share of Colombian exports of cocaine. The rest presumably is in the hands of small refining and smuggling entrepreneurs. Extrapolating from Zabludoff's data, the total number of Colombian cocaine traffickers is approximately 16,000 to 20,000, of whom 6,000 to 7,000 can be considered critical to industry functioning. Thus, total full- and part-time employment in the Colombian cocaine industry probably does not exceed 160,000, or 1.3 percent of the national workforce.[21] (By contrast, in 1991, the Colombian coffee industry employed at least 740,000 workers, or 6.1 percent of the workforce in that year.[22]) Cocaine's income effects are far more important to the Colombian economy than the employment effects, a point to be discussed later.

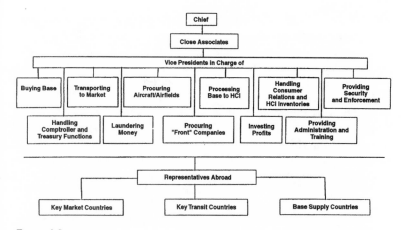

FIGURE 1.8

STRUCTURE OF "FULL SERVICE" COLOMBIAN COCAINE TRAFFICKING ORGANIZATIONS
Source: Sidney Zabludoff. "Colombian Narcotics Organizations as Business Enterprises." In U.S. Department of State, Bureau of Research and Intelligence and the Central Intelligence Agency, *Economics of the Narcotics Industry Conference Report.* Washington DC: State Department and CIA, 1994.

Gross and Net Revenue from Cocaine

The traffickers' revenue depends on several factors about which information is poor. How much cocaine they sell, where they sell it, or to what extent they are involved in selling directly to retailers as distinct from wholesalers is unknown. Each of these factors can make a major difference in the amount of money traffickers earn. For instance, if the traffickers sell in Central and Western Europe, they can make twice as much as if they sell in the United States: In 1994, wholesale prices there ranged from $35,000 to $50,000 per kilogram compared to $16,000 to $25,000 in major U.S. cities. As table 1.2 shows, cocaine's cost increases more than tenfold between Colombia and the United States. This means that Colombian entrepreneurs need to repatriate only a small portion of their revenues to cover their basic costs; the rest can be laundered or invested anywhere. Also, as the table shows, in Europe a kilogram of cocaine can sell for two to three times as much as the same amount sold in the United States, and the profit for the traffickers can be four times as much.

With regard to costs, we have no clear idea of how much gross revenue goes toward cocaine industry operating expenses. Those costs include much more than coca leaf purchases and lab worker payments. There are heavy security expenses, from paramilitary forces to payments to government informants. Trafficking to the United States requires a complex constellation of outlays for landing rights, refueling, loading, unloading, repacking, storage facilities, aircraft maintenance, and assorted payoffs to local officials and leaders. For example, in the 1980s, Medellín cartel leaders reportedly paid the Panamanian Defense Forces $1,000 for every kilo trans-shipped through Panama, in addition to the more routine expenses required to maintain the Panama route. Also during that time, the cartel paid officials in Cuba's Ministry of Interior $6 million to move 6 tons of cocaine through the island en route to the United States. In Mexico, which in the 1990s became an important conduit for South American cocaine entering the United States, some traffickers such as Juan Carlos Abrego, the leader of the so-called Gulf cartel, reportedly charged a 40 to 50 percent commission in kind (that is, in cocaine hydrochloride) to deliver cocaine to U.S. wholesale cells controlled by Colombian organizations. While possibly the most expensive smuggling option for Colombian traffickers, the Mexican route is almost certainly one of the safest, given the large-scale deployment of U.S. Customs, Coast Guard, and Department of Defense resources in the Florida Straits and the Bahamas and the extensive air surveillance systems in place along the U.S.-Mexico border and in the Gulf of Mexico.

Even if we could learn how much the Colombian cocaine industry makes, we then would have to try to determine how much makes its way back to Colombia and how much stays out of the country. Following orthodox economic theory, Colombian economists gener-

TABLE 1.2
COST AND PRICE STRUCTURES FOR COCAINE

	Per Kilo Price/Cost	
	U.S.	Europe
Prices in Major Markets	$13,000	$35,000
Transport from Colombia Laboratory to U.S. Wholesalers	$ 3,000	$ 4,000
Cocaine Hydrochloride shipped from Colombia	$ 1,000	$ 1,000
Money Laundering (15% of gross profits in U.S., 10% in Europe)	$ 2,000	$ 3,000
Miscellaneous Costs: Handling, Bribes in Major Market	$ 500	$ 1,000
Net Profit per Kilo	$ 6,500	$26,000

Source: Adapted from Zabludoff. In U.S. Department of State, Bureau of Research and Intelligence and the Central Intelligence Agency, *Economics of the Narcotics Industry Conference Report.* Washington DC: State Department and CIA, 1994.

ally consider that only the money that returns to Colombia constitutes income for the country. But, in fact, the billions held abroad by Colombian drug traffickers have enormous potential influence on the country, politically and economically. Indeed, drug money can have corrupting effects without returning to the country at all. (Consider, for example, a hypothetical situation in which a Colombian drug lord transfers money from his U.S. bank account to that of a Colombian official and the official then uses the bribe to buy a house or apartment in Florida or to pay for his children's education at an Ivy League college.) The issue is made more complicated by the Cali cartel's reliance on Colombian-born agents in the United States. Large numbers of Colombian residents in the United States traffic in drugs but are not necessarily members of the exporters' organizations. These Colombians, whatever their citizenship status, could still retain important family ties and other connections in their homeland. The Colombian resident population in the United States (including citizens, noncitizens, and illegals) ranges from 450,000 to 1 million; of this number, an estimated 10,000 are involved directly in trafficking drugs. The portion of earnings from people that flows back to Colombia, however, is virtually impossible to calculate.[23]

It is not clear whether their income should be counted as Colombia's income or as U.S. income, because it is not clear if these Colombian-born U.S. residents will stay in the United States or return to Colombia. Francisco Thoumi argued that these people may well return to Colombia,

TABLE 1.3
COLOMBIA: NET NARCODOLLAR EARNINGS, AS ESTIMATED BY COLOMBIAN ECONOMISTS

Economist	Period	Amount in billion dollars	Drug Type
Miguel Urrutia	1991	.17	Cocaine
Hernando José Gomez	1991	.28	Cocaine
Eduardo Sarmiento	1991	1.1	Cocaine
National Drug Council	1994	1.8 to 2.5[a]	Cocaine
Francisco Thoumi	1980s to early 1990s	2.0 to 5.0	All drugs
Solomon Kalmanovitz	1991	3.11	Cocaine
O'Byrne and Reina	1991	3.4[b]	Cocaine

[a] Gross income.
[b] 2.9 billion from European sales, $0.5 billion from U.S. sales.
Sources: Semana, April 13, 1993, pp. 34-39; Francisco Thoumi, Economía, Política y Narcotráfico, pp. 192, 208; Mauricio Cardenas S. and Luis Jorge Garay S., Macro Economía de los Flujas de Capital En Colombia y America Latina, p. 288.

because "In the United States, they would merely be well-to-do foreigners, only partially assimilated into mainstream society and faced with constant risk of detection; in Colombia, they could join the upper tiers of society, especially in small and medium-sized cities."[24]

Given the difficulties of estimating gross and net revenue, Colombian economists have attempted to estimate income from indirect evidence. The studies are ingenious but inconclusive, because there is simply not enough data. As indicated in table 1.3, the estimates of Colombia's income from cocaine vary by a factor of 20-to-1 among Colombian authors. Salomón Kalmanovitz estimated 1991 cocaine income for Colombians at $3.1 billion, while Miguel Urrutia argued that cocaine income that same year could have been as low as $170 million. Both are serious economists, now at the Colombian central bank, but they arrive at very different conclusions. In the Zabludoff model, 330 tons of cocaine are delivered, net of seizures and losses to foreign markets. More than three times as much cocaine is sold in the United States as in Europe, yet traffickers' total profits from U.S. sales are significantly lower than profits from European operations. Gross exports earnings from each of the ten core organizations earns an average of $600 million per year. Of that, traffickers' profits average $370 million, or approximately 60 percent of gross sales for each of the ten organizations. (See table 1.4)

TABLE 1.4
ANNUAL COCAINE EARNINGS TO CORE
COLOMBIAN ORGANIZATIONS IN THE 1990s

	United States	Europe	Total
Successful Cocaine Shipments	250 tons	80 tons	330 tons
Gross Export Earnings in $ billion U.S.	3.25	2.80	6.05
Net Earnings in $ billion U.S.	1.63	2.08	3.71

Source: Calculated from Zabludoff. In U.S. Department of State, Bureau of Research and Intelligence and the Central Intelligence Agency, *Economics of the Narcotics Industry Conference Report.* Washington DC: State Department and CIA, 1994.

If the major exporters account for 75 percent of Colombian cocaine sales, total Colombian export earnings from cocaine would equal $8 billion or approximately 90 percent of Colombia's total merchandise exports in 1994 (8.7 billion) and 380 percent of Colombian coffee exports (2.1 billion) in that year. The value-added portion of this $8 billion can be calculated at 4 to 5 billion, which is equivalent to 8 to 9 percent of Colombia's 1994 GDP of $53 billion.

Such estimates could be on the low side, however. The very large profits obtained from the cocaine trade inside the United States are a tremendous incentive for Colombian exporters to move operations "downstream" or closer to the consumer. (Within the United States cocaine may pass through five or six levels of distribution before being sold by the gram to users.) Accordingly, in the early 1990s, the Cali cartel established distribution cells in U.S. cities that sold 30 to 100 kilograms of cocaine at prices of $35,000 to $45,000 per kilogram, which was two to three times the U.S. port of entry price.[25] In Zabludoff's model, cocaine is sold to a U.S. wholesaler for $13,000 per kilogram. Hence, the cell operations might at least double the cartel's per-kilogram earnings. Colombians also have distribution cells in Europe, but little is known about their activities. Thus "core" organizations could earn twice what Zabludoff estimates as U.S. earnings. At the same time there are countervailing factors that may reduce the Colombian cartel's income closer to what Zabludoff estimated. Cartel representatives in the United States, for example, may offer large discounts to regular buyers—the cells' actual balance sheets are not known with certainty. Also, shipping cocaine to the United States through Mexico and paying Mexican traffickers a large percentage in kind could greatly reduce the Colombians' overall earnings picture. The calculation of $8 billion for Colombia's international cocaine sales thus seems a reasonable if somewhat conservative estimate.

Of course, not all of the income returns to Colombia. Indeed, quite possibly only $2 billion to $3 billion a year returns, a figure within the range used by some Colombian economists. However, traffickers' large cocaine surplus translates into a significant amount of money available for legal investments as well as lobbying and bribes. By all indications, Colombia's trafficking establishment is powerful, well connected, and capable of inflicting enormous damage on the country both economically and politically.

COCAINE AND NATIONAL DEVELOPMENT

Although cocaine is a fairly important industry in the Andean regions, it has had relatively little effect on overall economic performance. No evidence suggests that cocaine brought an economic boom to any of the Andean countries. Quite the contrary; Colombia, Peru, and Bolivia each experienced serious economic crises during the 1980s. In each country, the crisis took a different shape and had different causes, but there was one strong similarity: The cocaine industry did not propel the overall national economy into growth.

Cocaine's Contribution to Growth

Colombia's economy did well in the late 1970s. Perhaps cocaine had something to do with this, but there is another obvious explanation: a boom in coffee prices that raised coffee export revenue from $1.4 billion in 1974 to $3.9 billion in 1980.[26] The national economy began to decelerate in 1982, as the foreign debt crisis hit Latin America. Suddenly shut off from access to the foreign capital on which it had become unhealthily dependent, Colombia experienced a slow decline that ceased only a decade later. Legal per capita GNP fell from $2,000 in 1981 to $1,280 in 1991, ajdusted for inflation. (See figure 1.9.)[27] In other words, the average income expressed in constant dollars fell 36 percent during the coca-rich 1980s. (According to another measure, constant peso income per capita, the economy rose in the 1980s, although at half the rate of the 1970s.) The problems during the cocaine period contrast to the relatively rapid growth during the precocaine period (roughly, 1966

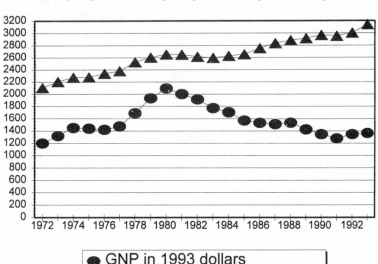

● GNP in 1993 dollars
▲ GDP in 1987 pesos (hundreds)

FIGURE 1.9
COLOMBIA: PER CAPITA INCOME
Source: World Bank, *World Tables 1995.* Baltimore: The Johns Hopkins University Press, 1995.

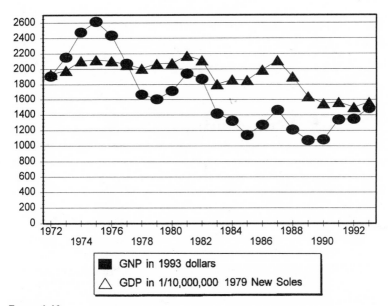

FIGURE 1.10
PERU: PER CAPITA INCOME
Source: World Bank, *World Tables 1995.* Baltimore: The Johns Hopkins University Press, 1995.

to 1978), when per capita income rose steadily. Of course, such a phenomenon lends itself to multiple explanations, such as government mismanagement or the rise of guerrilla terrorism, yet cocaine probably played some role in the decline. As Thoumi put it, "It is not surprising that the majority of Colombian economists argue that the negative effects of the [narcotics] industry clearly surpass the positive, and that they do not consider the [narcotics] industry benefits the country."[28]

In Peru, legal income per person was on the decline most years from 1975 through 1990. (See figure 1.10.) There was a temporary upturn in 1986-87 when the Garcia government adopted shortsighted policies of large-scale government spending and cheap imports, but then the economy headed steadily down until 1990. From a peak of $2,620 per person in 1975, legal income (adjusted for inflation) had dropped to just $1,080 in 1990.

In Bolivia, the coca boom was associated with a 40 percent decline in noncoca per capita GNP from the 1975 peak to the 1985 trough. (See figure 1.11.) In 1993 dollars, while income per person in 1975 was $980, in 1985 it was just $570. Those years mark the period of the deepest economic crisis in Bolivia's history. Of course, the country had numerous

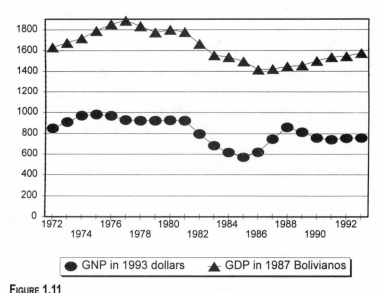

FIGURE 1.11
BOLIVIA: PER CAPITA INCOME
Source: World Bank, *World Tables 1995.* Baltimore: The Johns Hopkins University Press, 1995.

other economic problems at that time, including large government defi-
cits, rampant inflation, and declining prices for its mineral exports. However, the strong growth of coca production at the same time that the legal
economy was declining suggests that the cocaine industry had a negative
effect on the rest of the economy. Supporting this hypothesis is the fact
that legal agricultural output declined 25 percent per capita from 1980 to
1990 while coca leaf output grew about 250 percent.

Thus it is clear that the national economies went deeper into
crisis in the middle of the cocaine boom. That fact can be read in
several ways, which are not necessarily mutually exclusive. One way
would be to say that coca and cocaine provided a cushion when the
legal economy went into freefall; that coca provided a margin of sur-
vival for some. Yet, if so, the cushion was awfully thin. When legal
income per person drops $1,450 from 1975 to 1992, as it did in Peru,
the 1992 cocaine income of $67 per person does not look very impor-
tant. And in Bolivia, where the decline in legal per capita income
during the crisis was $360, the coca income—$77 per person at the
peak of the coca boom in 1988 and $30 per person in 1992—was not
much compensation.

Perhaps coca is a crop of desperation that is attractive only because of an economic crisis, and coca is not an economically desirable

industry in normal times. Bolivian Planning Minister Samuel Doria Medina, in an interview, spelled out this theory. When the currency was losing value by the hour, when imports could not be had, when there were few legal ways to make money, when the government was not to be trusted, Bolivians naturally looked for a way to earn dollars outside the formal economy. But once there were attractive legal alternatives, then fewer Bolivians chose the risks of being outside the law.[29]

A third explanation would be that the cocaine boom was caused in part by the crisis in the legal economies. That is, because of the crisis, thousands were thrown out of work (as when the Bolivian government dismissed 30,000 miners in 1985) and thousands of young men looking for their first job were unable to find any productive employment. So the jobless moved to the coca-growing regions, where land was readily available. Their labor made possible an expansion in coca production. In other words, the cocaine boom may not have been solely due to increased U.S. demand.

In the 1990s, the growth prospects for cocaine demand are poor. Historically, illicit drugs go in and out of fashion. David Musto of Yale University has described the first cocaine epidemic, which began after cocaine hydrochloride became available in cheap and pure form around 1885. At first, Sigmund Freud, the father of pschoanalysis, sang the praises of the new wonder potion, which was not controlled by any law; it was consumed in many forms, including the new drink, Coca-Cola. According to Musto, "The first epidemic lasted from 1885 until the 1920s, about 35 years. There were three stages: an initial euphoria about an apparently harmless, indeed, a valuable and helpful stimulant; a middle period of dispersion and multiplying instances of prolonged use; and, finally, a powerful rejection of cocaine as its popular image became as negative as it had once been positive."[30]

The pattern Musto describes seems to be repeating itself in part. The development of freebase and crack has made cocaine available to lower-income users. Author Mark Kleiman observes, "As cocaine became associated with unwed teenage mothers rather than with rock stars and yuppie greed-heads, it grew less fashionable. [At the same time,] the quantity consumed per user also rose, as compulsive binge users came to constitute a larger and larger proportion of the total user population."[31] A high rate of growth outside the United States plus a small decline in the United States could translate into flat world demand. The most likely prospect is that cocaine will be a slow-growth industry with uncertain price prospects.

Prospects for Economic Growth in the Andes

Meanwhile, Colombia, Peru, and Bolivia each have good legal growth prospects for the late 1990s. The future of the Colombian economy depends on the oil and gas industry, not on coca. Colombia is on the edge of an oil boom.[32] British Petroleum is leading a consortium undertaking a $7 billion development ninety miles northeast of Bogotá. Production, which was 90,000 barrels a day in early 1995, is expected to increase to 500,000 barrels a day when a two billion dollar pipeline to the Caribbean coast is completed in late 1997. Even at a modest $15 a barrel for its low-sulfur crude, Colombia's production would be worth $2.7 billion a year. And British Petroleum also found such large gas reserves that the Colombian government is undertaking a $3 billion program to pipe natural gas to all urban households by the end of 1997. Thus the hydrocarbon industry offers good prospects of overtaking illegal drugs as the largest industry in Colombia, especially since the income from the latter industry does not appear to be growing much. At the same time, Bogotá has much to do to ensure that its oil riches are developed: Taxes have to be made competitive with other oil producing countries, and oil companies need protection from guerrilla groups that regularly attack oil facilities unless bribed.

Peru's legal economy is on a fast track, with growth dwarfing anything that happens in the cocaine industry. From 1993 to 1995, the legal economy grew eight times as fast as the cocaine industry ($10 billion growth versus the $1.3 billion 1993 cocaine income). This amounts to 27 percent real growth in three years, the fastest growth of any economy in the world during that period—faster than China, faster than any East Asian tiger. Peru's main economic problem in 1995 was, in fact, an economy overheating with too rapid growth. In May 1995 the government agreed with the International Monetary Fund on conditions designed to slow growth to 6 to 7 percent per year.[33] Two dozen U.S. firms are drilling for oil or digging for minerals in the country. "Peru has truly become the mecca for the world's geologists and miners," said Ronald Cambre, president of Newmont Mining, one of the world's largest mining firms. In the decade 1994 to 2003, mining firms plan to invest $8.7 billion, increasing the value of annual mining output from $2 billion to $5 billion.[34]

Government policies account for these excellent prospects. Peru's government has been able to restore domestic tranquility with the taming of the Shining Path guerrilla threat, and it is strongly pro-business. For instance, it has already sold forty-nine state firms, netting $3.2 billion (with investors pledging to invest a matching sum in upgrading the firms), and it plans to sell another twenty-six, including the state oil company, water company, steel company, railroad, and mining conglomerate. The stock exchange has been revitalized by a scheme that encourages private pensions. Infrastructure is being improved, with a three-year, $1 billion road development program. Thanks to the turnaround in the business environment, old plans are being revived—for example, Royal Dutch/Shell announced plans in 1995 to invest $1 billion in a gas field it discovered in the mid-1980s.

In so vibrant an economy, the cocaine industry is of shrinking importance. It seems likely that the Peruvian cocaine industry will grow only slowly because, as explained in detail in chapter 5, a fungus has devastated production in the Upper Huallaga Valley, the main coca-growing area. As a $1.3 billion industry, coca accounted for 3.9 percent of the 1992 $33 billion GNP; however, that same $1.3 billion will account for only 2.2 percent of the projected $60 billion GNP in 2002.

Bolivia's economic prospects are not as clear as those of Peru and Colombia. The political atmosphere is good for growth. After seventy-six governments (or more, depending on how semicoups are counted) in the first 157 years of independence, Bolivia has had stable, democratically elected governments since 1983, with two peaceful transitions from one party to another. There is broad support for sensible government budgets and sound money; inflation, which was 23,000 percent in 1985, was 11 percent in 1995. There is also broad support for free trade; once heavily protectionist, the maximum tariff is 10 percent. To be sure, political strife continues about many other areas of economic policy, and the strong political lobby for restrictive trade union rules and for government ownership of key sectors will hold back growth. The current government has taken on the trade unions and is campaigning for privatization of the main government-owned firms. It may or may not succeed. No matter what happens, the issues will remain controversial, and investors will remain wary of policy reversals after the next election.

La Paz estimates that annual growth in the late 1990s will be 7.0 percent if structural reforms are made or 4.7 percent if they are not.[35] That sounds optimistic but possible; after all, annual growth averaged 4.5 percent from 1991 to 1995. The engines of growth will be hydrocarbons, mining, and tropical agriculture. The most important of these is hydrocarbons (oil and gas). While twenty-four oil firms were active in Bolivia in the 1970s, oil nationalism led most to leave. Yacimientos Petroliferos Fiscales Bolivianos (YPFB) could not fill the gap, especially because of its poor management, and crude output fell from 49,000 barrels per day in 1973 to 18,000 in 1987 before slowly rising to 27,000 barrels a day in 1995. Now, with new laws, foreign firms are returning. Sixteen foreign firms have signed exploration contracts. But hopes are pinned on natural gas, not oil. In December 1994, after protracted negotiation, YPFB signed a contract with the Brazilian state monopoly Petrobras to supply natural gas worth about $200 million a year for twenty years. More difficult negotiations remain to tie down the details of the pipeline financing and fees. Meanwhile, plans are well advanced for a similar size deal with Enap, Chile's state oil company. If both deals proceed, Bolivia's exports would increase by 45 percent (from $887 million in 1994).

As for mining, the *Financial Times* reported on April 16, 1992, "Excited mining analysts and businessmen claim that the country is on the threshold of a boom the like of which it has not seen since the days of the tin barons of the 19th century. A timely combination of pro-business legislation and important discoveries have attracted a swarm of international mining groups." The number of foreign companies operating in Bolivia increased from four in 1991 to forty in 1995. The success of the $160 million investment to develop the Inti Raymi gold mine, majority-owned by Battle Mountain of the United States, is attracting the interest of other firms. Meanwhile, a vigorous gold jewelry industry has developed, mostly in small shops in La Paz, with $54 million in exports in the first half of 1994.

Tropical agriculture offers good prospects, especially in the rich soils around the city of Santa Cruz (the best soils in tropical Latin America). Soya yields are 2.5 to 3.0 tons per hectare, compared to 1.5 tons in Brazil. However, the area is subject to variable weather—there were floods in 1992 and drought in 1994. Furthermore, transportation problems, especially dependence on the inefficient railroad to the Paraguay River, have limited exports, although transport costs should drop as new roads open and as river transport is extended into the producing areas.

PUTTING COCAINE IN PERSPECTIVE

Cocaine is big business. Most income in the cocaine industry comes from distribution inside the consuming countries, a sizable chunk of which is controlled by Andeans. Conceivably, they may earn $10 billion or more a year from cocaine, with the Colombian share amounting to $8 billion. To be sure, the amount brought back into the Andean economies is much less, perhaps $4 billion a year, of which the majority goes to Colombia. That is a lot of money, but nothing near the fantastic sums produced by multiplying the U.S. government estimate of potential output times the U.S. government figure for retail price.

Furthermore, cocaine income should be put into the context of the $90 billion GDP of Bolivia, Peru, and Colombia. Cocaine is an important industry in the region, equivalent to perhaps 7 percent combined GDP of the three countries, but it is not the heartbeat that sustains the body economic. Other sectors in the region offer better growth prospects than cocaine, a product for which the market at least in the United States is mature (as reflected in steady or declining price and quantity). The Andes has excellent prospects in mining and petroleum; it is expected that by 1997, Colombia will produce $3 billion a year in oil. After years of poor economic performance, the Andean economies appear to be taking off into solid growth—spectacular growth, in Peru's case in the mid-1990s. Under these circumstances, cocaine's share in the national economy looks certain to decline.

In sum, while cocaine is certain to remain part of the Andean scene for the foreseeable future, it seems unlikely to dominate the stage as it did in the economically troubled 1980s.

Part II

Cocaine Trafficking

2

The Medellín and Cali Cartels

EVOLUTION OF THE COCAINE INDUSTRY

The business of exporting cocaine first took shape in Colombia in the mid-1970s, according to most historical accounts. At that time, the industry was not organized to handle large volumes. Rather, cocaine was produced in makeshift laboratories with rudimentary technology; some operations were located in private homes on the outskirts of major cities. Human couriers—"mules"—smuggled small quantities of cocaine—a few grams or a few pounds in luggage as personal effects. Trafficking organizations typically were simple, comprised of a Colombian buyer, a smuggler-courier, and a point of contact in the United States who received the merchandise and sold it to a U.S. wholesaler. Trafficking entrepreneurs sometimes acted as their own mules. At one time most pioneers of the Colombian cocaine industry—Pablo Escobar, the Ochoa brothers, Carlos Lehder, the Rodríguez Orejuela brothers—personally carried small amounts of cocaine to the United States. While in the United States, they sought out distribution "persons who would make contact, find clients and guard the product."[1] Such formative experience exposed traffickers to the profit potential of the U.S. market and influenced the future development of the cartels' smuggling and distribution networks. Growing U.S. demand for cocaine in the early and mid-1980s precipitated major organizational changes in the Colombian cocaine industry. Production and transport were revolutionized. The "mule" system was discarded and replaced with fleets of aircraft that could carry loads of 400 to 1,000 kilograms of cocaine. By the 1990s, traffickers were using merchant shipping, cargo jet aircraft, and semisubmersible vessels to export multiton loads of cocaine to foreign markets. Carefully planned export routes required the complex coordination of many activities: air, sea, and overhead transport; aircraft trafficking and maintenance; drug loading and unloading and storage; delivery of bribes to appropriate officials in transit countries and—in recent years—intensive collaboration with trafficking organizations in transit countries. Traffickers, especially those associated with the Medellín coalition, also sought to realize economies of scale in production. Huge cocaine laboratories, some the size of industrial factories, were set up in remote jungle and plain regions. (In early 1990 Medellín traffickers turned over to the government, as a peace gesture, one gigantic complex of three interconnected laboratories apparently employing 150 workers and capable of producing 20 tons of cocaine per month.)

The requirements of large-volume smuggling also forced the industry to create new organizational forms. One crucial innovation was export collaboration among different trafficking groups, usually groups based in the same city or region. These patterns of collaboration did not constitute true cartels—that is, groups of independent producers who agree to maintain cocaine wholesale prices. (Prices dropped precipitously in the United States, from $45,000-$55,000 in 1982 to $10,000-$20,000 by the late 1980s: see figure 2.1.) Rather, they were designed to rationalize the system of transporting cocaine—to maximize export volumes while reducing the risk to each supplier. As Francisco Thoumi notes, traffickers established a "transport insurance mechanism that could be used by smaller participants to join in large shipments of cocaine that were insured by large drug entrepreneurs."[2] Risks were spread around by moving large amounts of cocaine to target markets via different conveyances and routes. Pablo Escobar Gaviria pioneered the insurance system in Medellín. Suppliers paid him a premium of approximately 10 percent of the U.S. wholesale price of cocaine; if a particular dealer's shipment was lost, Escobar would replace it—of course, at the purchase price of cocaine in Colombia. Assuming that the chance of seizure can be calculated at 10 percent, Escobar and other kingpins thus stood to make an enormous amount of money just by shipping cocaine to the United States for smaller operators and insuring them against loss.[3] This insurance system and variations of it shaped the development of the cartel structure in Colombia and remains a defining characteristic of the cocaine export business in that country today.

The system also was and still is used to attract outside investors to the cocaine business. Businessmen with clean records could purchase a stake in cocaine shipments. The stake, or *apuntada,* scheme offered investors exceptionally high returns with little downside risk. As Colombian author Mariá Duzan explains: "The drug dealer provided the cocaine and served as the shipping agent. If the shipment was successful everyone made money. If not they were insured."[4] The *apuntada* worked to erase the distinction between legitimate elites and the trafficking underworld in Colombia. The process was es-

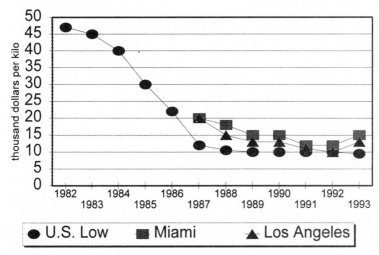

FIGURE 2.1
PORT OF ENTRY PRICES FOR COCAINE (LOW DOLLAR FIGURE FOR ONE KILO)
Source: Personal Communication with Peter Lupsha, University of New Mexico.

pecially advanced in Medellín, a city hit by a serious economic recession in the 1970s and early 1980s. According to Duzan, members of Medellín's most important families participated in the *apuntada.* A mocking account written by a Medellín drug trafficker observed that entrepreneurs and politicians "would approach us asking for a share in some shipment, always saying in subdued voices out of earshot 'but no one must know. This must be kept absolutely secret, do you understand me?'"[5]

As the cocaine traffic expanded, the industry became specialized and hierarchically organized. In the industry's early growth phase—approximately 1980 to 1984—trafficking organizations consisted of entrepreneurs, their close associates (usually family members), pilots, chemists, and money handlers. By the late 1980s, an integrated and efficient international marketing structure had developed: Trafficking organizations per se comprised principally top leaders, senior managers, and their staffs. These "core" organizations conducted the entire range of trafficking functions, working through layers of subcontractors and freelancers who provided key specialized services such as refining, smuggling, distribution, money laundering, and enforcement. Sophisticated patterns of collaboration developed among these organizations, albeit usually on a regional basis. The groups cofinanced and coinsured large shipments of cocaine, pooled information on law enforcement activities (such as planned raids against major leaders), developed joint counterintelligence and counterenforcement strategies and collaborated to improve their bargaining position vis-à-vis the state. In Cali, according to a *Miami Herald* report, major drug kingpins each contributed $200,000 per month to maintain a joint intelligence-gathering operation; much of the money went to bribe police, army officials, and politicians. For instance, Cali leaders such as the Rodríguez Orejuela brothers, José Santa Cruz Londoño, Helmer Herrera Buitrago and Juan Carlos Ramírez reportedly established a common $8 million fund to influence the outcomes of the 1994 presidential and congressional election campaigns.[6] Also, in the 1980s and early 1990s, leaders of the Medellín and Cali cartels negotiated as a group with the Colombian government in an effort to obtain collective judicial benefits such as sentence reductions, an end to extradition, and even amnesty for their crimes. (For a discussion of Colombia's drug negotiations see chapter 4.)

The core groups established elaborate networks of importers and regional distributors in the United States. In New York City, for example, Cali organizations reportedly maintained ten to twelve marketing subsidiaries, or "cells," each comprising ten to twelve salaried employees who earned anywhere from $2,000 to $20,000 per month. Cell directors reported directly to the home office in Cali, where the directors made all key decisions on the cell's activities—they set prices, determined the amounts of cocaine to be sold, and approved prospective buyers. This cell structure, which benefited from a large Colombian resident population in the United States, allowed Cali-based exporters to obtain per-kilogram cocaine prices two to three times higher than those realized by selling to a U.S. wholesaler at the point of entry. Trends in the industry dictated forward integration. At the beginning of the 1980s, cocaine dealers could realize a gross income of $40 million and a net income of perhaps $38 million (a 95 percent profit rate!) just by delivering a ton of cocaine to first-level wholesalers in the United States. By the beginning of the 1990s, lower cocaine prices and the necessity of shipping the drug via more complex and expensive routes (the result of stronger U.S. air and maritime interdiction efforts) had reduced smuggling profits to 50 percent or less of earnings.

Colombian traffickers also established cooperative relationships with a number of foreign trafficking organizations focused on various issues: organization of markets, trade deals (drugs-for-drugs, drugs-for-weapons, drugs-for-cash exchanges), smuggling logistics, and laundering or repatriation of trafficking proceeds. Some of these arrangements probably concerned exchanges of criminal expertise and joint business planning. For example, as noted in chapter 1, Cali-based organizations rely on the "Gulf cartel" and other Mexican traffickers to deliver cocaine to Cali distribution cells in the United States. (Mexican traffickers, however, are now setting up their own distribution networks in the United States, especially along the West Coast—a development that might engender rivalry with the Colombians in the long run.) Cooperation between Colombian traffickers and Italian organized crime groups to sell cocaine in Italy and Europe appears to be particularly advanced; the Cali cartel and the Sicilian mafia, for example, are experimenting with franchise arrangements that would allow the mafia to distribute large consignments of Cali cocaine to European buyers outside of Italy. Colombian traffickers also rely on Sicilian money laundering networks in Italy, Switzerland, Brazil, Venezuela and the United States to recycle the proceeds of cocaine sales in Europe. Further, the Cali group has established working relationships with organized crime figures in Poland, the Czech Republic, and Russia, with the aim of using these countries as a "back door" to ship cocaine to Western Europe. Three shipments recently seized by the Russians—1.1 tons of cocaine in Vyborg, in February 1993; 400 kilograms in St. Petersburg in April 1994; and almost 220 kilograms in Gdansk, Poland, in May 1995—were traceable to Cali trafficking organizations. Reports abound that Cali organizations have converted cocaine cash to Russian commodities such as diamonds and non-ferrous metals that can be resold for "clean" hard currency in the West. In general, international narcocooperation opens new markets for narcotics and other illegal products, exploits economies of scale in selling to those markets, finds new laundering outlets for illegal drug capital, and diminishes criminal formations' vulnerability to prosecution by national governments.

EXPANSION IN CENTRAL AMERICA AND THE CARIBBEAN

Colombian traffickers began cultivating ties with Caribbean and Central American countries with a vengeance in 1984, following the assassination of the Colombian justice minister Lara Bonilla. The resulting government crackdown forced many leading traffickers into exile in Panama. There, as Bruce Bagley notes, they "strengthened already existing relations with General Noriega."[7] They set up a large cocaine processing laboratory in Darien Province and transformed Panama into one of the world's foremost centers for laundering drug money. In return for $4.6 million in payoffs, Noriega allegedly allowed the Medellín cartel to move 4.6 tons of cocaine through Panama and to stockpile the merchandise with the protection of the government. (The general was convicted by a U.S. federal court in 1992 for drug trafficking, money laundering, and racketeering and was sentenced to forty years in prison. He is now appealing.)

The Colombians in Panama began planning new transshipment routes and money-laundering centers. They cultivated ties with both the Sandinistas and the Contras in Nicaragua and made deals with Mexican traffickers and officials to transship cocaine through Mexico. With the help of Juan Matta Ballesteros, a Honduran agent of the Medellín mafia who had escaped from a Bogotá jail in 1986, they subverted members of the Honduran military. In addition, they cultivated new official ties in Belize, Cuba, Haiti, and several smaller island countries. Today nearly every Caribbean and Central American has been tainted to some degree by drug money.

For example, in the Bahamas, Colombian kingpin Carlos Lehder converted the island of Norman's Key into a base for large-scale cocaine and marijuana smuggling between 1979 and 1982, earning a cut of all shipments passing through; apparently police and senior government officials connived in the operation. A 1994 Commission of Inquiry investigated several cabinet ministers and public officials, including Prime Minister Lyndon Pindling, for allegedly taking bribes from Colombian drug smugglers. The commission's report lead to a shuffle: Three ministers resigned and two were dismissed. Pindling, however, was never tied directly to any drug payoffs. In March 1985, Norman Saunders, then minister of the Turks and Caicos Islands, was arrested in Miami on drug trafficking charges; he subsequently was convicted and sentenced to eight years in prison. A U.S. Senate probe in 1991 reported evidence of a major arms trafficking scandal in Antigua; according to the investigation, the Antigua Defense Force had bought 400 Galil rifles and 100 Uzis in Israel in 1989 and then sold the shipment to the Medellín cartel in Colombia. Reportedly 232 Galils had ended up on cartel kingpin José Gonzalo Rodríguez Gacha's farm. One rifle found apparently had been used to assassinate Colombian Liberal Party candidate Luis Carlos Galán in August 1989. In April 1994 a convicted former member of the Medellín cartel testified that Haiti's then police commander, Joseph Michel François, had collaborated with the cartel in arranging the shipment of 70 tons of cocaine through the island in 1987. According to the informant, François had actually traveled to Medellín to discuss cocaine transshipment through Haiti with cartel members.[8]

Communist governments also were drawn into the pattern of hemisphere-wide corruption. First, consider Nicaragua in the 1980s. A U.S. government affidavit filed in U.S. District Court in Miami in July 1984 charged that two major Colombian traffickers, Pablo Escobar and Jorge Ochoa, and a Nicaraguan official were conspiring to smuggle cocaine. The official, Frederico Vaughn, was an assistant to Nicaraguan interior minister Tomás Borge. According to the indictment, these men conspired to smuggle roughly 1.5 tons of cocaine from Colombia to the United States via Nicaragua. Vaughn allegedly was paid $1.5 million for providing the traffickers with secure facilities. Photographs supporting the indictment showed Vaughn and Escobar loading a Miami-bound aircraft with cocaine-containing boxes with the assistance of Sandinista troops, which suggests that other Nicaraguan officials may have participated in the scheme as well. Furthermore, there are allegations that the Medellín syndicates funneled $10 million to the Nicaraguan Contras between 1982 and 1985 for fuel, landing rights, and other services in areas under Contra military control. Another purpose of this donation, according to unpublished testimony before the Senate Foreign Relations Committee, was to buy "a little friendship" from the CIA, which had supported the Contra rebels in 1982 and 1983.[9]

A particularly significant relationship developed in this period between the Medellín cartel and high officials in the Cuban government. Cuba, of course, occupied a key geographical position astride principal drug smuggling routes that link South American exporting countries to the United States. The cartel decided to exploit this potential. In early 1987 a Miami-based cartel representative, Reynaldo

Ruiz, met with Colonel Antonio de la Guardia, the head of the MC (*Moneda Convertible*) Department of the Cuban Ministry of Interior, a department charged with circumventing the U.S. economic blockade of Cuba, and a subordinate, Major Amado Padrón Trujillo. (Ruiz was a Cuban emigre whose cousin Miguel worked in the MC Department; Ruiz's wife, Ligia, was a native of Medellín who maintained a friendship with Gustavo Gaviria, Pablo Escobar's cousin.) At the meeting, an agreement was reached in which the Colombians would ship 400 kilograms of cocaine through Cuba's Varadero Airport in return for payment of $800 per kilogram. (In subsequent deals, the price was increased to $1,000 per kilogram.) The first operation took place in April 1987. Between then and 1989, the Cubans and the cartel conducted fifteen successful smuggling operations that moved approximately 6 tons of cocaine through the island and earned the MC Department an estimated $3.4 million.[10]

A concurrent smuggling scheme involved division general Arnaldo Ochoa Sanchez, who had headed the tenth section of the Ministry of Defense and the Cuban military mission in Angola and who was a decorated hero of the Cuban revolution. In April 1988 Ochoa sent his aide, Captain Jorge Martínez Valdez, to meet in Havana with Antonio de la Guardia and representatives of Pablo Escobar. Then in early May 1988 Martínez traveled to Medellín to meet Escobar, using a forged Colombian passport furnished by the cartel. Escobar and Martínez concluded an accord to traffic cocaine through Cuba for a fee of $1,200 per kilogram. (Escobar also proposed setting up cocaine laboratories in Cuba but the Cubans apparently rejected the idea.) Thereafter Ochoa's group orchestrated two failed smuggling operations. One, involving a Panamanian ship called *Jennifer*, never materialized because the vessel's captain was murdered. The other collapsed after the Cuban border patrol seized a boat loaded with about 500 kilograms of cocaine. After the second failure, which de la Guardia had failed to prevent, Escobar threatened to send a representative to Cuba to "complain to the authorities and to demand the return of the merchandise."[11]

Ochoa, de la Guardia, Padrón, and Martínez were arrested by Cuban authorities in June 1989 and executed the following month. A number of other Cuban officials, including de la Guardia's brother Patricio (also a Ministry of Interior official) and Interior Minister José Abrantes, were condemned to long jail sentences in connection with the scandal. Yet it is very possible that other top Cuban leaders were involved in drug smuggling through Cuba. Conceivably they believed infusions of drug capital would aid Cuba's economic problems. Significantly, at his trial Ochoa characterized his motives as altruistic and patriotic. "My main concern in this has not been for myself but for the revolution," he told the military tribunal. The general's stated intention was to use proceeds from narcotrafficking to invest in tourist enterprises in Cuba. "If tourism develops, Cuba benefits," he said. In a letter to two Cuban Politburo members that was smuggled from jail, Patricio de la Guardia claimed that drug trafficking in Cuba "was authorized at the highest levels" of the Cuban government.[12] Ruiz, who helped arrange the deal between the MC Department and the Medellín cartel, subsequently charged that Fidel Castro's brother Raul was fully informed of the cocaine shipments through Cuba from 1987 to 1989.[13]

Despite the 1989 purge, the Cuba connection apparently survived. A report by a Russian research group, "Feliks," composed of former KGB agents, claims that at the end of May 1990, Cali don Miguel Rodríguez Orejuela met with representatives of the Cuban Ministry of Interior in a ministry facility near Havana. According to Feliks, as a result of the meeting, "the role of Cuba as an important transit center for cocaine, severed after the execution of General Ochoa, was reestablished."[14]

The Colombian drug cartels also were active in Mexico. As mentioned, the Colombians depend directly on Mexican organized crime for stockpiling, protecting, and transporting the cocaine. The Mexicans also arrange payoffs to key officials in the Revolutionary Institutional Party (PRI), the attorney general's office, the Mexican State Judicial Police, and other important institutions. However, the Colombians may be attempting to establish their own ties to the Mexican power structure. An article in a Bogotá magazine, *Cambio-16,* claims that Miguel Rodríguez's former accountant, Guillermo Pallomari (now in custody in the United States, under a plea bargain arrangement), told DEA officials that the cartel "gave money to the electoral campaign of Ernesto Zedillo in Mexico, although the latter probably was unaware of this."[15] And, according to University of New Mexico scholar Peter Lupsha, usually reliable sources say that during the spring and summer of 1994, the Cali cartel sent $40 million in two shipments to Mexico to support the Zedillo campaign. They hypothesized that these funds were used to guarantee Cali a "superior, favored and protected position in the new administration."[16] However, the Mexican government vigorously denies these allegations.

REGIONAL BLOCS

The early growth phase of the cocaine industry, roughly from 1980 to 1984, was a period of relative harmony in Colombia's cocaine establishment. *El País* (Cali) reporter Luis Cañon, who wrote a biography of Pablo Escobar, argues that in those years "one grand cartel [existed] comprising all traffickers who held any power."[17] Kingpins who later affiliated themselves with rival power blocs pooled expertise and resources to ship large quantities of drugs and generally to ensure the success of the cocaine enterprise. During 1984—in a tangible example of such cooperation—Cali don Gilberto Rodríguez Orejuela and Medellín drug lord Jorge Luis Ochoa Vásquez jointly undertook to set up a cocaine distribution network in Spain. (Both were arrested in Madrid in November of that year and remained in jail until their extradition to Colombia in mid-1986.) In the early 1980s cooperation also extended to the political realm. The Cali mafia apparently sanctioned the formation of the vigilante group *Muerte a Los Secuestradores* (MAS, or Death to Kidnappers) in Medellín following the April 1981 kidnapping of Jorge Ochoa's sister by the M-19 guerrilla group. MAS announced its existence on December 2, 1981 when a helicopter flying over a soccer match in Cali's Pascual Guerrero Stadium dropped thousands of leaflets with the warning "Kidnappers will be hanged from trees in public parks or simply shot and marked with the symbol of our group."[18]

Yet this political and economic cooperation had begun to fade in the mid-1980s, in part due to market saturation in the United States. Port-of-entry U.S. cocaine prices declined almost 40 percent between January 1982 to January 1985 (see figure 2.1) and more than 70 percent from January 1982 to January 1989. Ruthless competition for external sales took place within Colombia's drug underworld. In a particularly egregious example, Medellín kingpin Pablo Escobar Gaviria and José Gonzalo Rodríguez Gacha took advantage of Gilberto Rodríguez's 1984 to 1986 sojourn in a Spanish prison to penetrate the cocaine market in New York City, traditionally a Cali preserve.[19] Important philosophical differences also divided the Colombian cocaine establishment. Medellín traffickers had personal political ambitions, harbored deep resentments against the Colombian elite and favored the use of violence as a political tool. By contrast, the group of traffickers based in Cali (and more broadly in Valle de Cauca department) preferred to advance their objectives through bribery and manipulation rather than through bullets and car bombs.

Such factors precipitated a major regional split in the cocaine industry. By the mid-1980s, two rival coalitions of criminal organizations centered in the cities of Medellín and Cali (but encompassing broader regional groupings of traffickers) accounted for perhaps 70 to

80 percent of cocaine exports. The remaining 20 to 30 percent lay largely in the hands of quasi-independent trafficking groups based in Pereira, Santander, Bogotá, and the north coast of Colombia. These independents apparently maintained a loose affiliation with the Medellín coalition and accepted Pablo Escobar as their leader and spokesman.

The Medellín and Cali cartels differ along several important dimensions. One concerns the structure of authority. In Medellín a single kingpin—Pablo Escobar—exercised a vast sway over trafficking operations—that is, Escobar's mantle of leadership, his access to the means of violence, and his ruthless domination of smaller exporters held the coalition together and established its identity. The Cali coalition, by contrast, is a relatively loose association of exporters; no single head or heart drives it. A second difference relates to the cartel's political style and impact. Medellín traffickers used their vast fortunes to bankroll political movements and (in the early 1980s) to seek elective office directly, while Cali leaders have stayed out of politics, except for buying politicians or contributing to political campaigns. A third difference concerned the use of the violence to achieve political ends. The Medellín coalition unleashed violence against Colombia state institutions and against Colombia's political elite, and also financed an armed crusade against the revolutionary left. The Cali cartel does not generally use violence as a political tool, although it ruthlessly persecuted nonstate actors who appeared to threaten its interests.

The Medellín Cartel

Escobar's ascendancy within the Medellín cartel has been well documented. While prominent cartel figures such as the Ochoa brothers and Rodríguez Gacha maintained personal trafficking empires, Escobar was by far the largest operator. According to Cañon, at least ten nominally independent organizations in Medellín exported cocaine in the 1980s. "Each had its own pilots, representatives abroad, cocaine packers and shipping routes"; however, "all revolved around Escobar." The trafficker administered some of the organizations directly (via his cousins, Gustavo de Jesús and Luis Hernando Gaviria); others paid Escobar a kind of export tax for the right to traffic in cocaine.[20] Beginning in early 1990 Escobar levied "war taxes" on Medellín cocaine shippers (ranging from $100,000 to $200,000 per organization per month) to finance the cartel's political-military activities. Following his surrender to justice in June 1991, Escobar tried to increase these taxes. Threats of reprisals from Escobar's hired assassins and enforcers ensured broad compliance with the trafficker's financial demands as well as acceptance of his overall leadership of the cartel.

Escobar's relations with the Galeano and Moncada brothers was a case in point. By the early 1990s, the Galeano-Moncada organization had acquired a significant position in the cocaine business, largely by default—because founding fathers of the Medellín cartel were mostly dead or in prison. Yet the Moncadas and Galeanos still were subordinate to Escobar in the Medellín hierarchy. Escobar demanded an increase in their war tax from $200,000 to $1 million per month. Apparently, the brothers agreed in principle to this demand, but Escobar subsequently ordered his associates to steal $20 million in banknotes known to be hidden in the organization's underground cellars. In July 1992 two chieftains of the organization, Fernando Galeano and Kiko Moncada, visited Escobar in La Catedral prison to complain about the heist. Escobar lectured the traffickers about his leadership of the industry, his pioneering role in establishing trafficking routes "so that others could benefit," and his success in demolishing the U.S.-Colombian extradition treaty. (Extradition of Colombian citizens had been banned under Colombia's 1991 constitution; reportedly Escobar had spent vast sums on bribes to members of the Constitutional Assembly to accomplish this objective.) The meeting did not end well. Galeano and Moncada were executed during the visit on Escobar's orders—the former apparently inside La Catedral and the latter in the vicinity of the prison. Later Escobar's assassins tracked down and murdered two other members of the organization—William Moncada and Mario Galeano.[21]

Also noteworthy were the Medellín mafia's forays into politics—an unusual and (some might say) unprofessional pattern of behavior for criminal elites. The early 1980s was a period of intense office-seeking and other overt political activity by drug dealers. Pablo Escobar himself established the political movement *Civismo en Marcha* (Good Citizenship on the March) in Medellín, which became the vehicle for his election to the Colombian Congress in June 1992 as an alternate deputy on the parliamentary list of Jairo Ortega Ramírez. As a politician, Escobar attempted to portray himself as a civic leader and as a protector of the poor. The traffickers sponsored some high-profile civic programs, including the donation of several hundred new housing units to poor slum dwellers and construction of some eighty illuminated sports arenas in Medellín and surrounding communities. Such programs and the populist philosophy underlying terms were publicized in an Escobar family newspaper, *Medellín Cívico,* directed by Escobar's uncle but financed largely by the capo himself. Articles contrasted Escobar's public-spiritedness with the indifference of local businesses and selfishness of the Colombian political establishment. According to a March 1994 article, Escobar's civic campaigns "frightened politicians and bureaucrats who had done nothing for the people." Another *Medellín Cívico* report analyzed the trafficker's accomplishments in the following terms:

> Fifty thousand trees planted in fifty barrios of Medellín . . . schools built with plenty of space, with an eye to beauty and pedagogical function. Broken sewers repaired to protect residents from contaminated water and from epidemics, [sewers that were] a health hazard that the government has ignored for years. Basketball courts, skating rinks, multi-sport arenas . . . thousands of bricks to expand the houses of poor families, to finish buildings, churches, and wings of schools. Illumination of barrios trapped in darkness because of indifferent bureaucrats or politicians who do not keep their promises. . . ."[22]

Another Medellín-affiliated mafioso who attempted to use drug money to launch a career in politics in the early 1980s was Carlos Lehder. Though not one of the cartel's inner circle, Lehder had, as mentioned, pioneered the transportation of cocaine to the United States through the Bahamas in the late 1970s and early 1980s. Lehder used the proceeds of this venture to establish a political party—the *Movimiento Latino Nacional* (MLN)—in his native Quindio in early 1983. The party's ideology combined populist and fascist themes (opposition to "communism, imperialism, neo-colonialism and Zionism")[23]; its aims included nationalization of banks, transport, and the assets of multinationals; an end to "foreign intervention" in Colombian life; the abrogation of the extradition treaty; and the creation of a united Latin American army to safeguard Latin sovereignty, culture, and frontiers. The MLN for a time maintained its own newspaper, *Quindío Libre,* which circulated in major Colombian cities. The party had limited electoral successes—winning approximately 12 percent of the vote in the regional elections in Quindío in March 1984. By 1986, however, the MLN's future had ebbed. Most of its followers had rejoined the traditional political parties or had affiliated themselves with the leftist *Union Patriotica* (Patriotic Union). Lehder himself, although a fugitive from justice, was the MLN candidate for the Colombian Senate from Quindío in the March 1986 congressional elections; he lost overwhelmingly.

For criminal organizations, power does not go hand in hand with electoral success; power is best exercised covertly. Colombia's cocaine capos clearly overreached themselves in their eagerness to handle power directly. The media attention proved devastating, and the traditional political establishment, feeling threatened, mobilized to oppose the newcomers. Government officials and the media called both Escobar and Lehder criminals. Also, Lehder publicly admitted that he had been involved in narcotrafficking, telling Radio Caracol in June 1983, "I myself have participated in the great Colombian bonanza." By late 1983 both traffickers had been forced into hiding. In May 1984 President Belisario Betancur signed an extradition request for Carlos Lehder, and in September the government issued a warrant for Escobar's arrest.[24] In February 1987 Lehder was captured in a police raid near Medellín and extradited to the United States, where he was convicted of smuggling 3 tons of cocaine into the country and sentenced to 135 years in a federal prison.

Such experiences doubtless were a salutary lesson for the traffickers. After 1984 the Medellín mafia mostly removed itself from the front line of politics. (Lehder's 1986 congressional bid was an exception.) Violent political participation became almost the norm until the early 1990s, when the cartel's leadership structure was largely destroyed. Still, the mafia sought a legal political voice. Drug money apparently found a new outlet in a political movement, the so-called *Movimiento de Restauración Nacional* (MORENA), which appeared on the Colombian scene in mid-1989 as the political arm of the rightist paramilitary groups that operated in the Middle Magdalena Valley and which was nominally supported by the local 1,400-member farmers' and cattlemen's association. Although MORENA denied links to drug kingpins, by the late 1980s Medellín traffickers controlled 40 percent of the land in the Middle Magdalena, according to a Colombian military estimate, and also funded most of the paramilitary operations in the region. Inevitably, traffickers contributed substantially to the movement's activities. José Gonzalo Rodríguez Gacha, reportedly the largest single landowner in the area and a long-standing enemy of guerrilla groups, was thought to be MORENA's main sponsor. MORENA aspired eventually to become a national political party to get votes of "all good citizens who opposed subversion." Its more immediate aim was to gain control over the forty-two mayoralty seats in the valley in the 1990 election. However, the movement disintegrated shortly after Rodríguez Gacha's death in December 1989—a coincidence that apparently underscores the movement's close links to its trafficker-patron.[25]

The Medellín cartel's principal hallmark was an addiction to the use of violence for political ends. The violent phase of traffickers' political participation postdated the electoral phase and no doubt partly was driven by traffickers' rage at the collapse of their hopes to achieve power legitimately. Some Colombians who perished at the hands of mafia assassins (for example, Justice Minister Rodrigo Lara Bonilla,

Liberal Party leader Luis Carlos Galán, *El Espectador* director Guillermo Cano) had publicly exposed Escobar's ties to drug trafficking in the early 1980s, thus destroying the trafficker's apparently promising career in politics. However, as the 1980s wore on, violence began to serve more calculated purposes: to influence judicial outcomes, to diminish national support for extradition and other major counternarcotics initiatives, to establish a framework for negotiating a political accord with the government, and to strengthen traffickers' rural power bastions by underwriting campaigns against Marxist insurgent groups and their leftist sympathizers.

One cartel target was Colombia's criminal justice system. The aim, of course, was to render the system ineffective. Judges trying drug trafficking cases in Colombia were offered the proverbial choices of *plomo* or *plata* (lead or silver)—death if they convict, a bribe if they set aside the charges. Not surprisingly, few judges opted to convict. In 1987 and 1988 one criminal court judge released from jail or dropped charges against four major cocaine dealers: Gilberto Rodríguez Orejuela, José Santa Cruz Londoño, Evaristo Porras (a Leticia-based trafficker), and Jorge Luis Ochoa. A mid-level trafficker arrested in Medellín in connection with the murder of Guillermo Cano was released after several days because no judge there was willing to try his case. Policemen and security officers faced the same options—they could serve on the cartel's payroll as informants (and earn handsome monthly salaries), or they could try to make drug busts and arrests and suffer retaliation. Almost 500 policemen and 40 judges were killed during the 1980s and early 1990s. In 1989, 20,000 Colombian judicial employees, 4,300 judges, and 50 magistrates of Bogotá's superior court went on strike to protest the government's failure to furnish them adequate protection against violent drug traffickers.

Trafficker-sponsored violence also targeted members of Colombia's political elite, including high government officials, political party leaders, and other prominent figures. Between 1984 and 1990 an astonishing number of high-profile Colombians—most outspoken opponents of the Medellín mafia—lost their lives to traffickers' assassins. Among the victims were, as mentioned, a minister of justice, the director of the Bogotá daily *El Espectador,* a Supreme Court justice, a leader of the leftist Patriotic Union (UP), a governor of Antioquia, an attorney general, and the leading Liberal Party candidate for president in the 1990 election. Two other slayings—of 1990 presidential candidates respectively from the Patriotic Union and the former M-19 guerrilla group (most of the group had laid down their arms by early 1990)—also have been attributed to the Medellín mafia, though less credibly. These assassinations did much to weaken the government's resolve regarding extradition, prosecution of drug kingpins, and other criminal matters.

Beginning in 1989, the Medellín "Extraditables" (a name adopted by the violent members of the Medellín coalition) escalated their campaign of antistate violence. Responding to a massive government onslaught against the cartel following the murder of Liberal leader Luis Carlos Galan, the mafia declared "absolute and total war" against the government and the Colombian political and economic elite. The emphasis of mafia strategy switched from selective assassination of prominent leaders (although killings continued) to indiscriminate terror attacks against the Colombian state and the society in general. Traffickers relied on weapons favored by terrorist groups—explosives. Some forty car bombs exploded in between 1989 and 1993, leaving 500 people dead, most of them civilians. One bomb that destroyed the facade of the Department of Administrative Security (DAS) headquarters in Bogotá in December 1989 killed 100 people, gravely wounded 250 more, and damaged 1,500 businesses in a radius of 30 blocks. Some bombs also were placed in hotels, political offices, banks, and commercial centers. A bomb aboard an Avianca flight en route from Bogotá to Cali killed 119 passengers. (Urban bombings reportedly caused $50 million in material damages in Bogotá alone between 1989 and 1993.)[26] Beginning in late 1989, the Extraditables employed another terrorist tactic—they took members of the elite as hostages and demanded ransom to finance their "war" against the state. By late 1990, political pressures stemming from the increased human and material costs of the drug war compelled the government to initiate indirect discussions with Medellín cartel leaders and to offer lenient terms for their surrender.

The Medellín mafia's violent behavior was not directed only against the government and the oligarchy but also against the revolutionary left. Traffickers orchestrated a number of attacks against the UP (considered the civilian branch of Colombia's main guerrilla group, the Revolutionary Armed Forces of Colombia, or FARC); some 800 to 900 UP members perished in these episodes. In rural regions, traffickers collaborated with traditional landowners, the military, and other elements of the local power structure to combat predatory guerrilla attacks and infrastructure. (This collaboration is described in chapter 7.) Traffickers were instrumental in financing and equipping armed self-defense groups that became a significant political and military force in some regions; for example, a paramilitary network centered in Puerto Boyacá (in the Middle Magdalena Valley) in the late 1980s had its own fleet of planes, helicopters, launches, jeeps and bulldozers, a printing press, clinic, and training schools, not to mention vast stores of ammunition and automatic and semiautomatic weapons.[27]

The Medellín cartel's cocaine income, which probably reached $5 billion to $6 billion or more by the late 1980s, provided the wherewithal to maintain enormous complements of sophisticated weaponry (AK-47s, Uzis, AR-15 and Galil rifles, and M-16 machine guns), grenades, rocket launchers, and ground-to-ground missiles. It also purchased ground-to-air and air-to-air missiles of French manufacturers from Cuba in 1989 or early 1990, although there is no evidence that the traffickers even deployed them. (Ten such missiles were discovered in an apartment in South Bogotá in February 1990.)[28] In April 1990 Colombians allegedly working for the Medellín cartel tried to buy 120 Stinger antiaircraft missiles and other U.S. military hardware in Florida but were foiled by the Federal Bureau of Investigation (FBI) and Florida police.[29] In the late 1980s, the Medellín mafia ran several training schools for paramilitary operatives—essentially for drug traffickers' private armies—in the Middle Magdalena Valley. Former Israeli Army and British Special Air Services (SAS) personnel were hired as instructors, and courses covered topics such as camouflage, self-defense, weapons, intelligence and counterintelligence, and communications. As of mid-1989, some 11,000 paramilitary commandos operated in Colombia, many, though not all, under the sponsorship of the Medellín cartel. It also supported bands of trained contract assassins, including the groups Los Quesitos and Los Priscos, recruited by Pablo Escobar. Some 3,000 hired killers reportedly worked on the cartel's payroll.[30] Some are unemployed teenagers or preteens from Medellín's poorest neighborhoods; others are former FARC (Fuerzas Armadas Revolucionarias de Colombia), ELN (Ejército de Liberación Nacional), or April 19th Movement (M-19) guerrillas who have deserted or retired from those organizations. According to Colombian police sources, Escobar even contracted with active ELN guerrillas to plant car bombs during 1993, when his own organization's capability to inflict terrorist attacks was waning. Outside specialists were enlisted for specific acts of violence. For example, the 1,100-pound bomb that exploded in front of the Colombian DAS building in Bogotá may have been fabricated by a Spanish terrorist who was a member of the Basque Fatherland and Liberty group.[31]

The Medellín mafia's violent strategy helped accomplish two of its immediate political objectives—the defeat of the U.S.–Colombian extradition treaty (which allowed Colombia to send traffickers to the United States for trial and sentencing) and the initiation of peace negotiations with the Colombian government. (For a discussion of such negotiations see chapter 4.) The shattering violence of the period from 1989 to 1993 also diminished Colombian enthusiasm for repressive law enforcement generally. Due to the problems it had dealing with the Medellín cartel, the government's policy toward the Cali cartel emphasized peaceful dialogue and negotiated surrender.

Yet violence also proved to be the Medellín mafia's undoing. Its war against the state and the deaths of innocent civilians isolated the traffickers politically. A government crackdown kept traffickers on the run and disrupted their business operations. By 1989 Pablo Escobar and Gonzalo Rodríguez Gacha became targets of intense manhunts, and large rewards—ranging from $600,000 for Rodríguez to several million dollars for Escobar—were offered for their capture. In December 1989 Colombian authorities, aided by a Cali cartel informant, tracked down and killed Rodríguez Gacha in Tolu, near the Caribbean port of Covenas. In August 1990 President Cesar Gaviria defined narcoterrorism as the principal threat to Colombian democracy and pronounced that "we will confront it without concessions."[32] The government opted to negotiate with traffickers in 1990 and 1991 and several drug lords, including Escobar, surrendered to justice. Yet following the kingpin's escape from jail in July 1992, the government pursued the trafficker and his associates without mercy. As of early 1993, bounties offered for Escobar included $7 million from Colombian government and an additional $5 million from a group called People Persecuted by Pablo Escobar (PEPES), comprised of Escobar's enemies and rivals in the cocaine business. In the seventeen months from July 1992 to December 1993, the Medellín Search Bloc (a government search team) undertook operations resulting in the killing of 209 "members" of the Medellín cartel, most of them apparently associated with the cartel's military and terrorist networks. An additional 52 drug criminals were captured, and 29 drug leaders turned themselves in under the government's surrender program.[33] All of Escobar's closest associates were either killed or went to jail during this period. In December 1993 the Search Bloc finally caught and killed Escobar himself—effectively delivering the coup de grace against the original Medellín coalition.

The trafficking arrangements that have replaced this dismembered structure are not clear as of this writing. Parts of the old coalition, including remnants of the Moncada-Galeano organization (now led by Rafael Galeano), continued to export cocaine as of 1995, but Medellín's overall market share has diminished drastically—to as little as 10 to 20 percent compared to 70 to 80 percent in the late 1980s. Importantly, the remaining Medellín godfathers have no appetite for

Escobar-type assaults against the Colombian oligarchy or for political adventurism generally. Also, according to numerous reports, the new leaders have set about mending relations with the Cali cartel. Some "organizational crossover from the fractured Medellín group to Cali" may have occurred in the post-Escobar period.[34] (The process of reconciliation began even before Escobar's death, as the foundation of PEPES, which apparently included Escobar's enemies within the Medellín cartel as well as Cali traffickers, makes clear.) The new Medellín leadership may look to Cali for overall strategic guidance; at least "they respect the Rodríguez brothers and listen to their suggestions," as *El País* reporter Luis Cañon observes.[35] In other words, the Medellín traffickers, like those in Cali, are avoiding political conflicts and blending into the traditional power structure.

The Cali Cartel

The trafficking coalition centered in Cali, which dominated Colombian cocaine exports after 1990, differed from its rival in important respects. As noted, effective power in the coalition is dispersed, not centralized. The Cali cartel, a loose confederation of exporting organizations centered in Valle de Cauca department, comprises at least three sizable core organizations in proper—those of the Rodríguez brothers, José Santa Cruz Londoño, and Helmer Herrero Buitrago; it also includes an indeterminate number of smaller organizations and factions in central and northern Valle. (Trafficking centers outside of Cali include the cities of Tulua, Buga, and Palmira in central Valle and Cartago and Roldanillo in northern Valle.) The Cali cartel does have leadership of a sort. Until his June 1995 arrest, Gilberto Rodríguez Orejuela retained what he called a "poder convocatoria" vis-à-vis other Valle traffickers—he served as the cartel's spokesman on matters affecting relations with the Colombian government. (Rodríguez, for example, defined the common position of the Valle group in surrender negotiations with the Colombian government in 1993 to 1994.) Also, Rodríguez reputedly played a pivotal role in arranging political cover and police protection for Cali drug operations. While he has hinted that his power extends to other regions of Colombia, the range of his influence cannot be ascertained.

Very little is known about the internal workings of the cartel's organization, especially about financial decision making, recruitment and promotion practices, and methods of ensuring compliance. Evidently top leaders and their closest associates often are related by family ties (as was the case in the Medellín cartel). Similar to Pablo Escobar in Medellín, the Cali leaders appear to be micromanagers who keep close tabs on their employees. "Every dollar and every kilo must be accounted for and personal contact, phone calls, daily operational supervision and involvement are required," notes researcher Peter Lupsha.[36] Strong incentives exist for good performance. For example, valued employees or contractors receive a share of a cocaine shipment—perhaps five to ten kilos—which translates into bonuses of $50,000 to $100,000 or more when the shipment reaches its international destination. The organization maintains close control over cocaine shipments, requiring overseas distributors to sell only to approved wholesale buyers. To discourage cheating, traffickers representing the organization overseas almost always have immediate family members—parents, sisters, or wives—in Colombia. As Cañon notes, "The Cartel knows exactly who they are, where they live and what they do. If the representative embezzles money or commits some indiscretion, the family in Colombia pays the price immediately. Thus loyalty is guaranteed."[37]

Dominant trafficking organizations within the Cali coalition probably charge smaller ones for insurance or transport services or for the use of smuggling routes. No Escobar-type "war taxes" are levied on members of the Cali coalition, but members probably pay prorated fees to maintain the elaborate system of political-administrative protection that benefits the group. The organizations also cooperate in noneconomic ways—for example, they share information on movements of police and security forces, maintain a common front against rival traffickers, and negotiate collectively with representatives of the Colombian government.

Cali's style of political participation, unlike Medellín's, has been low key. The group clearly does not equate power with electoral success. Cali traffickers have not sought political office directly or funded controversial political movements. (However, Cali campaign contributions flow to congressional and presidential candidates and generally grease the wheels of the system.) Also, unlike the Medellín traffickers, the Cali dons do not fund-high profile community projects—such as the Barrio Pablo Escobar in Medellín—to build a power base among the urban and rural poor. Cali's narcowelfare contributions, such as they are, probably are made in the name of legal businesses controlled by traffickers and flow through large, well-established networks of charitable organizations. A modern clinic in the city of Tulua in Central Valle, the Centro Diagnostico del Occidente, reportedly was financed by drug money. However, the clinic is a profit center requiring payment for its services, and its connection to drug dealers is not advertised. In general, Cali's protection strategy has relied on establishing good relations with the power elite, not in cultivating a following among the poor. The Cali leaders' failure to buy protection "from below"—to build a basis of effective political support—probably has increased their vulnerability to capture; at least it has lowered the political costs to the Colombian government of persecuting and arresting them.

Furthermore, the Cali cartel is not closely associated with the programmatic anticommunism of some Medellín leaders. While Cali leaders have contributed to self-defense forces in insecure rural areas and at least one paramilitary massacre in northern Valle was attributed to a Cali trafficker, a former associate of Gonzalo Rodríguez Gacha, they were less involved in organized counterinsurgency activities and in the "dirty war" against the Colombian left than was the Medellín cartel. In general, members of the Cali cartel, like most of the world's professional criminals, prefer to avoid taking political stands, to cultivate good relations with the nation's power brokers, and to concentrate on maximizing legal and illegal profits.

The issue of violent political participation also divided the Medellín and Cali cartels. Generally, the Cali coalition does not participate in or endorse acts of violence against high-level government functionaries or against the Colombian establishment. Colombian author María Duzan in *Death Beat* recounts a story in which a Cali drug dealer sent to jail decided to threaten the judge who indicted him. When Gilberto Rodríguez Orejuela found out about the threat, he sent a message to the trafficker saying that "we don't kill judges or ministers, we buy them."[38] The string of high-profile political assassinations orchestrated by the Medellín cartel in the 1980s antagonized the Cali leaders. According to Cali's Gilberto Rodríguez, Medellín-sponsored violence was the principal factor precipitating the open conflict that erupted between the cartels in the late 1980s; however, competition for cocaine sales in the United States—especially in the lucrative New York City market—also contributed to the conflict, which by the end of 1988 left approximately 500 people dead in Medellín, Cali, New York, and Miami and destroyed some 50 drugstores and 10 radio stations belonging to the Rodríguez brothers. With the escalation of hostilities between the government and the Medellín cartel in late 1989, Rodríguez converted his organization into "the principal source of information to the [Colombian] security agencies"—in effect, allying with the government to fight a common narcoterrorism threat.

Though politically nonviolent (at least until 1995), the Cali cartel—like other organized crime associations—targeted groups and individuals considered a threat to business operations. Traffickers associated with the Medellín cartel, for example, were murdered during the "war of the cartels" in the late 1980s. One important victim was Rafael Cardona Salazar, who oversaw Escobar's cocaine distribution operations in the United States; he was gunned down in December 1987. The cartel made at least two attempts on Escobar's life. One came in the form of a car bomb detonated in front of one of the trafficker's residences—an apartment building in Monaco—in January 1989. Also in 1989 the Cali cartel contracted with British mercenaries Dave Tomkins and Peter MacAleese to mount a helicopter raid to kill Escobar at his estate, Napoles, in the Middle Magdalena Valley. (The operation, in June 1989, failed when one of the helicopters crashed into a mountain in eastern Antioquia.)

The Cali cartel also participated in other violent episodes. During the 1980s, for example, Cali traffickers and other members of the local bourgeoisie backed vigilante organizations operating in Valle de Cauca and Risaralda—so-called *grupos de limpieza social* (social cleansing groups)—that targeted marginal urban dwellers such as vagrants, thieves, beggars, prostitutes, and drug addicts. The bodies of such unfortunate "expendables" were discovered in Cali bearing signs reading "*Cali limpia, Cali linda*" ("Cali clean, Cali beautiful"). In many cases, victims were dumped into the Cauca River, which by the early 1990s became known as the River of Death. (The municipal administration of Marsella, in Risaralda, apparently went bankrupt due to the cost of fishing bodies out of the river, performing autopsies, and burying the victims.) While the social cleansing groups were similar to the paramilitaries in the Middle Magdalena Valley and northern Antioquia— both were supported by a coalition of elites that included traffickers— the *limpieza* groups lacked a clear political agenda and did not target specifically guerrilla fighters and their civilian counterparts.[39]

The Cali cartel's relations with the extreme left were not cordial. In 1992 the Revolutionary Armed Forces of Colombia (FARC) kidnapped Christina Santa Cruz, the daughter of José Santa Cruz Londoño, and held her for $10 million ransom. (Recall that José Ochoa's sister was kidnapped by a leftist group, the M-19, in late 1981.) Cali traffickers retaliated by seizing at least twenty hostages, including several members of the Colombian Communist Party, the United Workers' Trade Union, and the Patriotic Union, as well as the sister of guerrilla leader Pablo Catatumbo, who had represented the Simon Bolivar Coordinating Group (the directorate for Colombia's active guerrilla organizations) in peace talks with the government. Intermediaries negotiated the release of Christina Santa Cruz and Catatumbo's sister, but the fate of the other hostages has not been reported.[40] Furthermore, although Cali traffickers were not self-described crusaders against communism, they clearly were capable of employing violence against leftist sympa-thizers. Consider, for example, the case of Henry Loaiza Ceballos, a Cali-affiliated trafficker who had once worked for Gonzalo Rodríguez Gacha in Putumayo. Loaiza was accused of involvement in killings by right-wing paramilitary groups in the Central Valle town of Trujillo in 1990. The massacre was especially grisly: 107 suspected unionists and guerrilla supporters were rounded up, tortured, and killed. The bod-ies were dismembered with chain saws and dumped into the River of Death as a warning to other pro-guerrilla elements.[41]

In addition, a number of murders of policemen and low-level judicial employees in Cali during the 1990s have been attributed to the Cali traffickers. Such incidents, however, are not typical of Cali's style of operations. In a bizarre pattern detected in the 1990s, several construction workers who had built and outfitted Cali leaders' urban residences were murdered possibly to prevent their leaking informa-tion regarding the location of secret passageways and hiding places. A similar concern for secrecy may have prompted the elimination of several employees of communication companies who tapped tele-phones and set up surveillance and countersurveillance systems for drug dealers. The murders, according to El Tiempo were "part of a macabre plan to silence people with knowledge affecting the security of their communications."[42]

Despite all this, however, violence and intimidation played a relatively small role in Cali's political strategy, at least to mid—or late 1995. The Cali group sought to advance its objectives principally through bribes, economic penetration, and legal manipulation. While the Medellín cartel also sought to buy political influence and immunity from prosecution, its offers of money frequently were accompanied by a death threat. While violence may have diminished with the as-cendancy of the Cali cartel, corruption of political and administrative life in Colombia appears to have reached new heights.

The cartel's influence on the Colombian economy also is perva-sive. Cali enterprises span many economic sectors: banking, commu-nications, construction, urban transport, light industry, agribusiness, and retailing. Some 30 to 40 percent of the building construction in Cali is said to be financed by Cali drug money. The cartel maintains extensive real estate and business holdings outside of Cali, for ex-ample, in or near the Pacific coastal port of Buenaventura and on the island of San Andres. (Cali traffickers own at least fifteen hotels, as well as several casinos and boat rental sites in San Andres; in Buenaventura they have invested in shipping and construction enter-prises and have established a large supermarket.) March 1995 police investigations uncovered complex configurations of holding companies used by Gilberto and Miguel Rodríguez Orejuela, José Santa Cruz Londoño, and Helmer Herrera to disguise their ownership of dozens of interrelated businesses, investment corporations, and pharmaceutical companies.[43]

Furthermore, the Cali group has lobbied hard on the legal front. Cali lawyers participated in the drafting of law 81 of November 1993 (discussed in more detail in chapter 4), which offers discretionary benefits—such as two-thirds reductions in sentences and the possibility of house arrest or social service in place of jail—to traffickers who collaborate with justice. Such "collaboration," moreover, does not require traffickers to incriminate themselves. The cartel reputedly contributed 90 million pesos ($100,000) to congressmen in 1994 to vote for modifications of the Colombian penal code that would largely eliminate penalties for illegal enrichment and for third-party representation of traffickers and also do away with a system of anonymous ("faceless") judges established under President Cesar Gaviria.[44] Guided by Valle Senator Gustavo Espinosa (now under arrest) the proposed "narcobill" sailed through the Senate but was killed at the last minute in the Chamber of Representatives. (Another narcobill introduced in late 1995 would have eliminated illegal enrichment as an "autonomous" crime—requiring that a guilty verdict be contingent on prior conviction of the criminal delivering the bribe. This provision,which would have frozen corruption investigations pending judgments against the Cali leaders also passed the Senate and was defeated in the lower house.) In December 1994 a lawyer, Guillermo Velez Calle, who reportedly serves as a regular defense attorney for drug dealers, petitioned the Colombia Supreme Court to void provisions of the Colombian penal code that allowing the use of evidence obtained abroad in Colombian criminal cases. Such a change would be devastating; Colombian prosecutors have relied extensively on evidence derived from law enforcement operations in the United States (including testimony of witnesses, wiretaps of traffickers' conversations, and seized records of cocaine distribution cells) to convict major kingpins. Proofs supplied by the United States have served to convict approximately twenty important traffickers, including the three Ochoa brothers and Gonzalo Mejia Sanin, a marketing agent for the Medellín cartel. The meager proofs possessed by the Colombian government, on the other hand, seldom permit convictions for serious drug offenses.

The Cali group's assimilationist strategy has made it a difficult target for a Colombian government and public that are weary of antidrug campaigns and decreasingly tolerant of the costs of repression.

Still, the group is not invulnerable. (As discussed earlier, one point of vulnerability is the cartel's inability to command wide popular support.) In 1995 the government mounted a major crackdown on Cali, sending a special squad of 6,000 soldiers to raid mansions owned by the drug lords, increasing rewards for capture of top leaders, and seizing Cali-owned properties, businesses, and financial records. The campaign was designed in part to assuage U.S. opinion—specifically those critics in the Clinton administration and in Congress who believe that the Samper administration is soft on drugs. On June 9, 1995, members of the squad captured Gilberto Rodríguez in one of his homes in northern Cali. Three other Cali leaders, Henry Loaiza, Victor Patiño, and Phanor Arizabaleta, surrendered to justice in June and July. In early July still another Cali kingpin, José Santa Cruz Londoño, was arrested while dining in a Bogotá restaurant. Finally, Colombian authorities captured Miguel Rodríguez in a raid on a Cali apartment in August. Rodríguez was the sixth major Cali kingpin to end up behind bars in two months. Still, U.S. State Department officials believe that the Cali kingpins continue to manage their criminal empires from prison.

While Colombian leaders may have finally recognized that the Cali cartel represents a threat to national institutions, until 1995 their preference was to negotiate with the Cali kingpins rather than to prosecute them (a point discussed in chapter 4). Whether Colombian courts will confer appropriately long sentences on those leaders in custody remains to be seen. (Santa Cruz, however, escaped from a Bogotá jail in January 1996 with the aid of corrupt officials.) The spreading corruption in Colombia suggests that the threat from Cali is more insidious than was that from Medellín's overtly violent drug lords. Yet the prosecutor-general Alfonso Valdivieso explained, "The corruption of the Cali cartel is worse than the terrorism of the Medellín cartel. . . . Terrorism can be fought and faced; corruption has no face."[45] In March 1996, the United States decided to impose aid sanctions on Colombia, partly on the ground that Colombian judicial and law enforcement systems are "significantly undercut by the corrosive impact of drug-related corruption."[46] A critical challenge facing Colombia is the destruction of the political, bureaucratic, and judicial influence that Cali traffickers have established to protect themselves and their operations.

3

The International Dimension:

Colombians, Italians, and the European Market[1]

Narcotics industries rank among the world's most successful illegal enterprises, generating annual resources of roughly $150 billion to $300 billion. Major production and trafficking complexes in the Andes, Southwest Asia, and the Golden Triangle of Southeast Asia thrive, apparently impervious to international enforcement efforts. Furthermore, with the end of the Cold War, the disintegration of hostile power blocs, and the emergence of global trading and financial systems, significant changes are occurring in the makeup and dynamics of international narcotics markets. As University of Pittsburgh scholar Phil Williams notes, such developments "have fundamentally changed the context in which criminal organizations operate and encouraged what had been predominantly domestic groups to develop into transnational criminal organizations."[2]

Criminal organizations are not simply developing tentacles abroad. A particularly alarming tendency in the global narcotics market is the development of strategic cooperation among criminal empires that deal in illicit drugs. This chapter focuses on one subset of the trend toward international narco-cooperation: the apparently expanding ties between Colombian trafficking coalitions and Italian criminal enterprises. Such ties are motivated by three principal factors: rapid development of the European market, market entry strategies, and logistics of handling the cash generated. The market for cocaine in Europe apparently has developed rapidly. Comparative seizure statistics (admittedly not a perfect indicator of market dynamics) suggest that cocaine demand in Europe is exploding, while demand in the United States is increasing more slowly or even stagnating. Between 1989 and 1994 cocaine seizures increased 320 percent in Europe while rising only 32 percent in the United States. Between 1992 and 1994 cocaine seizures almost doubled in Europe but actually declined in the United States. (See table 3.1.) In 1994 approximately 1 ton of cocaine was seized in Europe for every 3 to 4.4 tons seized in the United States. In 1989 the ratio was 1:14. Relatively high cocaine wholesale prices in Europe (two to three times the U.S. level) suggest that the proportion of European sales could grow in future years. Western Europe probably offers the best sales potential, but former East bloc countries also offer opportunities. For example, Russian criminal networks increasingly are peddling Western hard drugs to Russian consumers. Cocaine is now the drug of choice for the wealthy mafia elite in Russia. Indeed, the Russian market is very attractive from a seller's perspective: Cocaine prices in Russia's major cities in 1994 ranged from $200 to $300 per gram compared to a mere $30 to $90 per gram in New York.

A second consideration—a vital one from the Colombian perspective—concerns market entry strategies: The traffickers face the challenge of introducing large volumes of cocaine to European distributors while minimizing the risk of seizures, losses, and arrests. Colombian traffickers maintain extensive networks of contacts in Spain and (to a lesser extent, Portugal), which provide facilities—import-export fronts, warehouses, and stash houses—to receive and store cocaine shipments; however, Colombians generally have been less successful in establishing secure networks outside the Iberian peninsula. "Basically, Colombians don't feel comfortable operating in Western and Central Europe," notes Greg Passic, a DEA official specializing in international money laundering.[3] Colombians, furthermore, are relatively conspicuous; arrest statistics—some 300 to 400 Colombian nationals have been arrested every year in Europe in the 1990s—suggest that they are fairly easy targets for European law enforcement authorities. From the Colombian perspective, therefore, a strategic partnership with

Italian crime groups—which are better attuned than the cartels to local conditions and problems—might make eminent business sense.
The trade-off is that the Colombians part with their cocaine at very
low prices. A 1994 seizure in Turin in northern Italy of 5.5 tons of Cali
cocaine, much of it destined for distribution outside of Italy (specifically in Germany, Switzerland and Liechtenstein), may signal the beginning of this type of collaboration.[4] Participating criminal organizations
on the Italian side, the Sicilian Cosa Nostra and the 'Ndrangheta, a
criminal syndicate based in Calabria, paid the Colombians a mere
$10,500 per kilo for the cocaine, one-third or less the average Euro-
pean wholesale price for the drug.[5]

TABLE 3.1
COCAINE SEIZURES IN EUROPE AND THE UNITED STATES, **1989** TO **1994**
(IN KILOGRAMS)

Year	Europe (Calendar Year)	United States (Fiscal Year)
1989	7,109	99,407
1990	14,307	107,346
1991	14,747	111,733
1992	15,523	137,556
1993	17,178	110,701
1994	29,890	130,967

Sources: Interpol and Federal-Wide Drug Seizures System.

A third factor derives from the logistics of handling magnitudes
of cash generated by cocaine sales. Available evidence from court
cases, wiretaps, informants, and other sources suggests that the Colombians have experienced difficulties in collecting the proceeds from
these sales. Revelations from the 1992 "Green Ice" operation in Italy
indicate that the mechanisms for "recycling" money are cumbersome,
typically involving bulk cash transfer of small-denomination lire notes
through long chains of intermediaries. Payment cycles are extremely
long; in the case of a large shipment of cocaine to Sicily in 1987-1988,
the Colombian suppliers were not fully compensated for two years.
(This case is discussed later.) Emissaries from the five to six families that comprise the Cali cartel have sought direct assistance from
the Sicilian Cosa Nostra—the most powerful organized crime group
in Italy (and probably in Europe)—both in transporting cocaine
earnings back to South America and in laundering these earnings
through investments in Europe.

The actual state of cooperation between Colombian cocaine organizations and Italian organized crime groups is extremely complex.
The term "cooperation" itself comprises a multiplicity of relationships
that can be examined along several dimensions. One dimension concerns the partners or actors in the relationship—that is, which Colombian groups are cooperating with which Italian groups. Available data
suggest that Colombians have established ties with the four main Italian criminal groups, with local mobsters in central and northern Italy
who may or may not be tied to these groups, and with various Italian
crime families living abroad. A second dimension concerns the kinds
of transaction or exchanges in which these groups are engaged-sales
and shipping arrangements, distribution of cocaine in Europe, swaps
of cocaine for heroin, money laundering channels and methods, and
exchanges of favors involving acts of violence. A third dimension relates to the level or intensity of cooperation; here a distinction can be
made between simple buyer-seller transactions and business ties that
involve advanced planning, long-term arrangements, and the creation
of a dedicated infrastructure.

The subject of Italian-Colombian criminal cooperation (and of
international criminal cooperation generally) requires careful analysis.
A number of journalists, law enforcement officers and academics in
Italy and the United States have advanced the proposition that the
Sicilian Cosa Nostra and Colombian trafficking groups have formed an
"alliance" to distribute cocaine in Europe and to launder the proceeds
of drug sales. To be sure, the Colombians (especially the Cali families)
and the Sicilians have discussed business arrangements that would
rationalize the cocaine market in Italy and perhaps in Central Europe;
also, as noted, the two sides may be experimenting with franchise
arrangements. Cooperation, however, still falls short of a full-fledged
alliance. The Colombian organizations currently ship large quantities
of cocaine to Europe and Russia without relying on the Sicilian connection. Even in Italy Colombians and Sicilians have not established
an exclusive business relationship: Colombians rely on a variety of
different Italian networks to distribute cocaine and to launder money
there, and Colombians themselves are involved in the upper levels of
cocaine distribution in Rome and several northern Italian cities.

Furthermore, while economic forces and law enforcement trends
favor emergence of transnational business ties among criminal groups,
obstacles to such arrangements exist. Different groups have different
national roots, organizational cultures, recruiting practices, and no-
tions of what constitutes honor in a business relationship. Also,

conflicts can arise when one group invades the other's turf or when agreed-on terms of payment for merchandise are not met. The presence of Colombian distributors and even entire distribution cells in northern Italy is one possible source of tension between the Colombians and Italian organized crime groups. Another is the Colombians' continuing difficulties in getting their cocaine earnings out of Italy—problems exploited brilliantly by DEA and Italian police operatives in the 1992 "Green Ice" operation. (Green Ice was a DEA-coordinated undercover sting operation in 1990 to 1992 aimed at the financial workings of Colombia's drug cartel.) Yet it can be the argued that a stable, long-term cocaine venture between the main Colombian cocaine organizations and the Cosa Nostra would largely remove these irritants—in other words, that the net results of such an agreement would be fewer Colombian traffickers in Italy (and in Europe) and more efficient money-laundering and recycling mechanisms.

Taking these factors into consideration, the prospects that sustained cooperation or a full partnership between Colombian trafficking coalitions and the Sicilian mafia will develop in this decade seem fairly good. The two sides have established contact and have drawn up the basic outlines of their future relationships. Certainly, law enforcement officials and decision makers in the United States and Europe must be alert to the possibility of the "alliance" scenario and to its implications for international stability. As the late Palermo chief prosecutor Giovanni Falcone remarked at a meeting in Rome shortly before his assassination in 1992, "Direct contacts between Colombian drug dealers and the Sicilian mafia have already begun. These contacts are extremely dangerous because of the risk of solidified business linkages between criminal organizations of great economic power and enormous operational potential."[6]

This chapter examines the scope, dynamics, and implications of collaboration between Colombian and Italian organized crime groups, focusing especially on the Colombian-Sicilian relationship. First, we focus on two instances that illustrate the nature and dynamics of their interactions: one involved the shipment of almost 600 kilograms of cocaine from the Caribbean island of Aruba to Castellamare del Golfo in Sicily in 1987-1988; the other involved a 526-kilogram shipment from Ecuador to Livorno, Italy, in mid-1992. Second, we analyze different dimensions and levels of interaction between Italian and Colombian criminal formations. Finally, a concluding section assesses the significance of Sicilian-Colombian collaboration for the development of cocaine trafficking and other types of criminal enterprises in Europe.

CASE STUDIES OF ITALIAN-COLOMBIAN CRIMINAL COLLABORATION

The Sicilian Connection

Italian-Colombian criminal collaboration comprises a disordered patchwork of actors and commercial relationships. Colombian traffickers sell cocaine to a broad variety of Italian crime groups both inside and outside Italy. Also, no single Colombian group monopolizes the Italian cocaine market. However, the Medellín and Cali trafficking cartels and their subsidiaries have been the dominant suppliers of cocaine to Italy and other European countries (and Cali's share has increased dramatically relative to Medellín's in recent years). Furthermore, Colombian-Sicilian interactions have been the most extensive, the best documented, and—from a strategic perspective—possibly the most significant of the Colombian-Italian criminal connections. For example, the three largest cocaine shipments recorded in Italy to date were negotiated partly or entirely between Colombians and Sicilian trafficking organizations; these included a 596-kilogram load delivered from Aruba to Sicily in early 1988, a 526-kilogram shipment sent from Ecuador to the northern Italian port of Livorno in 1992, and a gigantic cargo of 5.5 tons shipped from Cartegena to Turin via the port of Genoa in January-February 1994. (Unfortunately, few details are available on the latter episode; hence, only the earlier shipments are considered here.) The potential effects of sustained business collaboration between the Colombian organizations and the Sicilian Cosa Nostra are vast and disturbing; these could translate into massive increases in cocaine sales in Europe, improved security for trafficking operations (measured in fewer seizures and arrests), and increased criminal penetration of economic and political structures in several European or Eurasian countries.

This section examines the dynamics and implications of the Colombian-Sicilian relationship, focusing specifically on the *Big John* and the *Cinta* deals, named after the ships involved in the smuggling operations. *Big John* and *Cinta* are case studies of the problems, pitfalls, and possibilities inherent in international criminal cooperation; hence, aspects of these cases are worth recounting in detail.

Big John

The *Big John* case represented the Sicilian mafia's first major foray into the European cocaine market. Police investigations and court records both indicate that the impetus and financial backing for this enterprise came from several families in Palermo Province (from Palermo itself and from the small nearby town of Corleone). Operational leadership was provided by the Madonia family from the Resuttana district in Palermo. Curiously, planning and negotiations for the consignment took place mostly in the United States, not in Italy or Colombia. One key link was a Miami-based Sicilian mafioso (a member of the Sicilian, not the American, Cosa Nostra) named John Galatolo, who, together with Sicilian colleagues from New York and Philadelphia, ran cocaine distribution networks along the U.S. East Coast. Galatolo was specifically entrusted by the Madonia family to prepare the consignment. The other link consisted of two Colombians, Waldo Aponte and Angel Leon Sanchez, who supplied Galatolo's cocaine operation and who maintained direct or indirect contacts with trafficking organizations in Barranquilla and Medellín. Following protracted discussions in Miami and New York, Galatolo, Aponte, and Sanchez finalized terms of the shipment on the Caribbean island of Aruba in October 1987. The *Big John* departed from Aruba with the cocaine in December 1987 (presumably the drugs had been shipped there from Colombia earlier), and the cargo was transferred to a fishing trawler off the coast of Castellamare del Golfo in eastern Sicily in January 1988.[7]

Although the shipping arrangements proceeded more or less according to plan, the *Big John* venture was hardly a model of successful criminal collaboration: In Aruba, the Colombian and Sicilians had negotiated a price of $21,000 per kilo for the consignment with payment to be completed within ninety days. The payment terms were not met, basically because no effective mechanism existed for handling and transferring bulk quantities of lire notes—the proceeds of cocaine sales in Italy. Colombian and Sicilian representatives met several times during 1988 in various locations—Miami, Rome, and Milan—to try to resolve the payment delays. Eventually a system for transferring cash from Italy to Colombian accounts in Switzerland and the United States did emerge from these discussions, but the procedures were circuitous and cumbersome. (Money-laundering channels are discussed later.) Indeed, the Colombians were not paid in full until February 1990, more than two years after the cocaine was delivered.[8]

Repatriation mechanisms had not improved significantly in Italy as of late 1992. Money still moved through long chains of intermediaries; payment cycles were lengthy, and payment itself was often a hit-or-miss proposition. As Alessandro Pansa, a top Italian police official, told reporters in September 1992, "Colombians have no difficulty at all getting cocaine to Italy but they have more difficulty getting back the money they make from it."[9] This situation effectively diminished the

Colombian traffickers' ability to exploit the lucrative Italian market (cocaine use in Italy is the highest in Europe in per capita terms); hence, the Colombians have gone to some lengths to rationalize their financial relations with Italian organized crime groups. Repatriation continues to be a choke point in Colombian cocaine operations in Italy, although representatives of Colombian trafficking groups are actively seeking ways to streamline the process.[10]

Cinta

The second important documented case of Colombian-Sicilian cooperation involved the transportation of 526 kilograms of cocaine hidden in a container of frozen fish (or shrimp) from Ecuador to the northern Italian port of Livorno. The shipment, carried aboard the Ecuadorean freighter *Cinta,* arrived in June 1992. The architect of the *Cinta* deal was a middle-ranking Sicilian hoodlum named Massimo Quadra, who had set up a seafood business in Ecuador as a cover for his cocaine operations and also had invested in an Ecuadorean airline—Saeta—that flew a regular route between Guayaquil, Ecuador, and the United States.[11]

Quadra acted as a middleman between several Cali trafficking organizations and major buyers in Sicily and in Rome. Most of the cocaine was destined for Sicily—indeed, the consignment was addressed to Brancagel, a frozen fish company in Palermo, in which Quadra was a partner. The Sicilian principals included the Cangemi family, based in Partinico in eastern Sicily, and possibly one or more Corleonesi families (families based in the town of Corleone). The powerful boss of the Corleonesi, the notorious Salvatore ("Toto") Riina, may have had a hand in the transaction.[12] The most important figures in the Roman group of buyers were Gaetano Sideri and his wife, Antonella Porcacchio. The Sideris were already linked to the Cali cartel through Antonella's brother, Giancarlo, who lived in Colombia, was married to a Cali native, and—possibly through his wife—had cultivated a successful association with Cali trafficking organizations. While reports suggest that in the *Cinta* transaction, the Sideris were fronting for a more significant trafficking group, the Calabrian 'Ndrangheta, this relationship has not been clearly established.[13]

The *Cinta* deal ran into problems from the start. The vessel was detained by Italian Customs in Livorno because the fish contained impermissibly high levels of mercury. Eventually the traffickers managed to salvage their investment. Massimo Quadra wrote a letter to the port authorities offering to send the contaminated fish to Bosnia as a humanitarian donation. After an ichthyologist appeared on the scene to certify that the fish was fit for human (if not Italian!) consumption and some payoffs apparently were made to Customs officials, the containers of fish were loaded onto trucks ostensibly bound for Trieste (at the border of the former Yugoslavia). However, first the trucks made a detour to Rome, where Quadra's associates extracted the cocaine, resealed the containers, and sent the load of fish—by now possibly rotten as well as contaminated—onward to Trieste. We can only wonder whether the Bosnians ever received the fish, or, if so, whether they enjoyed their repast.[14]

Difficulties with the *Cinta* shipment and more general concerns about the progress of Colombian cocaine operations in Italy prompted the Cali drug lords to take an unprecedented and risky step. While the *Cinta* was languishing in port, the Cali organizations sent three emissaries to Italy. One was Orlando Cediel Ospina-Vargas, alias Tony Duran, a trafficker from Colombia's Caribbean coast and a specialist in cocaine transport systems. Another was Pedro Villaquiran, an employee of the Grajales family (one of the five principal groups comprising the Cali cartel). A third was Bettein "Bettina" Martens, a Belgian or Dutch financial wizard whose general portfolio included manipulating and laundering the proceeds of Cali cocaine sales in Europe. Their immediate task was to secure the release of the *Cinta*'s cargo from the Livorno Customs authorities. The Colombians' Cosa Nostra partners were frantic—they had threatened to mount a commando-type raid on the port to retrieve the cocaine. However, Ospina-Vargas argued for a more manipulative approach; indeed, the actual rescue operation—the payoffs, the transport subterfuge, and the humanitarian gesture to the Bosnians—appear to have been largely his idea.[15]

After solving the *Cinta* problem, the Cali representatives turned to more important structural problems. The Cali group was anxious to expedite the payment cycle for the *Cinta* shipment and to establish a more coherent framework for their cocaine operations in Italy generally. Existing arrangements within Italy depended on a chaotic demimonde of financial operators, front companies, and assorted petty crooks. Ultimately, the system depended on Colombian couriers— who would arrive in Italy (usually in a northern Italian city such as Milan), pick up suitcases of small-denomination bills, and carry the money across the Italian frontier, typically to Switzerland and Austria. From there the money would be wire-transferred or sent by courier to cartel bank accounts in the United States, Brazil, Venezuela, and Colombia.[16] A further item on the Cali agenda concerned the importation of cocaine into Italy and Europe. The Colombians wanted the Italians to establish a network of legitimate container companies and import-export forms in Italy that could handle large-volume shipments. The network, to be extended to other European countries, would comprise storage facilities and commercial channels for the cover products (such as fruits, vegetables, or fish) that accompanied the drugs. In the past, the Colombians had lost huge loads of cocaine when they had to dump legal merchandise for which there were no buyers. In a notorious incident in Amsterdam in late 1991, Colombian traffickers extracted a three-ton cocaine shipment from containers of passion fruit juice, then dumped the juice in the city's canals. The Amsterdam police, alerted by the sudden change in color of water from muddy gray to bright orange, tracked the spill to the source and impounded the cocaine. As Ospina-Vargas told Massimo Quadra in a conversation wiretapped by police in Rome in September 1992, "We need a company that operates credibly in the market. . . . if it sells fish, it must really sell fish."[17]

Agents of Italy's Servizio Centrale Operativo and the DEA carefully monitored the visits of the Cali emissaries; at the time they were investigating money-laundering activities as part of a two-year multinational investigation known as Green Ice. The DEA and the Italians hit on an ingenious plan—to create an entire controlled mechanism for recycling cocaine money from Italy to the United States (to DEA front companies in San Diego) and from there to Cali bank accounts in Colombia. Undercover agents presented the scheme to Bettina Martens, who had been charged with the task of recycling part of the proceeds from the *Cinta* shipment. To Martens, who had told undercover agents that she "had no idea how to get the money back to Colombia," the offer seemed an answer to a prayer. Between July and September 1992, Martens made eight cash deliveries totaling about $4 million in lire bills—most of the money collected from the Sideri group—to a storefront set up by Italian police "money launderers." The Green Ice deception was so sophisticated that some of the money apparently did circulate through the DEA's pipeline, at least as far as San Diego.[18]

Ospina-Vargas's main mission was to discuss grand strategy with the Sicilians—to restructure fundamentally the Cali-Cosa Nostra business relationship. In meetings with Massimo Quadra in Rome and with one of Quadra's principals, Antonio Cangemi, in Palermo, Ospina-Vargas outlined the Cali cartel's strategic vision: The Sicilians would set up the legal fronts to import and distribute Cali-supplied cocaine in Italy and Europe; the Sicilians would invest the Colombians' earnings in legal businesses in Europe or use the (envisioned) network of transportation companies to transfer the money back to South America.

His hosts appeared to be receptive to these schemes,[19] and a new era in Colombian-Sicilian cooperation appeared to be dawning. Yet in late September 1992, police closed the trap, arresting Ospina-Vargas, Villaquiran, and Martens in Rome and Massimo Quadra in Palermo. A criminal conspiracy of major proportions had been thwarted, at least temporarily.

However, counterstrategies by the cartels can be expected. According to a DEA informant, the five principal Cali families have decided to set up a jointly funded counterintelligence unit, staffed by "outside" financial experts and former police operatives, to absorb the lessons of Green Ice and to forestall future penetration of their financial networks. In other words, the Green Ice debacle, though a setback to the Cali cartel, seems likely to spur further efforts by the Cali drug lords to rationalize their cocaine trading and money-laundering operations in Europe.[20]

Other Relationships: Non-Sicilian Organized Crime; The Sicilian Diaspora

As noted earlier, the Sicilian mafia made a strategic decision in the mid- or late 1980s to acquire a significant position in the European cocaine market. At the time, the Sicilian sought an unchallenged monopoly on the importation of cocaine into Italy. Under this scheme Colombians would sell only to Sicilian buyers. During the *Big John* negotiation, for example, John Galatolo warned the Colombian representatives, Waldo Aponte and Angel Leon Sanchez, that "if you guys are making a commitment to supply the Sicilian mafia with cocaine . . . make sure that there are no small couriers, Colombian couriers, coming to Italy." If the Colombians did send couriers, said Galatolo: "We would have to kill them and we are not going to be responsible for those actions."[21]

The Sicilians did not succeed in obtaining this monopoly. Today, as mentioned, Colombian cocaine suppliers deal directly with a multitude of Italian buyers and distributors. For example, the Colombians maintain extensive ties with the three principal non-Sicilian organized crime groups: the Calabrian 'Ndrangheta, the Neopolitan Camorra, and a relatively new group, the Sacra Corona Unita (SCU), based in the southeastern region of Apulia. (The organized crime centers of Calabria, Campania/Naples, Apulia, and Sicily rank among the most impoverished and least industrialized regions in Italy.) The Colombian ties with the Camorra are better established than those with the other two groups, largely because the Camorra boasts a fairly extensive trafficking network in central and northern Italy (mainly in Lombardy, Liguria, and Lazio); also, crime families with Camorra ties operate in a number of European and South American countries. Yet in the early 1990s the 'Ndrangheta maintained "a permanent representative in Colombia, protected by the Medellín cartel"; also, 'Ndrangheta-affiliated families have been identified in some Italian cities (Milan, Turin, and Florence) and in Argentina.[22] The SCU's operations in Italy are relatively localized; however, an important SCU trafficker with ties to both the Medellín and Pereira cocaine organizations was arrested in Riseralda Department in Colombia in March 1993. Oddly enough, certain Camorra and 'Ndrangheta representatives also are members of the Cosa Nostra. Indeed, according to Alison Jamieson, a longtime observer of the Italian criminal scene, "Some of the leading bosses of the 'Ndrangheta have now actually entered the highest level of Cosa Nostra, the Commission." Such intermingling may suggest a tendency toward the development of a single Italian criminal cartel—one in which the powerful Sicilian mafia would have the dominant voice.[23]

Beyond the major Italian criminal formations, there exists a second tier of criminals with whom the Colombians have established more or less regular commercial relationships. As Alessandro Pansa observed, commenting on Italian-Colombian criminal relationships, "Not all criminal activity takes place within the confines of major organizations belonging to defined criminal groups."[24] The Sideris and their associates in Rome fall into this category. This secondary tier of criminals interacts in various ways with the major syndicates, but the operators usually are not dedicated to one particular group—indeed, the larger operators (such as the Sideri group) may buy and distribute cocaine in their own right. The Colombians themselves are not particularly choosy about their business partners: The activities of "Carlo," a DEA undercover agent in Rome who, between December 1988 and May 1992, negotiated five separate "buys" of cocaine totaling 154 kilograms from two different Medellín suppliers epitomizes the disorganization of the Italian cocaine market. "If the Colombians are cooperating just with organized crime groups, why use me?" "Carlo" asked.[25]

The emigration of southern Italian and Sicilian crime families to Western Europe, North America, and various South American countries provided new outposts for criminal activities, as many of these families are involved in trafficking or money laundering. (Most of this movement occurred in the 1960s and 1970s or during the "mafia war" in Sicily in the early 1980s.) Since the mid-1980s, the trafficking networks of the South American families have been especially significant in facilitating exports

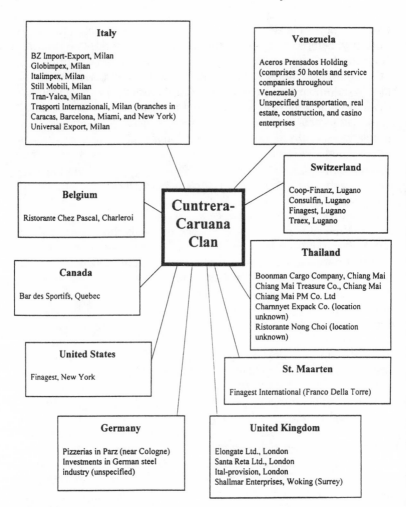

FIGURE 3.1

CUNTRERA-CARUANA BUSINESS EMPIRE

Sources: Personal Communication with Maria de Calabro, correspondent for *Corriera de la Sera;* Claire Sterling, *Octopus, the Long Reach of the Sicilian Mafia. New York: W.W. Norton, 1990.*

of Colombia's cocaine to Europe and Italy. These families provide transport covers and routes for narcotics shipments; they are involved only peripherally, if at all, in the business of cocaine or heroin refining. Overseas families act quasi-independently of "parent" organizations in Italy and Sicily (whether they are direct representatives of the Cosa Nostra,

Camorra, or 'Ndrangheta is a matter of interpretation); however, occasionally they act as intermediaries between the Colombians (or other South American suppliers) and parent groups in the homeland.

Prominent examples of the Italian-Sicilian diaspora include the Fidanzati and Mollica-Morabito families in Argentina, the Ciulla family in Chile, the Ammaturo group in Peru, and the Cuntrera-Caruana clan in Venezuela. (The Mollica-Morabitos and the Ammaturos are linked respectively to 'Ndrangheta and Camorra organizations; the others have Cosa Nostra ties.) The Cuntreras, the most important of these families, emigrated from Agrigento Province in Sicily to Venezuela in the 1970s and are linked by marriage to another Agrigento family, the Caruanas; in effect, the families comprise a single clan. The Cuntreras act as brokers in negotiations between Colombian and Italian crime syndicates; furthermore, clan-controlled transportation companies ship large quantities of cocaine to Europe and North America. In addition, the Cuntreras have been accused of trading illegally in chemicals used in cocaine and heroin refining. Yet the clan is best known as the "apex of the administrative-accounting phase" of the international drug trade—that is, it manages money derived from its own and (probably) other criminal organizations' narcotics businesses. The Cuntreras boast a global empire of legitimate businesses (see figure 3.1), which offers a wealth of opportunities for recycling and legitimizing illegally earned income. Over the years, the Cuntrera-Caruana clan has amassed invaluable technical and business expertise as well as a fortune estimated at $3 billion. Although three leading members of the clan, Paolo, Gaspare, and Pasquale Cuntrera, were extradited from Venezuela to Italy in 1994, the clans' companies, bank accounts, and money-laundering networks remain in place; demolishing this enormous criminal empire promises to be a lengthy and difficult undertaking for law enforcement agencies in a number of countries.[26]

FORMS AND LEVELS OF COOPERATION

Italian and Colombian trafficking groups cooperate in a variety of ways, particularly in sales arrangements, distribution of cocaine in Italy, exchanges of cocaine for heroin, recycling and laundering of narcotics earnings, and (less well documented) mutual assistance in acts of violence. Furthermore, different levels of cooperation can be identified, ranging from simple buyer-seller relationships to complex arrangements that involve long-range planning and possibly "umbrella" agreements covering several transactions.

Sales arrangements require negotiations over such matters as price and payment schedules, shipping methods and routes, delivery schedules, and methods of concealment. (The latter are extremely varied; for example, cocaine may be hidden as legal produce, in the walls or support beams of containers, or in the transport vehicles themselves.) In general, such arrangements reflect a "market entry" strategy for the Colombians. For example, Colombians generally provide the transport and concealment of large shipments of 50 kilograms or more. (Massimo Quadra's *Cinta* venture, in which he was left to ship 526 kilograms on his own, was an exception and, of course, the cover used—mercury-contaminated fish—nearly torpedoed the enterprise.) More important, Colombians have been willing to accept (or to live with) extremely liberal payment terms from their Italian partners; for example, in the *Big John* and *Cinta* cases, the Colombians asked for no downpayments on the transactions, even though the shipments involved were very large. In addition, the negotiated prices for the loads seemed low—respectively $22,000 and $21,000 per kilogram—well below the prevailing European wholesale price for cocaine of $50,000 and up.[27]

Distribution of cocaine in Italy is another important—and potentially sensitive—area of collaboration. According to Italy's Servizio Centrale Operativo, Colombians have managed to penetrate upper levels of cocaine distribution in at least some Italian cities, including the major port cities of Genoa, LaSpezia, Livorno, and Salerno and important political or industrial centers such as Milan, Bergamo, and Rome. To do so, it is almost certain that the Colombians have made ad hoc financial arrangements with local crime bosses, possibly paying them a percentage of each kilogram sold. Colombians also have established or helped to establish several cocaine hydrochloride refineries in Italy. One such laboratory was discovered in Filaccione near Rome in 1993, and another—a huge operation—in Savona Province in Liguria in northern Italy was shut down by Italian authorities in 1989. (The Savona laboratory reportedly was a cooperative venture of Colombian, Calabrian, and Sicilian traffickers; the police arrested 150 people and seized 200 kilograms of cocaine in the bust.)[28]

The presence of Colombian distributors in Italy raises a number of interesting questions. As Italian police frequently point out, not a single Colombian dealer has yet been killed in Italy; hence, whatever arrangements the Colombians have made with local mobsters appear to be relatively amicable.[29] Some observers argue that the major organized crime groups have approved or at least condoned these agreements. The fact that the Colombian presence is concentrated mostly in central or northern Italy—i.e. outside the home bases of the major syndicates—may be working to reduce conflict. Also, the Colombians are still playing a relatively minor role in trafficking within Italy. There is no firm evidence that they are stockpiling cocaine or setting up distribution cells to handle large-volume transactions. The temptation to do so is, of course, considerable—Colombians can realize much larger per-kilogram profits selling cocaine to mid-level distributors in Italy than they can selling to importers. Yet by expanding their distribution networks in Italy, the Colombians incur larger risks, including the risk of detection by the authorities and the risk of reprisals from Italian organized crime groups.

Exchanges of cocaine for heroin represent another dimension, though a relatively minor one, of Italian narco-cooperation. By and large, such exchanges appear financially insignificant: So far cocaine-for-heroin swaps have occurred only sporadically and involve very small quantities of drugs. For example, U.S. intelligence sources report that Italian-Colombian couriers occasionally bring 2- to 3-kilogram lots of heroin to Colombia to exchange for cocaine; however, as a U.S. narcotics expert in Bogotá puts it, "there is nothing worth opening a case on."[30] Major cocaine deals, such as the *Big John* and *Cinta* ventures, were purely cash transactions. While Sicilian traffickers probably have raised the issue of drug-for-drug exchanges in negotiation with their Colombian partners, so far the Colombians seem to have preferred to accept long payment delays to being paid in narcotics. According to a witness in hearings on the *Big John* case, "when the entire load of cocaine reached Sicily, [John Galatolo] wanted to take part of it, trade it for heroin, bring it back to the United States and spread it through pizza parlors."[31]

To be sure, Galatolo and his colleagues had arranged a few cocaine-for-heroin deals between the United States and Italy in the mid-1980s. According to *Big John* witnesses, the Sicilians bought cocaine from Colombian suppliers in the United States, transported the drugs to Sicily, and exchanged them at a rate of 3 kilograms of cocaine for 1 kilogram of "low-grade" heroin.[32] These, however, were small-scale transactions—essentially cases of petty entrepreneurship by Galatolo and his colleagues; they hardly reflected a conscious strategy on the part of either the Sicilian Cosa Nostra or the Colombian cartels.

Furthermore, drug-for-drug exchanges seem likely to diminish with time for two reasons. First, Colombia's domestic heroin industry is growing rapidly. Today Colombia ranks as the world's fifth largest cultivator of opium poppy, with 6,000 to 7,000 hectares reportedly under cultivation in 1995. Colombian police seizures of heroin and morphine have risen from none in 1991 to 50 kilograms in 1992 to 419 kilograms in 1995.[33] Colombian entrepreneurs are rapidly upgrading the quality of domestically produced heroin, hiring Southwest Asian chemists for this purpose and even mobilizing university students and chemistry professors to run laboratories.[34] Second, by all indications, the Sicilian Cosa Nostra is beginning to withdraw from the world heroin market, concentrating more on its traditional businesses such as extortion, contraband, and padding of government contracts.[35] Even within Italy, foreigners—Turks, Nigerians, and Chinese have taken over the business of importing and distributing cocaine and other drugs. Abroad, the Sicilians are clearly winding down their operations. While in the mid-1980s the Sicilian mafia was bringing 3, 4 or even 5 tons of heroin per year into the United States, after 1988 this traffic dwindled to almost nothing, according to DEA officials. (As of 1993, the Sicilian connection probably accounted for 5 percent or less of the U.S. heroin market.)[36] Today cocaine distribution in Europe and related money-laundering activities represent the principal focus of the Cosa Nostra narcotics business—and the principal raison d'être of the Sicilian-Colombian criminal connection.

Money laundering is an increasingly important area of Colombian-Italian criminal collaboration. As noted earlier, the laundering process sometimes has been slow and laborious. One reason is the Cosa Nostra's evident unwillingness to rely on interbank transfers of funds within Italy. "We have found no banking traces of Cosa Nostra activities since the early 1980s," noted a Palermo prosecutor in a 1993 interview.[37] The *Big John* venture is a classic case study of cocaine money management, Italian-style. Figure 3.2 shows the steps in the process. Bulk cash (lire) proceeds of cocaine sales were loaded into TIR (international highway transport) trucks belonging to the Madonia family in Palermo, packed with oranges, lemons, tomatoes, and other produce. The trucks were driven from Palermo to Milan, over circuitous routes to avoid possible police searches and roadblocks. Vincenzo Galatolo, John Galatolo's cousin from the Acquasanta district of Palermo, personally drove some of the shipments. The trucks were unpacked in the local vegetable market in Milan and the cash was transferred to an independent financial consultant, Giuseppe Lottusi, who, according to testimonies in the Big John case, had extensive previous connections to the Medellín cartel.

From Milan, Lottusi transported the money by car or taxi across the Italian-Swiss frontier to a financial company, FI. Mo., in Chiasso.

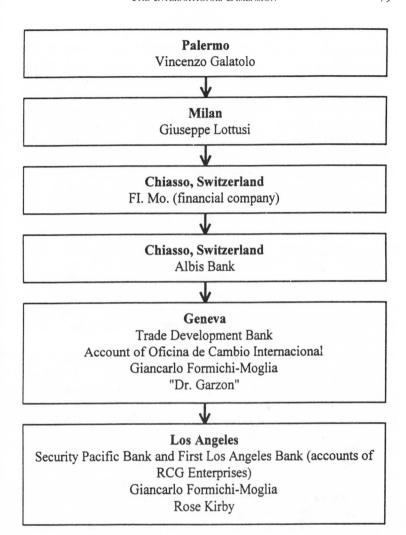

FIGURE 3.2

MONEY LAUNDERING NETWORK IN THE BIG JOHN CASE.

Sources: Servizio Centrale Operativo, Italy; Request from Haly Pursuanb to the Treaty between the United States and the Italian republic in Criminal Matters in the Matter of Aponte et al., Hearings, U.S. Disctrict Court, Washington, D.C., July 16, 1992 through July 27, 1992, pp. 131-144; Attorney's Office at the Law Court of Palermo, Request to Extradition to Italy of Giancarlo Formichi-Moglia N48865/91 N.C., pp. 6-8.

FI. Mo. then delivered the money to the Albis Bank there, which converted the lire notes into U.S. currency. The cash then was placed in boxes and sent via the Swiss postal system to the Trade Development Bank (TDB) in Geneva, where it was deposited to the account of a company called Officina de Cambio Internacional, controlled by Giancarlo Formichi-Moglia, a close associate of Lottusi's. According to Lottusi's instructions to TDB, one "Dr. Garzon," reputedly an important Colombian contributor to the *Big John* shipment, should have access to the funds. After Geneva, the money trail becomes harder to follow. Italian police investigators believe that some of the funds were transferred by wire or by courier to another Formichi-Moglia enterprise—RCG Enterprises—in Los Angeles. RCG, purportedly in the gold jewelry business, was a money conduit: The company would make up fake invoices for nonexistent jewelry purchases to export money to traffickers' bank accounts in Colombia and elsewhere. Yet RCG—the target of a DEA "Polar Cap" investigation—went out of business in late 1988 after the principals, Formichi-Moglia and his partner, Rose Kirby, fled to Australia.[38]

Since the *Big John* deal, the process of recycling cocaine income has come to depend on a chaotic assortment of commercial fronts and financial companies, operating in concert with corrupt bank officials and various self-employed money traders. Figures 3.3 and 3.4 depict elements of this system uncovered during the Green Ice investigation. Most of the actors operated independently or quasi-independently of the main Italian organized crime groups. Their actual financial manipulations are obscure; as in the *Big John* case, the money typically was transported out of Italy in bulk cash form. The main difference is that the final pickups—the last link in the money chain in Italy—commonly were handled by Colombian couriers, most of them direct emissaries of Colombia's principal trafficking coalitions.[39] An exception to this pattern was the case of Vera Romagnoli—an eighty-year-old retired schoolteacher from Mantova who handled criminal funds for the Camorras and possibly for other Italian organized crime groups. Romagnoli wire-transferred narcolire received in her accounts from Sirio Construction, a Camorra-controlled company in Naples, to Rotary Corporation, a New York company, controlled by her nephew, Sebastiano Sampietri. From New York the money was sent to a Rotary branch in Sao Paolo, Brazil, and from there to a jewelry company, Ourobras, identified as a business front for cocaine trafficking interests.[40]

Most of the drug-related financial transactions identified in the *Big John* and Green Ice cases involved movements of cash out of Italy

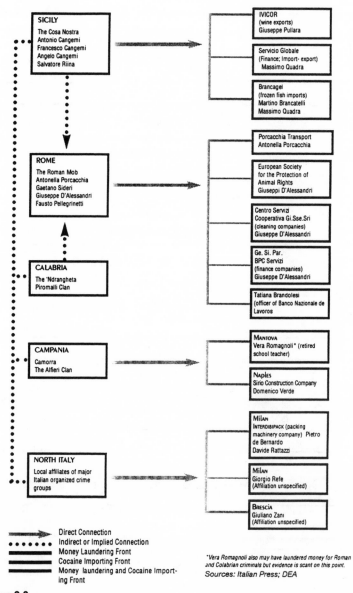

FIGURE 3.3

COCAINE IMPORTING AND MONEY LAUNDERING FRONTS IN ITALY UNCOVERED IN OPERATION GREEN ICE, SEPTEMBER 1992.
Sources: Italian Press; DEA.

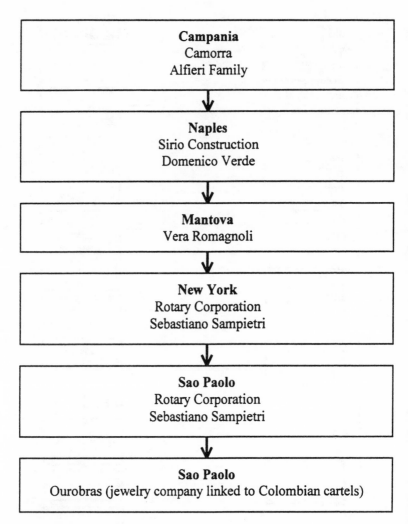

FIGURE 3.4
CAMORRA MONEY LAUNDERING NETWORK.
Source: Italian press articles.

to accounts in Europe, the United States or South America, where the funds would be accessible to Colombian trafficking organizations. This was money laundering in its most primitive form. However, Italian police investigators did detect one unusual pattern of financial cooperation: Colombian organizations apparently were transporting narcodollars from the United States to Italy (especially to financial centers in North Italy) and commissioning Italian money managers to convert the dollars to lire. The lire were then recycled in the same fashion as cocaine proceeds in Italy. The main purpose of this complicated transaction was to avoid a tax of 15 percent imposed by the Colombian government in the exchange of dollars to pesos. (One such currency operator was Giuliano Zani, who is identified in the bottommost frame of figure 3.3.) Still, little hard evidence has been uncovered of cooperation at higher levels of laundering—of "integration" as opposed to "layering" of narcotics funds. Speculation abounds, however, that the Cuntrera empire served as a vehicle for moving Colombian (as well as Italian) drug money into legitimate businesses. Furthermore, Italian police investigators believe that Colombians and Sicilians have discussed broader money-laundering ventures inEurope, ventures that might include purchases of real estate and banking and commercial enterprises in Central and Eastern Europe. Another laundering option would be to convert narcodollars or narcolire to rubles, buy commodities (such as strategic metals or oil) in Russia, and resell these commodities in the West at enormous profits. No proof yet exists, however, that the Cosa Nostra and the cartels are actually engaged in such ventures.[41]

A final area of possible criminal cooperation concerns exchanges of favors outside the sphere of narcotics trafficking. Of specific interest here is whether the Colombian and Sicilian (or other Italian) groups have established pacts of violence—mutual assistance arrangements to abet each others' terrorist agendas. For example, in mid-1992 Italian officials were speculating about a possible Colombian connection in the slaying of Palermo chief magistrate Giovanni Falcone. Top Italian officials such as Italy's "drug czar" Pietro Soggiu and Falcone's (and Paolo Borsellino's) successor, Giancarlo Casselli, now discount this possibility. The assassinations "possibly represented an adaptation of Colombian methods but were carried out by locals," Casselli said in an interview.[42]

Yet pacts of violence are a distinct possibility. Medellín traffickers, for example, may have relied on Sicilian (or other Italian organized crime) assistance in one important violent action—the near assassination of Enrico Parejo Gonzales, former Colombian justice minister and then ambassador to Hungary, in early 1987. Information on the affair is sketchy but the sequence of events, provided by a Colombian intelligence source, appear to be roughly as follows. In planning this operation, Medellín kingpin Pablo Escobar telephoned an Italian criminal acquaintance in New York who in turn contacted an organized crime group in Italy. (The group was not identified.) Essentially, Escobar wanted the Italians to provide cover for the Medellín cartel's assassin in Europe. When the assassin arrived in Italy, the Italians furnished him with a weapon and false documentation and actually drove him directly to Budapest to carry out the attempted hit. (Parejo was shot several times but survived and recovered.) What the Italians expected from the Colombians in return for this favor is not clear. While the Parejo affair may not presage a pattern of violent cooperation, the alleged events are a chilling commentary on the workings of international criminal organizations.[43]

Different levels as well as different forms of cooperation characterize Colombian-Italian criminal ties. At the lowest level are simple buyer-seller deals involving relatively small investments, little advance planning, and relatively little interaction between the parties. Larger, more complex transactions such as *Big John* or *Cinta* represent a higher level of cooperation: Planning for the *Big John* venture, for example, took more than two years. Completing the shipments (in the *Cinta* case) and working out payment arrangements (in both cases) required extensive cross-national communication, including a number of face-to-face meetings between the Italian and Colombian representatives. Possibly a third level of collaboration might include "umbrella" agreements covering price and payment terms for several drug shipments within a specified time frame or establishing mechanisms and terms of reference for recycling cocaine income. According to the representative of Italy's Servizio Centrale Operativo in Bogotá, such agreements now exist; they tend to last one or two years in the case of cocaine shipments and longer in the case of money-laundering arrangements.[44]

At the highest level is what might be called strategic cooperation, which encompasses the principles of long-term agreements, large-volume shipments of both drugs and money, and the creation of specialized infrastructure to facilitate these flows. Clearly, both the Colombians and the Sicilians would like to move in this direction, as evidenced by information from Italian police and DEA wiretaps of Ospina-Vargas conversations in Rome. As noted earlier, Sicilian container companies and import-export cover firms in Italy (and later elsewhere in Europe) would receive both cocaine shipments and the associated legal "cover" products. The same containers that transported the cocaine to Europe would be used to transport bulk cash proceeds back to South America. DEA officials believe that such arrangements would be expensive for the Colombians, as they could forfeit to the Italians a hefty percentage of their cocaine up front and also pay a substantial money-laundering fee (currently around 25 percent in Italy). While suffering a cut in profits, however, the Colombians would benefit from streamlined and relatively secure transport arrangements and from an accelerated repatriation of profits.[45]

Moreover, a strategic agreement with the Sicilians also could provide the Colombians with access to new investment opportunities and outlets in Europe. Ospina-Vargas discussed this with Massimo Quadra in Rome, albeit in very general terms. Some Italian investigators believe that the principal target areas for money-laundering cooperation are likely to be the former East Germany, Eastern Europe, and the former Soviet Union. The Sicilians could funnel narcodollars or narcolire through Eastern European banks, form business partnerships with the Colombians in the East, or use the Colombians' drug money to speculate in Russian ruble or commodity markets. Sicilian and Italian-American mafiosi are collaborating businesswise in the former Soviet Union (both groups reportedly hold interests in the South Russian International Bank in Yekaterinburg, for example); there is no reason why the Sicilians and Colombians could not do likewise.[46]

At the present time, though, Colombian-Italian criminal ties remain disorganized and chaotic. Their ties are fraught with irritations and potential conflicts of purpose. One such problem mentioned repeatedly concerns the laboriously slow payment cycles for cocaine transactions. While the cartels have resorted to sending their own agent to Italy to expedite payment, in so doing they run considerable risk. A second problem, at least potentially, is the presence of Colombian distributors in Italy; the more intrusive their presence, the greater the potential for conflict with local criminal groups or even with the major syndicates. A third problem concerns what the Colombians must perceive as a terribly risky and uncertain business environment in Italy. As mentioned, an undercover DEA agent attached to the U.S. Embassy in Rome was able to make successive cocaine deals with Medellín traffickers and the DEA and the Italian police successfully interposed a false link in the chain of money-laundering intermediaries in Italy. Equivalent successes would be far more difficult for the Colombians to manage-the cartels maintain better security on their turf than the Italian syndicates do on theirs.

Yet a more "strategic" level of Colombian-Sicilian cooperation might address these problems, especially if combined with expanded Cosa Nostra control over the importation of cocaine into Italy. The proposed transportation networks discussed in the text could expedite transfers of funds to the Colombians. Franchise arrangements to distribute cocaine in Western Europe may likely be under way, as the large Turin cocaine shipment suggests. A strategic alliance with the Sicilians could encourage (or force) the Colombians to withdraw most of their distributors and money couriers from Italy and to reduce their presence in other Western European countries. Finally, once the Sicilians control cocaine imports, they might be more willing and more able to provide adequate security for drug and money transactions. Such factors and prospects seem likely to produce more intensive and (possibly) more successful Colombian-Sicilian cooperation over the long term.

What can be done to disrupt the emerging strategic relationship between Colombia and Sicilian organizations? This relationship may contain vulnerabilities that can be exploited by police and intelligence agencies. As Phil Williams at the University of Pittsburgh explains, criminal cooperation "depends on mutual confidence regarding the ally's reliability rather than on formal agreements and legal contracts; hence the potential for creating suspicion and soaring discord is very considerable." A counteralliance strategy might seek to undermine this framework of trust, to "make it look as if one of the organization involved is betraying its partner for short-term gain."[47] For example, a carefully contrived series of incidents—cocaine shipments that go astray, cargo containers that are mislabeled, cocaine that arrives at its destination diluted or spoiled, cash deliveries that consistently add up short, money-laundering schemes that mysteriously go sour, and law enforcement successes that suggest a pattern of duplicity by the other partner—could introduce uncertainty and conflict into the partnership. (Indeed, problems in the relationship can arise from losses resulting from a single major seizure, such as that in Turin.) Of course, specific approaches must be configured to fit specific market frameworks and political and geographical circumstances. Yet more forceful measures against global criminal schemes are necessary. The prospect that criminal empires can pool their resources, rationalize markets for drugs and other dangerous substances, and even make common cause against governments presents a qualitatively new kind of threat to the international system—a threat that the U.S. and other Western governments can no longer afford to ignore.

NEW FRONTIERS: EASTERN EUROPE
AND THE FORMER SOVIET UNION

In addition to the Sicilian connection, the Cali cartel has established ties with trafficking groups in Eastern Europe and Russia. As mentioned, the cartel views former East bloc countries as a logistical "back door" to Western Europe and to a lesser extent as a future consumer market for cocaine. (As noted, cocaine is already beginning to catch on in Russia's major cities.) Two examples of Cali drug deals in the East can be cited. In September and October of 1991, Czechoslovak and Polish authorities impounded two 100-kilogram loads of cocaine hidden in bean shipments. The cocaine was destined for a Czechoslovak-Colombian agricultural import company based in Prague, for further transshipment to the Netherlands. A Colombian national and, interestingly, two former intelligence officers from Czechoslovak security forces jointly owned the shipping company—perhaps a harbinger of organized crime's future in the East.[48] In February 1993 Russian police and customs seized almost 1.1 tons of Cali cocaine in Vyborg, just across the border from Finland. That shipment had a remarkable history. It was shipped in a cargo container to Göteberg, Sweden, then offloaded onto a different vessel and transported to Kotka, Finland; from there it was moved by truck to the Russian frontier. The eventual destination of the cocaine was the Netherlands. (See figure 3.5.) The deal had attracted wide international collaboration—the principal actors included Cali traffickers, an Israeli national residing in Bogotá, Russian mafia figures, expatriate Russians in Belgium and the Netherlands, and an Israeli trafficking group in the latter country.

To date, no single criminal enterprise in Eastern Europe and the former Soviet Union has developed a scope and reach comparable to that of the Cali cartel or the Sicilian Cosa Nostra. Yet ominous changes may be occurring in the makeup of Russian drug syndicates. Consider, for example, a claim by the earlier-cited Feliks research firm that in the fall of 1991 several former KGB officers established a so-called Moscow narcotics group, centered in Moscow but comprising representatives in Afghanistan, Laos, London, and the Cayman Islands. (As mentioned, Feliks is itself composed of KGB veterans.) The Afghan and Laos affiliates were responsible for procuring drugs, principally opium and morphine. The London and Caribbean branches had two functions: to arrange delivery of narcotics to foreign criminal organizations (Colombian, Italian, Mexican, and others) and to invest the proceeds of narcotics sales in legal businesses. In other words, the Moscow narcotics group possessed the rudiments of an international

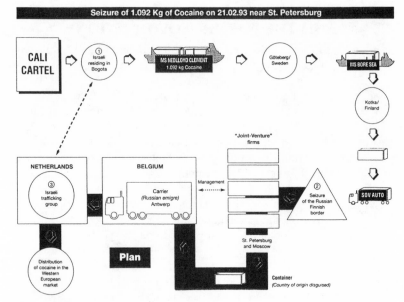

FIGURE 3.5
SEIZURE OF 1,092 KG OF COCAINE ON 21/02/93 NEAR ST. PETERSBURG.
SOURCE: BUNDESKRIMINALAMT.

trafficking and money-laundering structure.[49] The Feliks report makes no mention of a partnership or alliance between the Moscow narcotics group and other international trafficking organizations; yet the possibility of coordinated arrangements to distribute drugs, recycle drug money, or share criminal expertise obviously cannot be ruled out.

CONCLUSIONS

Undoubtedly more, not less, transnational collaboration will occur among criminal groups. The increasing integration of the global economy compels legal and illegal businesses alike to exploit new business opportunities abroad. As the dynamics of modern criminal operations emphasize increasing economies of scale to minimize smuggling risks and recycle bulk cash proceeds, they therefore encourage criminal groups to form partnerships with their foreign counterparts. Of course, the overall effect is to increase the wealth and strategic reach of South America's cocaine syndicates and other transnational criminal groups. Western Europe, Eastern Europe, and the former Soviet Union have become new targets of opportunity for the Cali cartel. While the market for cocaine in the United States stagnates, the cartel's working relationships with crime groups in Europe and Asia have provided access to millions of new consumers as well as a multitude of new opportunities to invest and launder the proceeds of drug sales.

A related point is that transnational criminal alliances are essentially fungible—they can be used to transport virtually any commodity. Western societies today are afflicted by an astonishing array of illegal outflows emanating from Communist or former Communist states: These include heroin and other hard drugs; heavy weapons such as tanks, fighter aircraft, and submarines; nuclear materials; counterfeit money; human body parts; illegal aliens; prostitutes; and professional hitmen. Moreover, a considerable number of the tens of thousands of mainland Chinese who enter the United States illegally each year do so via Mexico—a phenomenon rooted in a complex alliance between Mexican smugglers (specialists in moving people and goods across America's southwestern border) and Asian Communist and non-Communist criminal organizations. This alliance could be configured to move heroin, weapons, or any other illegal commodity. Indeed, drug trafficking routes created "by agreement" among transnational criminal entities can be harnessed to more lethal purposes, such as transporting teams of contract assassins across international boundaries or smuggling missiles, chemical weapons, plutonium, and atomic mines and warheads to terrorist nations and groups. In sum, transnational crime networks established to move drugs conceivably could have serious consequences for Western security and stability.

4

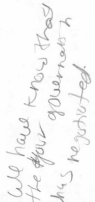

We have known that the four government has negotiated.

Colombia's Drug Negotiations

The Colombian government has negotiated periodically with the leaders of trafficking syndicates since mid-1984. Since September 1990, a legal structure has been in place that encourages traffickers to surrender and collaborate with the authorities in return for judicial leniency. From Colombia's perspective, the principal aims of such negotiations have been to reduce the incidence of societal violence (especially violence against state institutions) and to diminish the importance of the drug trade in Colombia. The traffickers, on the other hand, have sought to obtain amnesty or reduced jail time and the opportunity for reintegration into Colombian society. In an unusual situation, the government has had to negotiate with criminal figures who are not in custody and who command trafficking empires that have enormous political and economic influence. This chapter evaluates the history and societal impact of these dealings and their accomplishments and failures.

CONCEPTUAL ISSUES

Andean governments today confront powerful narcotics lobbies and populations weary of the cocaine war and consequently have opted to negotiate with participants in the trafficking chain. Drug negotiations have become an integral part of the political process in Andean countries. This trend is particularly obvious in the upstream phase of the cocaine industry, where governments have no real means of compelling 250,000 or 300,000 coca-farming families to eradicate their illicit crops. However, much to Washington's discomfort, governments also negotiate with drug kingpins, the refiners and exporters of cocaine. In Colombia, negotiations with traffickers have occurred as an extension of a peace process originally targeted at the nation's various guerrilla groups. Colombia's negotiations with Medellín cartel leaders date to May 1984, when former president Alfonso Lopez Michelsen and attorney general Carlos Jiménez Gómez held separate meetings with Pablo Escobar Gaviria and other kingpins in Panama. Since 1990 Colombia has offered sentence reduction and other legal inducements to traffickers who submit to justice, confess, and turn state's evidence. Colombian officials such as Gustavo de Grieff regarded negotiated surrenders as an alternative to traditional law enforcement. "I believe strongly in the surrender policy and consider that repression has failed," de Grieff admitted in a January 1994 interview with *Semana* magazine.[1] In Bolivia, the Paz government also sought to entice traffickers to surrender in return for legal benefits under a repentance decree issued in 1991, but the policy ended later that year when the decree expired.

The cocaine industry has amassed substantial economic, political, and military clout in the Andean countries—sometimes challenging government authority, sometimes performing quasi-governmental functions in regions where state authority is weak or nonexistent. However, the drug lords are not serious contenders for power nationally, and they exercise power in part by default in rural areas, because the government's political and military authority is weak or absent. In such areas, traffickers perceive leftist guerrillas, not the government, as the main enemy. In that respect, the traffickers' political concerns are indistinguishable from those of local landowners, businessmen, politicians, and military commanders. They all want to combat and destroy the guerrillas' political and military infrastructure. (Admittedly, trafficker-financed paramilitarism became fused with demands for regional autonomy in the Middle Magdalena region.) Traffickers *qua* traffickers do not have much of a political agenda. Colombia's nearly ten-year dialogue with the Medellín and Cali drug lords essentially has focused on matters of judicial and criminal procedures: extradition (the primary issue to mid-1991), penalties for drug trafficking and terrorist crimes, alleged violations of traffickers' human rights, and terms of imprisonment for drug traffickers. Of course, the vindictive campaign of the Medellín Extraditables against the state and the ruling elite from 1989 to 1991 produced destabilizing complications for Colombian democracy. Yet the traffickers' principal aim in unleashing violence—aside from manifesting generalized hostility toward the oligarchy—was to establish a favorable environment for negotiating with the Colombian government. The traffickers wanted the same treatment as that accorded to the M-19 and other insurgent groups, including amnesty and a judicial pardon. Indeed, they even imitated guerrilla terrorist practices in order to qualify as political criminals and win their freedom.

The idea of negotiations with drug dealers as a tool of social policy acquired broad official and public support in Colombia in the late 1980s. The Gaviria administration's peace initiatives vis-à-vis traffickers in 1990-1991 (to be discussed in detail later) produced important results: the incarceration of Medellín Extraditables and an overall reduction in drug-sponsored violence. Later, government leaders viewed negotiated surrenders of Cali leaders as insurance against a renewal of the narcoterrorist bombings, kidnappings, and executions that plagued Colombia in earlier years. "In no way will we allow the nation again to fall into episodes of war," declared defense minister Fernando Botero in a speech defending the surrender policy in September 1994.[2] Yet Colombia's narcodialogues never successfully addressed the vital questions of dismantling the trafficking coalitions' infrastructure and reducing production and exports of Colombian cocaine. Negotiations with the Cali cartel, in progress since early 1993, have proved abortive and even embarrassing for the government.

The Gaviria administration's chief negotiator, prosecutor-general Gustavo de Grieff, held multiple meetings with lawyers for the Cali dons (and conferred three times with traffickers themselves) in 1993 and 1994. The discussions focused largely on Cali traffickers' surrender terms and on their proposals to shut down networks for shipping drugs abroad. However, no coherent plan or timetable for accomplishing this goal emerged. Indeed, de Grieff seemed inclined to grant leniency to drug dealers without pressing them to reveal their business secrets. Moreover, he was a strong proponent of legalizing drugs "to break the economic backbone" of drug traffickers, as he wrote in an April 1994 letter to U.S. Senator John Kerry, a stance that undermined his credibility as a negotiator and as a prosecutor.[3] Critics charge, with some justification, that Colombia's drug negotiations progressively undermined the moral basis of the Colombian state, made a mockery of its justice system, and aggravated tensions between the Colombian government and the United States. Nevertheless, the idea of a peaceful negotiated solution to the drug traffic (an idea obviously subject to different interpretations) retains political currency in Colombia and continues to guide the government's drug control strategy.

A COMPARATIVE NOTE:
NEGOTIATIONS WITH GUERRILLAS

Colombia's policies toward drug traffickers presents a useful contrast to those initiatives designed to end its decades-long conflict with Marxist guerrilla groups. Of course, guerrillas constitute the second chief source of antistate violence in Colombia, and they represent as intractable a problem for the government as the Medellín and Cali cocaine mafias. The peace process has produced clear successes: Approximately 5,000 guerrillas from seven groups—the majority from the M-19 and the Army of Popular Liberation (EPL)—returned to civilian life between 1989 and 1994. Yet some 10,000 guerrillas—principally FARC and ELN, but including roughly 1,200 and 1,300 remnants of the EPL and the M-19—still rampage through Colombia: kidnapping, blowing up oil pipelines, and extorting money. Attacks on a major oil pipeline leading from Arauca in the eastern plains to the Caribbean port of Caracas have cost Colombia an estimated $100 million in lost oil revenues since 1986. In addition, almost two people per day were kidnapped by guerrillas in 1994—600 for the year—according to police sources. While the FARC and the ELN are engaged in a dialogue with the government, a succession of peace agreements and cease-fires have not held together.[4]

For reasons that, in the mid-1990s, may be more economic than political, the guerrillas clearly are unwilling to lay down their weapons and rejoin society. As an ELN spokesman remarked in a September 1990 interview, "Surrendering our arms is not even a consideration. These words are not in our vocabulary. We demand a new government and a new constitution."[5] In recent years, however, the guerrillas' declared sociopolitical agendas have become less overtly Marxist and more reformist in tone. Their current demands include land reform, reduction in poverty, respect for human rights, protection against paramilitarism, and lower military spending. More important, the lines between armed insurgency and common crimes are becoming increasingly blurred. Guerrillas earn enormous profits from shaking down ranchers, oil companies, drug farmers and processors, and other sources of wealth. For example, Colombia's National Planning Department estimates that in the period 1990 through 1994, Colombian guerrilla organizations raised $701 million from drug trafficking compared to $482 million from robbery and extortion and $328 million from kidnapping.[6] The FARC traditionally have participated more than other insurgent groups in the drug bonanza; yet as of late 1994, at least five ELN fronts comprising 400 to 500 guerrilla fighters collected taxes from different phases of the trade: cultivation, processing, and transport. Disarming and surrendering to the government would mean abandoning these lucrative extortion businesses, which may be an unattractive option for many guerrilla fighters.

Colombia's marathon negotiations with guerrilla groups have included wide-ranging discussions, not only on the mechanics of demobilization, but also on issues such as democracy, human rights, national sovereignty, elections, monopolies and oligarchies, and economic and social policy. Furthermore, the reintegration of guerrillas into civilian society poses a major problem for the Colombian government. Most guerrillas lack the skills and training to pursue civilian occupations. As one top EPL commander explained, "Demobilization is extremely difficult, because we were trained for war and not for peace. After 23 years, you cannot make the change overnight."[7] In contrast, if the cocaine industry disappeared tomorrow, its upper and middle echelons would not be destitute. The drug kingpins have their ranches, farms, sports clubs, discotheques, and department stores. Moreover, the cocaine business itself demands professional skills that parallel those found in the legal economy: The business requires chemists, chemical and industrial engineers, managers, pilots, communication specialists, security guards, accountants, and lawyers. Such people could adjust, albeit with some sacrifice of personal luxury, to a legal way of life. On the other hand, guerrillas are mostly violence professionals, comparable to the Extraditables' *sicarios* (assassins) or paramilitary commandos, whose opportunities for a successful civilian career are circumscribed at best.

To be sure, the picture is not entirely bleak. To date, the seven guerrilla groups that have surrendered have received significant political and economic advantages from demobilization. The government has granted the guerrillas amnesty for their political crimes. The M-19's legal political existence is now indisputable—the group managed to win nineteen out of seventy seats in the Constituent Assembly elected in December 1990. The M-19 fielded a presidential candidate and several congressional candidates in the 1994 presidential election (all of them lost) but later captured the mayoralty of Pasto in the southern Colombian department of Nariño. The economic benefits have been less widely publicized. As of 1994, such benefits included:

- A $200 living allowance for one year
- A $4,000 small business loan for each guerrilla
- Programs to teach guerrillas a variety of civilian skills, such as agriculture, baking, or automobile repair
- A clean legal bill of health
- Initiation of community development projects in areas held by guerrillas[8]

Still, political considerations, the lure of easy money, and apprehensions about civilian life have kept two-thirds of Colombia's guerrillas from reaching a peace accord with the government.

Obviously, the problems of guerrilla violence and narcotrafficking have different dynamics and implications, requiring different methods of resolution. The government has treated the drug lords far less magnanimously than it has treated the guerrillas, offering the *narcotraficantes* no amnesty, no pensions for retired mafiosi, and no provisions for granting formal political representation. On the other hand, the government's generosity toward guerrillas seems partly misplaced. Drug dealers cannot qualify as true political criminals, but many guerrilla fighters are themselves little better than bandits. At this time demobilization of guerrilla organizations and of related violent threats (such as paramilitary groups and roving bands of hitmen) and the establishment of peace and order in the Colombian countryside thus seem extremely remote prospects.

RATIONALE FOR NEGOTIATIONS

Drug negotiations have become an integral part of the political landscape in the Andean countries, but whether they can serve useful law enforcement objectives is less certain. Andean governments view negotiations more as a means of resolving conflicts with the cocaine industry—"bringing about a climate conducive to peaceful coexistence," as one Samper administration official put it—and hence reducing societal violence than as a way to curb the cocaine traffic per se. For example, Colombia has not yet evolved a coherent concept of plea bargaining: The Medellín cartel figures who are now in jail successfully extracted significant concessions from the government without revealing any details about their businesses. Government representatives and interlocutors for the Cali cartel talk about dismantling laboratories, routes, and other infrastructure, but concrete steps to realize these goals have not emerged. Furthermore, bargaining approaches require an institutional context in which to work effectively. Weak judicial systems, pervasive institutional corruption, and a weak popular consensus for antidrug efforts (narcotics trafficking consistently ranks as a relatively unimportant national problem in Colombian opinion polls) all work to undermine the bargaining position of governments vis-à-vis the cocaine industry.

Under ideal conditions, negotiations can extend the reach and effectiveness of conventional law enforcement activities; that is, they can furnish strategic intelligence about the drug trade and conceivably enable the authorities to dismantle some elements of the existing cocaine business. The structure of the cocaine industry might favor such an approach. An important chokepoint is the high level of geographic and organizational concentration of refining and export operations. According to the Zabludoff study cited in chapter 1, ten Colombian core organizations comprising approximately 500 entrepreneurs handle at least 60 percent of the cocaine reaching U.S. and European markets. Combined gross revenues of these organizations may total $6 billion annually. Below the top tier, approximately 6,000 people manage the day-to-day businesses of transport, overseas distribution, money laundering, and provision of security. This suggests that the cocaine trade is dominated by an elite and subelite of approximately 6,000 to 7,000 people. This group occupies a vital middle ground between the hundreds of thousands of Andean farmers and small processors and the roughly millions of street dealers and cocaine consumers in the industrialized countries.[9]

Cocaine enterprises function through an intricate system of contracts and subcontracts. Boundaries between the leadership core and lower echelons of the business are necessarily fluid. Access to information, however, is a key defining characteristic of the cocaine hierarchy. Below the top tier, information is highly compartmentalized horizontally and vertically. Transporters, wholesalers, and money launderers typically possess little or no knowledge of each others' operations. The manager of a cocaine storage site in the United States typically does not know the identity of shippers or wholesale distributors of the product. On the other hand, first-tier players in the industry almost certainly know the identities of the firms and skilled professionals who furnish critical services to their organizations. (In addition, a single contractor, such as a shipping firm or container company, might handle cocaine for several different trafficking organizations.) In other words, leaders who coordinate trafficking functions retain a vast store of knowledge about the workings of the industry. Such considerations suggest that the top tier could devastate cocaine operations by retiring en masse and by withdrawing protection from (or incriminating) the 6,000-odd lower-echelon actors who constitute the building blocks of the trafficking infrastructure. Viewed in these terms, in theory a negotiated settlement could cripple existing drug operations and could provide information necessary to strengthen the fight against future drug operations. Of course, critical variables in such a settlement would be the number of leaders surrendering, the share of the cocaine business that they represent, and the quality of their collaboration with the authorities.

The motivations of drug dealers also need to be considered. Most Colombian drug lords want a comfortable life in Colombia, and many probably would abandon the cocaine business if given the opportunity. (Pablo Escobar was an apparent exception, as is discussed later.) Traffickers' prospects for reintegration into society have been a recurring theme of Colombia's narcodialogue since the Panama meetings in 1984. According to a former government minister, Joaquín Vallejo, who served as an intermediary between the government and the Medellín cartel in 1988 and 1989, "They have much money, but they are not free men. They are capable of anything, even retirement, provided they can get their freedom."[10]

Orchestrating a shutdown of the industry, however, would expose major kingpins to reprisals from fellow criminals. This reality is reflected in traffickers' bargaining positions with the government. For example, traffickers perceive retirement from the business and surrender to justice as collective decisions. Their idea probably is to seek safety in numbers: The larger the group surrendering, the smaller the risk of retaliation from remaining traffickers. Surrender offers over the years have included 100 top-level Medellín traffickers in May 1984; "the so-called cartels of Medellín, Bogotá, and the coast" in September 1988; 200 to 300 Medellín Extraditables in November 1990; 200 Cali cartel members in early 1993; 300 traffickers representing organizations in Valle, Antioquia, Santander, and the north coast in October 1993; and 200 Valle traffickers in September 1994.

Traffickers have been reluctant to provide information about their businesses and their criminal associates. For instance, Cali leader Gilberto Rodríguez wrote in a letter to President Cesar Gaviria in January 1994, "My willingness to collaborate with justice is unalterable," but added, "with all respect, denunciations of fellow traffickers is not the best way." At the same time, Rodríguez offered to use his "power of assembly" (*poder convacatoria*) to guarantee that "the multiple groups identified as Valle [that is, from Valle de Cauca Department] traffickers would abandon their business and submit to the law."[11] Similarly, Rodríguez told *Time* reporter Tom Quinn in September 1994 that he could arrange the surrender of a "large percentage" of Colombian drug dealers: "They would get out of the business and stay out and dismantle their infrastructure, their labs, and their routes without tricks, without ratting on each other, and without violence," he promised.[12] Fulfillment of this ambitious agenda would be reflected in increased cocaine prices, which "should be four or five times higher on U.S. streets," and also in reduced international seizures of the drug.[13]

Drug kingpins' bargaining strategies, however, failed to win acceptance in Bogotá or Washington. The Cali proposals were short on specifics—the idea that traffickers could simply shut down their drug businesses without confessing or implicating associates was simply too much to swallow. In a conversation in early 1993, Colombian Attorney General Carlos Arrieta asked Gilberto Rodríguez's lawyers if the traffickers' surrender would represent "a process of surrender consisting of the massive surrender of routes, laboratories, and assets." One of the lawyers responded, "Some of the people interested in surrendering are thinking about doing this, but others are not." Clearly any surrender deal would have to involve forfeiture of trafficking assets and corroborating information about the drug trade. (Even the Medellín cartel leaders had offered repeatedly to give up their laboratories and airstrips as part of the dismantling process.) Otherwise, drug criminals could simply reactivate their cocaine enterprises after some years and blame resulting supply increases and price declines on new entrepreneurs entering the business.

From a law enforcement perspective, the mass surrender concept promoted by the Medellín and Cali traffickers offered both risks and possibilities. The retirement of much of the leadership core could indeed disrupt trafficking operations for a time. Yet both Bogotá and (especially) Washington have been cool to the concept of collective bargaining with traffickers, fearing that such negotiations would confer a political stature on drug criminals and even indirectly legitimize the narcotics business itself. Of course, elements of collective bargaining pervade Colombia's drug negotiations. (For example, in 1990 and 1991 Medellín cartel kingpins sought and got government guarantees against extraditions as conditions for surrendering.) Yet the Colombian government, like others, has imposed penalties on and greater benefits to dealers as individuals, not as members of a group. In contrast, in dialogues with insurgent organizations, Colombia has sought their mass demobilization and has structured its negotiation package accordingly.

Because of such constraints on both sides, serious negotiations to diminish the drug trade have not been possible in Colombia to date. Furthermore, because of corruption or ineptitude, the Colombian government has largely botched its surrender policy. President Ernesto Samper noted in 1994, "It is more important to dismantle the cartels than to incarcerate their leaders."[14] But in many instances the government has granted leniency to traffickers without demanding serious collaboration from them in return. To be sure, negotiations have contributed to some Colombian successes—such as the incarceration of dozens of high-level and medium-level Medellín capos and the demarcation of the cartel's political and military structure. Moreover, the diminishing returns and high political costs of repressive strategies have compelled the government to experiment with negotiated solutions. The question, however, is whether the government has gained or lost headway against the drug trade by adopting such approaches. This issue is explored in detail in the following sections.

The Limits of Repression

After the August 1989 assassination of the Liberal Party's presidential candidate, Luis Carlos Galán, the government of Virgilio Barco unleashed a wide-ranging crackdown on the Medellín cartel. The government invoked an emergency decree that paved the way for the administrative extradition of drug dealers—that is, extradition not authorized by a prior court decision or by a functioning international treaty. (In June 1987 Colombia's Supreme Court had effectively invalidated a 1979 extradition treaty between the United States and Colombia.) Between August 1989 and December 1990, the government sent more than twenty suspected drug traffickers to the United States for prosecution. (The principal rationale for this procedure is that major traffickers have been able to avoid prosecution or to negotiate or buy their way out of jail in Colombia.) Another emergency decree enabled the government to confiscate drug traffickers' real estate, aircraft, money, weapons, and other assets. At least $125 million of drug trafficking assets—including 1,800 buildings and country estates, 470 planes, and 600 vehicles—belonging mostly to leaders of the Medellín cartel and their associates were seized under this decree.[15] The government also launched a massive manhunt for Pablo Escobar, José Gonzalo Rodríguez Gacha, and other Medellín kingpins. Such hardline policies were backed by almost $200 million in military and law enforcement aid from Washington in fiscal years 1989 and 1990 and were initially successful in disrupting the cartel's trafficking operations. In addition, these policies undoubtedly made a high-level career in cocaine less attractive to many Colombians.

Developments in Colombia produced important effects on cocaine markets upstream and downstream. Wholesale cocaine prices in New York, the largest U.S. market, increased on average by approximately 40 percent between 1989 and 1990, and U.S.-wide purity levels decreased by 8 percent—an indication that less cocaine was being shipped to the U.S. market. Prices of Andean coca leaf and coca paste plummeted as Colombian buyers reduced their expeditions to Peru and Bolivia. In April-June 1990, prices of leaf in Peru's Upper Huallaga Valley and the Bolivian Chapare were more than 65 to 75 percent lower than those in July-September 1989. During 1990 many Bolivian coca farmers voluntarily eradicated their coca fields, receiving cash payments and other incentives from their government (ultimately from U.S. economic support funds) to switch to legal cash crops.

The pace of Colombia's anticocaine offensive slackened in late 1990 and early 1991, allowing the cartels to rebuild and reconfigure their trafficking network. In the end, Colombia's war against drugs had only a negligible effect on world cocaine markets. By spring 1991 Colombian cocaine exports had almost reached 1989 levels. Correspondingly, coca leaf prices had largely recovered from their 1990 lows, and the New York wholesale price of cocaine had fallen below the prevailing price when the crackdown began; in addition, according to DEA reports, by 1991 cocaine purity had increased 8 percent compared to the average level in 1990.[16]

Clearly, the cocaine industry had regrouped: U.S. and Colombian officials theorize that the Medellín cartel suffered from its clashes with the Colombian authorities and that the door was opened for the rival Cali coalition and other trafficking groups to capture a larger share of the cocaine business. Nevertheless, the Medellín coalition proved resilient enough to rebuild some of the supply and distribution networks that were disrupted during the crackdown—for example, by moving refining capacity to less restrictive neighboring countries, such as Brazil, Ecuador, and Peru. In addition, its leaders remained at large, both supervising cocaine trafficking operations and mounting terrorist attacks against the state.

Particularly worrisome was the conspicuous failure of the Colombian government to apprehend Pablo Escobar Gaviria. Widely regarded as the top figure in the Medellín cartel, Escobar consistently eluded the authorities, despite a series of encirclement campaigns conducted by thousands of Colombian soldiers, the Department of Administrative Security (DAS), and elite police troops. These egregious fiascos, as well as the failure to capture other major kingpins, suggests that the traffickers had established an extensive informant network in the command and control system of the military and the national police. A former associate who turned enemy of Escobar remarked sarcastically in April 1991, "They could not capture Pablo Escobar, because half of those who work for the government are protecting him, while the other half are pursuing him."[17]

From Colombia's perspective, the drug war was a losing proposition politically, economically, and militarily. A poll in five major cities, published in the Bogotá weekly *Semana* at the end of December 1989, found that 58 percent of the respondents favored negotiations with traffickers and 64.3 percent favored pardons for traffickers if they decided to retire from the drug business. A poll conducted for *Semana* in November 1990 concluded that more than 60 percent of Colombians were in favor of granting amnesty to traffickers and that more than

80 percent were disposed to accept an Extraditable as a cabinet minister, if such steps would bring peace to the nation.[18]

In addition, some Colombians questioned the military wisdom of the crackdown, pointing out that it served to invigorate the country's insurgent groups. In 1990, for example, the FARC and the ELN launched major offensives to expand their power bases in the Middle Magdalena Valley, northern Antioquia, the Peru-Ecuador border region, and elsewhere. The deteriorating state of Colombia's internal security was partly explained by the assignment of roughly 10 percent of Colombia's 117,000-man army to 1,800 *narcotraficante* buildings and estates, where they performed housekeeping functions, such as feeding the animals in Pablo Escobar's zoo.[19] Thousands more undoubtedly were chasing Escobar and his colleagues and guarding people and installations targeted by the narcoterrorists. The government crackdown also helped the guerrillas by undermining some of the anti-Communist paramilitary groups organized and funded by Medellín drug lords. A few paramilitary groups have disbanded since the early 1990s, creating a power vacuum of sorts and enabling guerrillas to filter back to their former strongholds.

Considering the limited success of crackdown tactics, and with the August 1990 election of President Cesar Gaviria Trujillo, Bogotá opted to seek a peaceful settlement of the drug conflict. The government's peace plan, originally announced in early September 1990, did not envision granting drug dealers the same political treatment accorded to guerrilla groups. Colombian law categorizes traffickers and rightist paramilitary groups as ordinary criminals, subject to prosecution and incarceration. Thus the Gaviria government's aim was to coax the traffickers to surrender, confess their crimes, and serve jail sentences in exchange for legal concessions, such as reduced prison terms and guarantees against extradition to the United States. The government's willingness to drop extradition proceedings constituted a major concession. Because of the notoriously porous character of Colombia's criminal justice system, extradition—which results in almost certain sentencing and punishment in the United States—has long been both a cornerstone of U.S.-Colombian antidrug policy and the law enforcement weapon most feared by drug dealers.

The immediate results of Barco's initiative were that the Extraditables toned down their campaign of antistate violence and began a process of reconciliation with the government. In November the government reviewed a surrender offer from 200 to 300 Medellín capos. The three Ochoa brothers turned themselves in between December 1990 and February 1991. To be sure, there were occasional reminders that the Extraditables were still willing to employ violence as a political tool. Yet with the surrender of Pablo Escobar on June 19, which followed by hours a 50 to 13 vote by the Colombian Constituent Assembly (a body elected in December 1990 to revise Colombia's constitution) to ban the extradition of Colombian citizens, the Extraditables' military raison d'être seemed to collapse. On July 3, 1991, the group issued a communiqué saying "We have decided to dissolve our entire military organization—we will end all action against those whom we consider enemies because of their stance against extradition."[20] By mid-1991 some twenty to twenty-five leading Medellín traffickers had submitted to justice under the government program; and by the end of 1993, this total had increased to at least forty. With the weakening of the Medellín cartel, leadership of the cocaine business shifted to Cali, and the primary focus of Colombia's narcodialogue shifted from the dismantling of trafficking enterprises to the containment of narcoterrorism.

HISTORICAL OVERVIEW
OF DRUG NEGOTIATIONS

The following sections describe the course and implications of Colombia's narcodialogues with the Medellín and Cali cartels. In neither case did negotiations yield a reduction in drug trafficking. However, the government's surrender policy vis-à-vis the Medellín cartel did result in a reduction of drug-sponsored violence (as measured by the numbers of murders, kidnappings, and urban bombings) and in the incarceration of most of the cartel's top leaders—important achievements in themselves. By contrast, the government's dialogues with the Cali leaders to date have produced no visible success; indeed, they have embarrassed the government domestically and damaged Colombia's relations with the United States.

Medellín[21]

On four occasions—in May 1984, September 1988, January 1990, and November 1990—leading Medellín drug traffickers made formal offers to abandon the narcotics business and relinquish assets used in the industry (such as laboratories, planes, and airstrips) to the Colombian government. In exchange, they sought concessions, including revisions in the U.S.-Colombian extradition treaty, an outright end to extradition, and a general amnesty.

    The traffickers communicated the first offer to the government in successive meetings with former President Alfonso Lopez Michelsen and with Colombian attorney general Carlos Jiménez Gómez in May 1984. Lopez happened to be in Panama then as an observer for that country's presidential elections. (Traffickers were on the run at that time because of a massive government crackdown mounted after the April 30, 1984 assassination of Rodrigo Lara Bonilla, Colombia's justice minister.) At the first meeting, in the Hotel Marriott in Panama City, Pablo Escobar and Jorge Ochoa told Lopez that they represented 100 top Colombian mafiosi—"the dome" of the Colombian cocaine establishment—whose international operations extended to Brazil, Bolivia, Peru, Ecuador, and the United States. The traffickers said they were ready to "dismantle everything" and repatriate money held in Swiss bank accounts provided that the government discontinued extradition and agreed not to confiscate their wealth. (According to one disputed version, the traffickers also offered to pay off Colombia's $10 billion national debt.) Lopez communicated the offer directly to Colombia's president, Belisario Betancur, who had just initiated a peace dialogue with the country's guerrilla groups. Betancur found the traffickers' plan intriguing and authorized his attorney general to travel to Panama to contact Escobar and his colleagues.

The traffickers gave Jiménez a long written document addressed directly to President Betancur in which they proposed "to eliminate once and forever any drug trafficking in our country" and asked the president to "consider the possibility of our reinstatement in Colombian society in the near future." The traffickers claimed to control 70 to 80 percent of the Colombian cocaine business and to earn an annual income of $2 billion. Their multinational enterprises were qualitatively different from "simple and traditional forms of trafficking such as personal transport of small quantities by tourists in briefcases or in false-bottomed shoes." They proposed to dismantle their enterprises by turning over laboratories and airstrips and by selling off their aircraft. In addition, they agreed to cooperate with the government crop substitution and demand-reduction projects. They expressed willingness to repatriate their wealth "if the right formula can be found to do this." Referring to their persecution in Colombia, the traffickers denied responsibility for the murder of Lara Bonilla and affirmed their support for the Colombia's democratic and republican system of government. In a "Suggestions" section at the end of the document, the traffickers requested revisions in the extradition treaty, an exemption for crimes committed before the revision, and the right to appeal extradition decisions to the Colombian Supreme Court.[22] The document was the first and perhaps the last of its kind—no such detailed surrender proposal has been submitted to the government since that time.

Nothing ever came of the traffickers' initiative, in part because of the overwhelmingly negative reaction of Colombia's political establishment. Leaders from every political party—liberals, new liberals, and conservatives—almost unanimously expressed open and categorical opposition to a dialogue with drug traffickers. Carlos Holguín Sardi, the conservative president of the Colombian Senate, summarized the view of the majority when he observed, "[Negotiations] where criminal law is concerned . . . would mean the total disintegration of our legal order and institutions."[23]

Furthermore, the U.S. Embassy in Bogotá and the U.S. Department of State were unsympathetic to the idea of negotiating with traffickers. According to *Semana,* Jiménez Gómez informally communicated the substance of the drug lords' offer to Alexander Watson, then the deputy chief of mission, who replied, "I will send the message [to Washington], but I see no possibility of an arrangement." Several days later, Jiménez received via the Embassy a State Department telex outlining U.S. objections to the proposal. The Betancur government in effect capitulated to strong domestic and international pressure, and the president announced in July 1984 that there never would be "any kind of understanding" between the government and the signers of the Panama memorandum.[24]

In retrospect, the United States and Colombia may have sacrificed an opportunity to strike a major blow against the cocaine industry. The drug lords were offering to shut down trafficking networks that they estimated had taken ten years to build. As Bruce Bagley, one U.S. observer, commented, "The intelligence about the industry's structure and money laundering operations would have been extremely useful to both Colombian and U.S. law enforcement in opposing a resurgence." Furthermore, Bagley notes, a deal might have "saved the country from the orgy of terror, corruption, and murder" unleashed by the traffickers in the mid-1980s.[25]

The traffickers drafted a second proposal in response to a September 1988 speech by President Virgilio Barco, who outlined a peace initiative that seemed to offer the possibility of a government-trafficker accord. The initiative called for "resolving all of the different forms and manifestations of violence, not only those generated by guerrillas."[26] However, later the government claimed that this message was directed at paramilitary organizations, not the Medellín cartel per se. For about a year, from mid-September 1988 until presidential candidate Galán's funeral on August 20, 1989, the Colombian government conducted an indirect dialogue with the leaders of the Medellín cartel. Germán Montoya, the secretary of the presidency (in effect President

Barco's chief of staff) and Joaquín Vallejo Arbelaez, a former cabinet minister who acted as an intermediary for the drug lords, reputedly held ten meetings that year to discuss the traffickers' proposals, which had hardened perceptibly since 1984. Now the traffickers were demanding an end to extradition and a pardon as the quid pro quo for retiring from the drug business and handing over weapons, explosives, laboratories, and clandestine airstrips.[27] They did not repeat their 1984 offer to repatriate their large fortunes to Colombia. In conversations with Vallejo, traffickers claimed to represent the "cartels of Medellín, Bogotá, and the coast," which controlled the majority of the Colombian cocaine business. The Cali group, they said, accounted for only 10 percent of the business and would have to make its own agreement with the government.

These talks did not progress very far, partly because of Montoya's insistence that the United States must be a party to any substantive negotiations or peace agreement with the drug dealers. "We must take into account the United States reaction in the event that Colombia implements this proposal. We cannot discard the possibility of political and commercial reprisals," he told Vallejo.[28] Montoya apparently also suggested or hinted that the cartel should conduct its own lobbying effort in U.S. power circles. In this Montoya may have been stalling his adversaries: While the conversations with Vallejo were proceeding, the Colombian army and police were conducting a campaign called Operation Primavera, which was highly effective, against the Medellín cartel's cocaine infrastructure. That operation destroyed hundreds of cocaine laboratories and seized more than 30 tons of cocaine hydrochloride and more than 2 million gallons of chemicals used in manufacturing cocaine, such as ether, acetone, and methyl ethyl ketone.[29] Some Colombian observers believe that the Medellín drug lords arranged Galan's murder because of what they perceived as the government's insincerity during the Montoya-Vallejo dialogue. Montoya himself suffered personally from the failure of the narcodialogues. Pablo Escobar subsequently told a cartel lawyer, Guido Parra, "That guy made a fool of us." In retaliation, the Extraditables ordered the kidnapping of Montoya's son, Alvaro Diego, in December 1989 (he was released a month later) and the kidnapping and brutal murder of the official's sister, Marina Montoya, a year later.

Nevertheless, the Medellín cartel did take seriously Montoya's insistence on a Washington connection in the negotiations. (Gilberto Rodríguez took up this same theme in a November 1994 letter, saying that the United States should participate even unofficially in Cali's talks with the government to help achieve "a fair juridical-political

agreement for the parties.")[30] In 1988, the drug lords reportedly attempted to hire the services of the New York firm Kissinger and Associates to mount a public relations campaign on behalf of the proposed
trafficker-government accord. No agreement was reached with the firm,
however.[31] In another episode in 1989, traffickers dispatched Vallejo to
Miami to discuss their proposal with a lawyer who had at one time "sorted
out legal difficulties" for Jorge Ochoa in the United States and who just
happened to be working with a team of corporate attorneys headed by
Jeb Bush, the then-president's son. According to one account, the lawyer
listened to Vallejo's presentation and "did not rule out the possibility that
the President would be receptive to the idea" of the traffickers' surrender
strategy. He promised to raise the matter with Jeb Bush, but only on the
condition that Jorge Ochoa pay off an outstanding debt of $25,000 for the
lawyer's past services. Vallejo returned to Colombia from the meeting
elated and optimistic that a solution to the drug issue was at hand. Negotiations, however, were overtaken by events. On the morning of August
18, 1989, the police commandant of Antioquia, Franklin Quintero, was
gunned down; that evening, Luis Carlos Galán, the front-running Liberal
Party candidate for president, was assassinated. On the same night, the
government issued the previously mentioned emergency decree against
the narcotics industry, and the traffickers responded six days later with a
declaration of "absolute and total war against the government and the
industrial and political oligarchy." In this turbulent atmosphere, the
Montoya-Vallejo channel no longer could function, and the negotiations
broke off.[32]

The traffickers' third and fourth offers came during the bloodiest
phase of Colombia's drug war, when the government was applying
intense pressure on the Medellín mafia and the traffickers were esca-
lating their campaign of violence against the state. The Extraditables
delivered both offers to the government after consultations via intermediaries with a group of Colombian political figures, the so-called
Los Notables, listed in table 4.1. Apparently, ex-president Alfonso Lopez
Michelsen played a leading role in these discussions. In both cases,
the Notables, presumably with the government's blessing, were trying
to accomplish two tasks: negotiating terms for the Extraditables' surrender and effecting the release of approximately twenty hostages,
among them sons and daughters of prominent Colombian families,
abducted by the traffickers between December 1989 and January 1990.
Most Colombian observers believe that these hostages were seized to
strengthen the traffickers' negotiating position, although the
Extraditables justified their actions as a way "to finance our war and to
provide housing to the less favored classes."[33]

TABLE 4.1
LOS NOTABLES

Alfonso Lopez Michelsen	Ex-president of the Republic
Misael Pastrana Borrero	Ex-president of the Republic
Julio Cesar Turbay Ayala*	Ex-president of the Republic
Monseñor Mario Revollo Bravo	First Archbishop of Colombia
Diego Montaña Cuéllar	Leader, Unión Patriótica

*Turbay, whose daughter Diana was kidnapped by the *Extraditables* in August 1990, apparently did not participate in the round of negotiations leading to the *Extraditables'* offer of November 23.

Source: Rensselaer, Lee, "Policy Brief, Making the Most of Colombia's Drug Negotiations," *Orbis,* Vol. 35, no. 2 (Spring 1991), p. 242, © Foreign Policy Research Institute, 1991.

The Notables issued a statement on January 15, 1990, hinting at "less rigorous treatment than the law prescribes" for traffickers if they liberated their hostages and suspended exports of drugs. Days later the Extraditables responded with a communiqué outlining their surrender terms—a document that, according to one high-ranking Colombian military source, had been reviewed and approved previously by the Notables and by Germán Montoya.[34] In the January peace initiative, the traffickers announced their acceptance of "the triumph of the state and of the existing legal order" and promised to end drug shipments and turn over their weapons and laboratories in return for unspecified "constitutional and legal guarantees."[35] They declared a unilateral truce and released several hostages, including Alvaro Diego Montoya. On January 29 the mafia turned over in Medellín a bus loaded with a ton of dynamite. In February, just before the Cartagena summit (a meeting of leaders from the United States, Colombia, Peru and Bolivia to discuss antidrug policy, held in Cartagena in February), the traffickers made an additional conciliatory gesture: They handed over to the Colombian authorities three of their most modern cocaine laboratories, located in the Urabá region of Chocó and Antioquia departments, not far from the Panamanian frontier. Together these laboratories could produce some 20 tons of cocaine per month and reportedly contained production plants for ether and acetone as well as chemical recycling facilities. (Although, not a single gram of cocaine was discovered in the laboratories.)

The Virgilio Barco government, however, was not of one mind on how to deal with the Extraditables' peace offers. Indeed, the negotiations issue and the hostage crises precipitated an intense debate within the administration. Miguel Gómez Padillo (head of the National Police),

Miguel Maza Marquez (DAS head), and government minister Carlos Lemos Simmonds strongly argued against a rapprochement with traffickers. At one meeting with the president, Maza stated, "We must not talk with criminals who have converted the national territory into a sea of blood—these criminals represent a mortal threat to our democracy." Barco himself and his secretary, Montoya, were inclined to be more flexible. Barco responded, "General Maza, please be quiet! We must listen to these people to have a sufficient basis for judgment and later express our opinions!"[36] The president subsequently told the directors of *El Tiempo* and *El Espectador,* "The policy of the government is flexible, because the law itself offers alternatives without violating the constitutional order." By way of clarification, Barco said that the government hoped to steer a path between "blind and obstinate repression" and "infinite and open dialogue with criminals."[37] In another more concrete gesture, the president postponed a final decision on the extradition to the United States of eight medium-level drug capos, even though all of the procedural work on the cases had been completed and the warrants were awaiting his final signature. Such positive overtures on both sides brought about a temporary truce in the drug war. The traffickers halted their campaign of bombings, kidnappings, and assassinations for approximately two months, from mid-January to late March 1990.

Yet these peace feelers did not produce serious negotiations, much less an accord between the government and the Extraditables. As noted, powerful members of the Barco administration opposed any peace negotiations. In addition, Bogotá always had to consider Washington's position. According to a close Barco advisor, during the Cartagena summit, Barco asked George Bush's opinion about the traffickers' surrender offer. Bush dismissed the offer, saying that the traffickers' sole objective was to avoid the threat of extradition. Bush impressed on Barco the White House's interest in Colombia maintaining a hard line against the drug traffic.[38] Still, Barco personally was probably open to negotiations. A letter of resignation by government minister Carlos Lemos provides additional evidence—the letter complained about "moral deterioration at the very core of the Colombian government" and noted, "The attitude of the government has changed imperceptibly and is no longer as decisive, intransigent, and firm as it was this past December."[39] The drug peace broke down in late March because of the murder of the presidential candidate of the Patriotic Union, Bernardo Jaramillo and because of the Colombian government's decision to resume extraditions of drug capos. Escobar issued a plausible denial of the assassination: "Why kill someone who was an enemy of extradition and a supporter of dialogue?" he asked in a letter to Diego Montaña.[40] Nevertheless, the window of opportunity for negotiations was closed for the remainder of the Barco presidency and narcoterrorism again plagued Colombia for several months. In August and September, the Extraditables kidnapped more members of the Colombian elite, including Diana Turbay, Marina Montoya, and Francisco Santos (the news editor of *El Tiempo*). In October the Notables once again offered to serve as intermediaries, effectively unofficial negotiators, on behalf of the Colombian government. However, Turbay and Montoya were both brutally murdered in January 1991.

Like the Bentacur administration in 1984, the Barco administration may have also missed an opportunity to strike a favorable bargain with the traffickers. If Barco had acceded to the Extraditables' offer when it was released, former President Lopez Michelsen remarked, "Many deaths would have been avoided." Rodrigo Lloreda Caicedo, the Social Conservative candidate for president in 1990, observed in a *Semana* interview in April of that year that "The government should have taken advantage of this opportunity to fix the conditions under which it would have been possible to produce the surrender of the authors of the crimes, the dismemberment of the criminal organizations of drug dealers, and the indemnization of victims of terrorism. The government did not do this."[41]

Lloreda's program for resolving the drug problem in Colombia, which he outlined during various campaign appearances, included four elements:

- Dropping extradition ("The treaty is too broad and too inflexible and is generally unfair to Colombia," he said in an interview in February 1991)
- Trying drug trafficking, terrorism, and kidnapping cases in military courts in front of military judges, who are considered to be better insulated than civilian judges from traffickers' bribery and intimidation
- Totally dismembering narcotics organizations and all the elements of those organizations
- Indemnifying victims of narcoterrorism by having the Extraditables compensate them[42]

Lloreda's ideas did not offer enough positive incentives to drug dealers (and included no mention of reduced sentences or pardons for them). However, he was correct in emphasizing that extradition was a credible threat to the traffickers. In his view, dropping extradition proceedings should be contingent on shutting down the organizations that produce and export cocaine. Unfortunately, when the Gaviria administration later did strike a bargain with the drug lords, this linkage was lost. All that traffickers had to do to avoid extradition was turn themselves in and be sentenced to jail for just one crime. As the following discussion shows, the extradition weapon was effectively sheathed well before extradition was finally voted out of existence in June 1991.

In early September 1990, the Gaviria government announced a major new peace initiative. The government would offer drug dealers the option of accepting sentences reduced by one-third and guarantees against extradition to the United States on the condition that they surrender to the authorities, confess to all their crimes in Colombia and abroad, and identify criminal assets and proceeds—laboratories and bank balances, for example. These conditions were stipulated in government decree 2047, issued on September 5. If they cooperated in "identifying the other perpetrators of or participants in the confessed crimes" and in revealing "the value of the property reported to the judges," their sentences would be cut by an additional one-sixth.[43] Thus, the government signaled its willingness to strike a bargain with the Medellín drug lords.

In November 1990 the Extraditables delivered a fourth offer: Approximately 200 to 300 Medellín traffickers would surrender to the authorities and would cease their trafficking and terrorist activities. In return, the traffickers demanded:

- Trial by appropriate Colombian courts (in effect, no extradition to the United States)
- An end to the requirement that traffickers confess to their crimes and denounce one another
- A special detention center where they could be protected against revenge or reprisals, relying on third parties for protection— the Colombian army or navy, Medellín municipal police, or aninternational human rights agency[44]

In another communiqué published just a day later, the Extraditables promised to release their hostages if the government respected their human rights and the rights of their families. The Extraditables' demands for special treatment stemmed from a novel legal argument: Drug trafficking and narcoterrorism are collective concerns, similar to political acts such as rebellion, so traffickers cannot be punished as ordinary criminals.[45]

The Colombian government's new, flexible stance toward the drug dealers reflected a significant shift in the attitudes of the nation's political establishment. For instance, Joaquín Vallejo, who represented the Medellín cartel in the 1988-1989 conversations with the government, had written in

El Tiempo in May 1984 that "no possible justification" could be cited for a dialogue with traffickers. "Apart from the problems of moral principles," he noted, "there remains doubt about whether they [the *narcotraficantes*] would keep their promises."[46] Similarly, Juan Gómez Martínez, the former mayor of Medellín, wrote as the director of the Medellín newspaper *El Colombiano,* "Colombia is shuddering to learn about the proposal for a dialogue between the lords of vice and the government. This is an insolent, immoral, and destructive proposal. The entire society repudiates the possibility [of such a dialogue]."[47]

By late 1989 and early 1990, however, most polls documented that Colombians were increasingly disenchanted with the Barco government's hardline policies. As noted, a consistent two-thirds of all respondents opposed extradition, and Colombians also were increasingly open to the possibility of a negotiated solution to the drug war. In the 1990 presidential elections, Cesar Gaviria apparently was the only candidate who ruled out the option of negotiating with the traffickers, and he won with only 47.5 percent of the vote. Yet, pressured by overpowering public sentiment for peace, Gaviria's government later would abolish extradition and make further concessions to halt the narcoterrorist violence.

The traffickers' new proposals produced a near euphoria in Colombia. Lopez Michelsen observed in a radio interview, "The country has never been so close to peace." The Colombian justice minister declared, "I believe we are at the threshold of a transcendental occurrence that will bring peace to Colombia."[48]

The Colombian government seemed willing to meet the traffickers halfway. In a letter published on November 23, the justice minister reassured the traffickers that informing on their colleagues was not a necessary condition for receiving the benefits of decree 2047. More important, the minister declared that traffickers would be spared extradition and would receive reduced sentences merely by confessing to one of any crimes committed inside or outside the country. (This latter point was later formalized in decree 3030, issued on December 17.) In yet another benevolent gesture, the government announced on January 27, 1991, that its offer of shorter jail terms and immunity from extradition extended until the moment of a trafficker's surrender. (The original offer only covered crimes committed before September 5, 1990.) Thus the government furnished the strongest assurance to date that traffickers who surrendered and confessed could escape extradition.

On December 18, 1990, the government's coaxing strategy landed its first major catch: Fabio Ochoa turned himself in to a Medellín judge. Ochoa's comment that day testified to the relentless and exhausting pressure on an outlaw executive: "I feel the same happiness entering jail as someone else feels when leaving it—I only wanted to end the nightmare my life had become."[49] Just eighteen days later, Jorge Luis Ochoa, the chief executive officer of the family cocaine business, surrendered to the authorities, and on February 16, 1991, Juan David Ochoa, the third member of the cocaine trafficking family, followed his brothers into custody.

Finally, on June 19, Pablo Escobar Gaviria—the reported leader of the Medellín cartel, who was under indictment in Miami, Los Angeles, and Atlanta—also surrendered. He was transported in an Antioquia government helicopter to the La Catedral prison located on a hill 8,000 feet above his hometown of Envigado, near Medellín. Reportedly Escobar himself contributed $2 million for the construction of the prison—the money was funneled through the Envigado municipal treasury. Indeed, Escobar apparently was the original owner of the estate on which La Catedral stood, but he deeded the land to Envigado fifty days before his surrender, receiving in return property of equivalent value elsewhere in the municipality.[50] The conditions of Escobar's incarceration, established after marathon negotiations with the government, were quite favorable to him. Of course, the one condition was that the prison be located in a city where the trafficker enjoyed great influence. Thanks in part to donations from Escobar, Envigado boasted the highest per capita city budget in Colombia (the budget had increased tenfold between 1983 and 1989) for public education, subsidies for school transportation, the most extensive water and sewer services in the country, and subsidized payments for medicine amounting to $40 per inhabitant.[51] Another condition was that Escobar and his representatives be allowed to screen the guards who would be responsible for internal security in the prison. In fact, the selection was made by a committee comprising the mayor of Envigado, the regional prosecutor of Antioquia, and the Colombian director general of prisons. The director general was the Bogotá representative, but the other two committee members were probably allies of Escobar.[52]

Escobar described his submission to justice as "essentially an act of peace."[53] A few days before his surrender, the Extraditables released their last hostages, Francisco Santos and Maruja Pachón (the director of Colombia's National Police Foundation, who was captured the previous November 7). As mentioned, on July 3, the Extraditables expressed their intention to disband their military structure, although much of it remained intact until Escobar's death in December 1993.

The Colombian government deserves some credit for its unorthodox tactics in ending narcoterrorism and bringing the *narcotraficantes* to justice. Apparently, the government's coaxing succeeded where manhunts and dragnets had failed. Nevertheless, these dramatic developments hardly represented a victory in the drug war. For example, even though the founding fathers of the Medellín coalition surrendered, no trafficking assets—laboratories, aircraft, records, money, names of accomplices—were turned over to the Colombian authorities.

Furthermore, surrender did not necessarily mean retirement from the cocaine business. Pablo Escobar apparently had no such intention. The security arrangements at the Envigado facility were designed to allow Escobar to continue running his illicit businesses while in custody. Known drug dealers and assassins freely visited La Catedral. The prison itself was equipped with fax machines, cellular telephones, and computers, which allowed Escobar to manage bank accounts and business transactions and to communicate with subordinates. The Colombian and international press have been reported widely on the luxurious accommodations of "Envigado's five-star hotel." (The prison had a bar, a lounge, a sauna, and other amenities. Prison guards even served drinks to inmates, according to one account.)[54] More startling, Escobar periodically slipped out of the prison to attend local special events and celebrations. For example, on June 19, 1992, he commemorated his first year in prison by drinking with friends in an Envigado nightclub, returning to La Catedral at four in the morning. A recent biography records Escobar's visit to a soccer match in the city: "When the soccer [fútbol] stadium of Envigado, which Escobar had built years before, hosted a classic game . . . the Patrón left the prison, protected by a powerful security apparatus. The automobile traffic in the area was vigorously controlled. Agents of the transit police offered their collaboration, demanding identification papers from suspicious cars—groups of two or three armed men formed a security cordon around the playing field."[55]

Escobar's antics at La Catedral eventually forced the government to demonstrate that "it retained control over the famous prisoner."[56] In July it decided to move Escobar to an unspecified maximum security facility, and on July 21 the army's IV Brigade in Medellín was ordered to occupy La Catedral. The operation was poorly conceived and executed. Sometime during the fifteen hours that the army commander, Gustavo Pardo, unaccountably waited before carrying out the order, Escobar escaped with nine of his fellow prisoners. High-level corruption possibly contributed to the escape. Six days later the Gaviria government issued a decree firing Gustavo Pardo, Hernando Navas, the national director of prisons, and Manuel José Espitia, commander of the Medellín military police.

Following his flight, Escobar still expressed interest in continuing the peace process and in returning to La Catedral. However, the

Colombian government—which had lost tremendous face as a result of his escape—now devoted its energies to tracking down and eliminating the capo.

Escobar's escape was followed by a partial recrudescence of the narcoterrorist violence prevalent between 1989 and 1991. From August 1992 to April 1993, eleven car bombing episodes in Bogotá, Medellín, and other cities left at least 60 people dead and another 400 wounded. Violence again served as Escobar's negotiating tactic. In January 1993 he wrote a letter to Prosecutor-General Gustavo de Grieff outlining his intention to create an armed insurrection force, the *Antioquia Rebelde* (Antioquia in Rebellion). Although he affirmed his commitment to peace negotiations, Escobar demanded that "From to-day on, the conditions of dialogue will be the same as those accorded to all rebel groups."[57] Antioquia Rebelde, however, had no political coloration whatsoever. (Indeed, Escobar's letter stated specifically that the group did not intend to fight for the independence of Antioquia.) The government's reaction was predictable. Government minister Fabio Villejas Ramírez declared, "In no way are we going to allow these criminal organizations to act now in political roles for the purpose of receiving judicial benefits."[58]

Meanwhile, Escobar's credibility and support within the Medellín underworld were deteriorating. The capo had been levying huge war taxes—$200,000 per month or more—on other trafficking organizations in the city. Some traffickers who refused to pay were murdered on Escobar's order. Escobar's enemies decided to retaliate. In February 1992 the People Persecuted by Pablo Escobar (PEPES) inaugurated its existence by burning down a farm belonging to Escobar's mother. PEPES subsequently incinerated an estate and ceramics gallery owned by Escobar's wife and blew up a warehouse in Itagüi a town south of Medellín, that contained the trafficker's collection of antique cars. In addition, PEPES liquidated at least seven of Escobar's close associates between April and June 1993. The apparent leader of PEPES was a veteran paramilitary leader, Fidel Castaño Mejia, who had been involved in confrontation with guerrillas in Córdoba and northeastern Antioquia. A government investigation implicated Castaño in the murders at the *fincas* Honduras and La Negra (see chapter 7). In addition, he reputedly had a long association with the cocaine trade. PEPES received significant financial support from Escobar's rivals in Cali; some observers even claim that Cali leaders were de facto members of PEPES. PEPES apparently was linked to another anti-Escobar group, *Colombia Libre* (Free Colombia), that also emerged in early 1993. *Colombia Libre,* which was composed of former Escobar associates and assorted businessmen and industrialists, offered a reward of $5 million for Escobar's head, which compared favorably to the more than $7 million that the Colombian government was offering at the time.[59] Escobar's enemies collaborated enthusiastically with the Colombian government. *Colombia Libre* claims to have provided intelligence to the authorities to support forty operations against Escobar's organization. Similarly, leading Cali traffickers maintained a network of informants in Medellín and—according to several accounts—also deployed high-tech tracking devices to intercept Escobar's communications. The information obtained from these channels was passed on to the police and to the DAS. Colombia's current prosecutor-general, Alfonso Valdivieso, acknowledged the Cali cartel's contribution of "valuable information" to the search for Escobar and his enemies. In sum, the government's successful liquidation of Escobar on December 2, 1993—ten years after the trafficker had become a fugitive from justice—owed much to the efforts of Colombia's cocaine establishment. This irony not only diminishes the government's achievement in coping with Escobar and the Medellín cartel but also casts a shadow over its subsequent dialogues with the Cali cartel.[60]

Cali

Despite the government's dismal experience with Pablo Escobar, the surrender policy initiated by the Gaviria administration in 1990 remained in place. Indeed, the policy was amplified and made more beneficial to traffickers. Decree 264 in February 1993 allowed prosecutors to grant benefits such as house arrest for crimes for which the minimum penalty was less than eight years (a category including most drug crimes); reduced jail time for study, education, and work; suspensions of jail sentences and outright elimination of sentences and other penalties for crimes; nonimposition of fines; and the opportunity to enter witness protection programs. To qualify for leniency under the decree, offenders would need to improve the "efficiency of the administration of justice" by helping the authorities dismember criminal organizations and identify intellectual authors of crimes. Colombia's constitutional court modified the decree in mid-1993, objecting mainly to provisions that would grant de facto amnesty for crimes. Nevertheless, points in the decree pertaining to house arrest, work-study, and witness protection were codified in law 81 of November 1993, which established a new legal scheme for reducing penalties by collaborating with justice. Unlike decree 264, the law did not offer the prospect of escaping punishment entirely. However, criminals who turned themselves in could earn at least a two-thirds reduction in prison sentences, at the discretion of a prosecutor or a judge. The law also offered provisional liberty (pending completion of investigations), the substitution of social work for jail time, and, the possibility of house arrest. Like decree 264, law 81 conditioned judicial benefits on offenders' willingness to inform on colleagues and to provide information on criminal structures. Confusingly, though—in a section no doubt inserted at the insistence of Cali lawyers—the law stated that benefits would not be contingent on the confession of the person collaborating. It is not clear what information the government could extract from criminals under this stipulation. The Cali leaders assured the government that they could "consensually" dismantle their businesses without confessing and without denouncing criminal associates.[61]

The Cali dons initiated surrender negotiations with the Colombian government in January 1993. The first offer was presented to Prosecutor-General Gustavo de Grieff by lawyers representing 200 Cali traffickers who claimed to oversee 60 percent of the cocaine business in Colombia. In October 1993 some 300 traffickers from Valle, Antioquia, Santander, and the Atlantic coast made a coordinated surrender offer to the Colombian Congress that included separate messages from each regional group. The 300 traffickers claimed to control 70 percent of the Colombian cocaine exported to the United States and Europe. The Valle traffickers' message read, in part, "We do not believe that surrender to justice—that is, not to choose the road of rebellion—must be linked to a sentence, confession or charge." Furthermore, as noted, the Cali group appeared divided on whether to surrender infrastructure such as laboratories and shipping routes to the authorities. Such uncertainties hardly provided a suitable basis for negotiations. Still, government representatives held multiple meetings with Cali lawyers (and on three occasions with important traffickers themselves) to discuss possible surrender options.[62]

In January 1994 Gilberto Rodríguez, the apparent spokesman for the Cali cartel, further detailed the group's position in a letter to then-president Cesar Gaviria. In the letter, Rodríguez denied exercising leadership over the drug trade but offered to use his influence—power of assembly—to convince the multiple trafficking groups in Valle de Cauca to "abandon the cocaine business and submit to the law." Rodríguez refused to confess, saying "I have maintained my innocence for 9 years before tribunals in Colombia and Spain. I will not declare myself guilty now just to get a few less years in prison." Rodríguez also refused to implicate fellow Cali traffickers. Instead, he cited his past "collaboration with the prosecutor-general and the Search Bloc" in the fight against Pablo Escobar as justification for receiving judicial benefits as prescribed in the law. Specifically, Rodríguez demanded house arrest in lieu of a jail cell. "My life would be in danger in any prison in Valle as in the country," he reported.[63] This demand eventually was modified. According to the Bogotá newspaper *La Prensa*, the traffickers negotiated with de Grieff to secure a maximum prison term of only four years, but this arrangement was overturned under pressure from government colleagues and from the U.S. Embassy in Bogotá.[64]

De Grieff, the Colombian government's pointman for surrender talks with the Cali cartel, favored dialogue as an alternative to repression. However, his controversial views did much to undermine the credibility of the surrender process. For example, his open support of legalization of drugs was essentially incompatible with his position as Colombia's chief law enforcement officer. "The way we are waging the war against drugs is unsuccessful," he wrote to President Gaviria in March 1994. "We should study the possibility of legalizing drugs in the long term to reduce drug traffickers' profits."[65] (De Grieff had articulated similar views at a conference in Baltimore hosted in November 1993 by the city's pro-legalization mayor Kurt Schmoke.) Furthermore, de Grieff favored extremely lenient surrender terms for drug dealers. At one point, he "stated his intention of allowing house arrest for members of the Cali cartel," according to a 1994 *Semana* article.[66] The deal with Gilberto Rodríguez represents another case in point. At the same time, de Grieff did not press hard for concessions from the Cali leaders. Moreover, a year of conversations with Cali lawyers failed to yield a coherent concept for dismantling cocaine enterprises. Indeed, in a *Semana* interview on October 18, 1994, de Grieff articulated a far less ambitious goal. "If they collaborate so that the business moves to other countries, too bad for those countries, but if they leave Colombia, that's wonderful."[67]

For these various reasons, de Grieff soon became an embarrassment to the Colombian government and a target of U.S. hostility. Washington always had viewed Colombia's surrender negotiations with suspicion—as possible sellout to trafficking interests. De Grieff's behavior seemed to confirm these fears. The prosecutor's difficulties increased after he held successive private meetings in mid-January 1993 with three recognized Cali traffickers: Helmer Herrera Buitrago, José Olmedo Ocampo Duque, and Juan Carlos Ramírez. Herrera reputedly had run one of the cartel's largest distribution operations in New York City in the early 1990s, and Olmedo Ocampo was considered a key figure in the growing Colombian opium-heroin trade. Reportedly the traffickers wanted de Grieff's help in clarifying their legal status. As a result of their meetings, the traffickers received certifications signed by the prosecutor conferring temporary immunity from arrest pending the results of an investigation. In this De Grieff apparently had acted on his own, for the Colombian government learned about the meetings three weeks later via an intelligence report. Nor was the United States informed of the talks as they occurred.[68]

De Grieff's status declined rapidly thereafter. In March U.S. Attorney General Janet Reno sent the prosecutor a letter saying that "appeals for legalization of cocaine and clandestine discussions with cartel leaders" did not advance the course of U.S.-Colombian cooperation against drugs. The letter also objected to de Grieff's weak bargaining stance toward traffickers. "You have continued to suggest that recent offers of cartel leaders to present frankly useless information about the structure of the cartels should be rewarded."[69] In early April Colombia's attorney general, Gustavo Arrieta, accused de Grieff of making "isolated decisions" that adversely affected the country's criminal policy.[70] Later that month President Gaviria told *El Tiempo* that de Grieff "has made decisions which, unfortunately, he has not explained sufficiently to either the Colombian government or the U.S. government."[71] A letter that month to the *Washington Post* from Massachusetts Senator John Kerry said that the prosecutor's recent actions and statements "threaten to bring about his nation's capitulation to the Cali cartel." De Grieff's positions, asserted Kerry, were "nearly identical with those of the cartel itself," which, in the senator's view, demonstrated the cartel's increasing influence in the "very office of Colombian law enforcement that is supposed to protect society against the cartel."[72] In another slight to de Grieff, the World Bank, under direct pressure from the U.S. Treasury Department, abruptly cancelled a workshop on the Illicit Drug Trade in Latin America and the Caribbean, scheduled for May 18 and 19, 1994 in Washington. The prosecutor general was to have been the featured speaker at the workshop. Evidently Washington could not tolerate discussion of legalization in such a forum.

Colombia-U.S. relations also were deteriorating on another front. In February-March 1994, the United States suspended an agreement with Colombia to share evidence in criminal cases. In the past, the United States had furnished important information, such as testimony from U.S.-based traffickers and telephone intercepts of conversations between Cali cartel members. A significant factor in the U.S. decision was widespread corruption at the upper reaches of the Colombian prosecutorial system. (In an interview in June 1994, de Grieff admitted that corruption in his office was responsible for the failure of at least one field operation to capture Cali cartel leaders in 1994.)[73] For the United States, though, the principal problem was an incident in late 1993 and early 1994, when the U.S. Justice Department facilitated the deposition of two Colombian witnesses in Miami by representatives of de Grieff's office. The case concerned a trafficker named Hernán Angel Warner, a member of the Urdinola Grajales organization, centered in northern Valle de Cauca. The Colombians managed a Miami distribution cell for the organization. Shortly after the debriefing, though, the witnesses' close family members in Colombia were murdered. Due to this incident and to general mistrust of de Grieff, the United States decided in early 1994 to suspend a 1991 agreement on evidence sharing with Colombia. As of early 1996, judicial ties between the two countries still had not been fully restored.

Because of these problems and pressures, surrender negotiations with the Cali cartel came under fire in Colombia in the spring and summer of 1994. Attorney General Arrieta suggested that existing surrender procedures created a "feeling of impunity" among drug dealers and should be scrapped. He also argued that the government in general was unprepared to negotiate with traffickers. Dependence on "what the traffickers tell us" and on "disorganized and unclear" proofs furnished by the United States placed the government in a weak position, he declared.[74] Meanwhile, de Grieff struck back at his domestic and U.S. critics. He defended legalization on grounds that "the traffickers do not deserve the economic utilities that we are helping them to have." He called the negotiations a "useful instrument" to diminish the drug trade; and he hailed the overall surrender process as a way of "bringing peace to the nation and reintegrating people into society."[75] At the same time, de Grieff told the Cali lawyers that the climate for surrender negotiations was no longer opportune and that their clients should wait for the next presidential administration to take office (in August) before reactivating discussions with the government.

In September 1994, following Ernesto Samper's inauguration, the Cali traffickers announced a new surrender offer. In a meeting with *Time* reporter Tom Quinn in Cali, Gilberto Rodríguez remarked, "We have a plan that will significantly reduce narcotics trafficking out of Colombia." Under the plan, some 2,000 Colombian traffickers would cease operations and shut down their enterprises in stages that Rodríguez said would cut supplies of cocaine to the United States by 60 percent. As usual, the Cali proposal provided no specific plan of action. However, the Samper administration seemed notably sympathetic. "The door is open on the surrender program again," observed a Samper aide. "It is verifiable, manageable, and politically saleable."[76]

Colombia's inability to prosecute traffickers effectively, however, remained a point of contention in U.S.-Colombian relations. The system was so ineffective that at least 33 percent of convictions for drug-related crimes did not result in imprisonment. In the celebrated cases of two North Valle kingpins, Julio Fabio Urdinola and his brother Ivan Urdinola

Grajales, the traffickers prevailed on prosecutors and judges to reduce seventeen-year sentences down to slightly more than four years. (In comparison, the Medellín Ochoa brothers had been sentenced to 8.5 years, a term still considered too low by many U.S. law enforcement officials.) Ivan Urdinola, whose various confessions were published in late 1994 (the traffickers were arrested in 1992), admitted only to exporting cocaine to the United States. He supplied no details about supplies or routes and the names of leading Cali figures associated with him. Colombia's prosecutorial institutions clearly need major reforms. A bill introduced by the U.S. Senate Foreign Relations Committee that would impose economic sanctions on Colombian cities cited as one of the justifications "an ineffective plea bargaining system that leaves law-abiding citizens entirely unprotected against crime."[77]

In fact, the United States was dissatisfied with Colombia on a number of counts: its failure to capture major drug kingpins, the increase of drug money flows into Colombia in the 1990s, and allegations of drug-related corruption at high political levels, including reports that Samper's 1994 presidential bid was bankrolled partly by the Cali cartel. U.S. perceptions of the weakness of Colombia's criminal justice system prompted Washington's decision not to grant Colombia full certification in early 1995 for its counternarcotics efforts. Certification, a procedure established in Article 490 of the Foreign Assistance Act, requires the president to determine whether major drug-producing and drug transit countries have taken adequate measures to suppress drug trafficking or have cooperated fully with the United States in combatting drugs. Full decertification would have exposed Colombia to U.S. economic retaliation, including the loss of most foreign assistance and possible increased tariffs on Colombian products; Colombia instead received a partial certification—a so-called "national interest waiver" that indicated U.S. dissatisfaction with Colombia's performance against drugs but that avoided sanctions. Such pressures and concerns prompted a number of Colombian moves to demonstrate greater resolve toward the Cali cartel. In late 1994, the government issued new arrest warrants against the Rodríguez Orejuela brothers and began a trial in absentia against Miguel Rodríguez. The safe-conduct passes issued to high-level traffickers in January were revoked. In November 1994 and again in February 1995, President Samper promised to strengthen sentencing procedures and to reduce benefits offered to surrounding traffickers. (In reality, though, such changes will depend on modification of law 81 of 1993, modification that would require congressional action.) In March 1995 the government arrested the younger brother of Miguel and Gilberto Rodríguez, Jorge Eliecer—touted by police as an important cartel leader, but in reality an insignificant figure in the cocaine business. In May the National Police disseminated leaflets from helicopters in Cali and Bogotá announcing rewards of $1.8 million for help in capturing the Rodríguez brothers and $625,000 for information leading to the arrest of five other top cartel members. (In mid-1994 the government had offered relatively modest rewards of $125,000 to $250,000 for principal Cali leaders.) In May-June the Colombian Congress passed, and President Samper signed, a law that for the first time makes money laundering a felony in Colombia and that also establishes severe penalties for official corruption. Finally, between June and August, Colombian authorities succeeded in capturing Gilberto Rodríguez, José Santa Cruz and Miguel Rodríguez; the government's offensive also apparently encouraged three other Cali leaders, Victor Patiño, Henry Loaiza, and Phanor Arizabaleta, to turn themselves in.

Yet the spirit of negotiations was not completely dead. A Catholic priest and ex-mayor of Barranquilla, Bernardo Montoya Hoyos (possible candidate for the Colombian presidency in 1998) met with Miguel Rodríguez, Helmer "Pacho" Herrera, and two unidentified traffickers in mid-June, evidently with the prior approval of the president and DAS director Ramiro Bejarano. Hoyos recounted his conversation with Samper to the Bogotá weekly *Cambio 16.* "I told the president that I hope that they will give themselves up and that I was going to talk to them. It would be great if they surrender. The president said yes, let's hope that they do. Then I went to talk to Bejarano from DAS and told him the same thing."[78]

Hoyos carried a three-part message back from the cartel leaders. The traffickers said that they were willing to surrender under "the most just and honest conditions"—that is, with guarantees of leniency. They noted that while they were "men of peace," some of their more violently inclined colleagues might unleash a new wave of narcoterrorism if the government does not "change its attitude" and discontinue its offensive against the cartel. Most important, the Cali dons asserted that a large number of political leaders were involved on some level with the drug trade and that the dons possessed evidence of this involvement—tapes, documents, and photographs. The message was a clear blackmail threat.[79] Apparently the threat did not succeed as the government's achievement in putting Miguel Rodríguez and other Cali leaders behind bars demonstrates. Yet that achievement was offset by a spate of accusations of political corruption against top Samper administration officials that began in July and that are continuing to date (May 1996). Some Colombian observers, including Samper himself, believe that the offensive against the cartel precipitated the corruption allegations. "Moral terrorism" by the cartel was Samper's explanation but the imprisoned Cali leaders may have sought revenge against Samper and his colleagues leaking details of their financial contribution to the 1994 presidential campaign.[80]

EVALUATION

Andean governments have viewed negotiations more as a tool of social policy than as a technique for diminishing drug flows or dismantling trafficking enterprises. While negotiations doubtless helped reduce narcoterrorist violence in the 1990s, they have produced few successes against the cocaine traffic per se. Important traffickers, such as the Ochoa brothers and the Urdinola Grajales brothers, negotiated relatively short sentences ranging from four to eight years while providing little information on the workings of cocaine enterprises. Ivan Urdinola, for example, refused to name major accomplices, saying that to do so would place him in mortal danger, and his confessions were full of fatuous statements. "Aside from being a drug trafficker, I am an admirable person," he told a judge at one point.[81] Of course, the late Pablo Escobar was the most notorious abuser of the surrender policy. Escobar's confession was disingenuous to say the least: For instance, he admitted to knowing fellow Medellín drug lords Jorge, Fabio, and Juan David Ochoa, but only as partners in real estate deals; he also acknowledged merely an indirect connection to a sizable cocaine deal, the 1987 export of 400 kilograms of cocaine to France and the Middle East; and he fingered his dead cousin, Gustavo Gaviria, as the intellectual author of that crime. (The Bolivian government's repentance program also produced disappointing results: The repenters primarily characterized themselves as simple cattle farmers who only dabbled in cocaine or lent money to traffickers, and the three most important traffickers who surrendered under the program received sentences of only four to six years.)

Traffickers' peace offers appear to have become progressively more favorable to them over the years. While the fear of extradition prompted the traffickers to offer far-reaching concessions—for example, when in 1984 the Medellín drug traffickers proposed to withdraw definitively from the cocaine industry, to surrender planes, airstrips, and laboratories, and to dismantle the "total infrastructure" of their enterprises, and when in February 1990 traffickers actually turned over a sophisticated cocaine-refining complex to the Colombian authorities—this fear greatly diminished over time. When the Medellín kingpins surrendered in the early 1990s, most of the basic machinery of the cocaine business remained in place. Under the Gaviria plan, surrendering trafficking assets and dismantling infrastructure were not required to avoid extradition, and the Constituent Assembly voted extradition out of existence. Although putting the leaders of the Medellín cartel behind bars constituted a victory of sorts for the Colombian government, the basic machinery of the Colombian cocaine business has not been affected greatly. In addition, although the Extraditables' offer of November 1990 discussed the possible surrender of 200 to 300 members of that group, only between 20 and 25 traffickers actually turned themselves in under the Gaviria decrees.

Of course, Bogotá's drug-fighting objectives were not the same as those of Washington: The chief U.S. goal is reducing the flow of Colombian cocaine into North American markets. For Colombia, as President Cesar Gaviria reportedly emphasized, ending narcoterrorism—"the principal threat against our democracy"[82]—represented a much higher priority than terminating the drug traffic per se, which Colombia defines as an international problem that will abate only when the consuming countries lower their demand for narcotics. Still, the peace settlement with the Medellín drug kingpins was a major disappointment, especially in light of previous trafficker offers to the Colombian government.

Cali cartel leaders recently offered to implement a plan to reduce cocaine exports from Colombia by 60 percent (their estimate of their share of the business), provided they spend little or no time in jail. Such an offer, however, invites skepticism. For example, are the Cali dons capable of controlling or directly influencing a sufficiently large percentage of Colombia's refining and exporting capacity to accomplish such a reduction? Much recent information suggests that the Colombian cocaine industry as a whole is more decentralized and balkanized than it was in the 1980s—Gilberto Rodríguez Orejuela himself noted in a November 1994 letter to *El Tiempo* that "there are many cartels"—and it depends on a multitude of subcontractors and freelancers.[83] Rodríguez's "power of assembly" also reportedly has been challenged by a younger group of Cali traffickers who are not interested in giving up the cocaine business until they themselves have accumulated illicit fortunes.

Of course, drug kingpins may possess considerable leverage with colleagues and lower-level operators. For example, they can cease purchasing of products or services or simply withhold protection from laboratories, transport companies, distribution cells, laundering operations, and other key trafficking entities. However, the Cali traffickers have offered no blueprint or timetable for dismantling their multibillion-dollar enterprises, and the government never forced the cartel to clarify the terms of its surrender offer. Moreover, a number of factors—the size of the illicit drug industry, the prevalence of official corruption, and the weakness of Colombia's criminal justice and judicial institutions—suggest that Colombia would not be up to the task of implementing such a deal. In addition, the constitutional ban imposed in 1991 on the extradition of Colombian citizens has greatly diminished the government's leverage over major drug kingpins.

In sum, negotiations with drug capos have done little to downsize the cocaine business and possibly have compromised the integrity of the Andean criminal justice systems. Since 1984, Colombia's cocaine industry has become a much more formidable foe—exports have increased at least 300 percent (according to U.S. estimates); earnings have at least doubled; and traffickers have greatly expanded their landholdings, investments, military capabilities, and influence within the bureaucracy. Controlling drug traffic today will be much more difficult than it would have been during the mid-1980s. Still, narcodialogues and voluntary surrender programs enjoy wide political acceptance in the Andes. Such realities should guide U.S. counternarcotics policy in the area. The United States traditionally has taken a dim view of Andean drug negotiations; indeed, left to their own devices, Andean governments have tended to strike bad bargains with cocaine traffickers. An active if unofficial U.S. role in the negotiation process—shaping the agenda of discussions and providing corroborating evidence and proofs—might help to ensure that the terms of a drug deal would contribute to U.S. law enforcement objectives. Conversely, without U.S. participation, a negotiated settlement could become either a comfortable retirement program for drug lords (who might serve little jail time or keep their fortunes intact) or a prelude to de facto legalization of drugs and drug trafficking.

Negotiations constitute a variant of plea bargaining, and in the United States prosecutors' ability to plea bargain has been a significant weapon in the struggle against organized crime. The cases of Barry Seal (a notorious drug dealer and pilot turned DEA informant) and Max Mermelstein (a transportation organizer for the Ochoa and Escobar organizations) illustrate how leniency in sentencing can be credibly exchanged for vital intelligence, even in U.S. courts. By his own admission, Seal smuggled more than 30 tons of cocaine into the United States in the early 1980s. Nevertheless, in 1984-1985 he helped the DEA secure indictments against the Medellín cartel and a corrupt prime minister, Norman Sanders, of the Turks and Caicos Islands. Seal eventually negotiated a plea bargain with federal prosecutors that enabled him to avoid a prison sentence. (Seal was murdered in February 1986, apparently the victim of an assassin hired by the Ochoa family.) Mermelstein organized the shipment of 56 tons of cocaine to the United States and the repatriation of $300 million in drug proceeds to Colombia between 1981 and 1985. After furnishing important testimony on big figures in the Medellín cartel, he was released into a witness protection program after serving only two years in jail. However, the U.S. concept of plea bargaining differs from the type sporadically attempted in Colombia. U.S. prosecutors generally strike deals with criminals who are already in custody, and collective bargaining with criminals as an inducement to turn themselves in (the type practiced by the Colombians with the cartels) is almost unknown. More important, plea bargaining in the United States is designed to extract testimony from lower-level criminals (for example, Seal and Mermelstein) to implicate higher-level criminals or crime bosses (for example, Escobar and the Ochoa brothers). Negotiating with top crime figures to dismantle a particular criminal enterprise or line of activity is essentially an uncharted area of law enforcement in the United States and most other countries.

Still, as the world's largest cocaine-consuming nation, the United States has an interest in the success of the narcodialogue in Colombia and elsewhere. At the least, Washington should press Andean governments to seek worthwhile agreements that cripple existing drug enterprises and supply the knowledge necessary to strengthen the fight against future organizations. The incarceration of Gilberto and Miguel Rodríguez, José Santa Cruz, and other leaders presents a possible opportunity for Washington and Bogotá to negotiate the dismemberment of powerful Cali organizations. What, then, should a surrender package include? What should traffickers be forced to relinquish in return for reduced jail time and other benefits? A negotiated settlement probably should focus on the following issues.

First, traffickers should furnish U.S. and Colombian authorities with information on cocaine supplies, laboratory sites, smuggling networks, transportation systems, overseas bank accounts, and cocaine distribution centers in the United States and Western Europe. Traffickers also should describe the inner workings of their organizations, such as cartel techniques for recruiting members, paying off public officials, making business decisions, and planning acts of violence. In other words, traffickers should produce a more comprehensive picture of cocaine trafficking organizations and their allied enterprises.

Second, traffickers should relinquish most of their illegally obtained wealth. The most appropriate use of this money would be repairing the damage caused by their illicit trade—for example, funding crop substitution programs and drug rehabilitation centers and compensating the families of traffickers' victims. By implication, drug funds stashed in foreign banks would be repatriated. In their 1984 proposal, the traffickers offered the "return of our capital to Colombia as soon as formulas enabling this to be done have been worked out."[84] Unfortunately, subsequent offers did not include this provision. If they are able to keep their huge caches of money stashed abroad, traffickers could continue funding cocaine laboratories (perhaps locating new refining operations outside of Colombia), managing distribution networks, and purchasing weapons.

Third, a system of verification is essential, because the United States and Colombia have no basis for believing that the traffickers would keep their promises. A newly established international commission of law enforcement and intelligence expert possibly could monitor the dismantling of cocaine laboratories and transportation systems, document the transfer of trafficker capital from foreign tax havens, and oversee the surrender of arms stocks. Sustaining the drug peace would depend largely on the effectiveness of new technologies—applied in conjunction with the newly acquired knowledge of drug trade operations—in detecting hidden jungle laboratories, drug-smuggling aircraft, cocaine in cargo containers, flows of drug profits, and the like. Colombia's dialogue with traffickers so far has virtually ignored the verification issue, which constitutes a very serious—and for the United States, unacceptable—omission.[85]

Of course, the benefits side of the package would have to be negotiated: the length of jail terms, the physical conditions of incarceration, and protection of traffickers who turn state's evidence. The issue of sentencing, of course, is critical. Current procedures in Colombia constitute an open door to immunity. For instance, the Cali leaders certainly desire maximum sentences of only five to ten years, but such penalties should be increased if they do not comply with the surrender terms just outlined.

Negotiations can extend the reach and effectiveness of conventional law enforcement, but they should not be seen as a miraculous solution to the South American cocaine problem. A "Panama scenario"— a negotiated shutdown of most of Colombia's cocaine business along the lines proposed by the Medellín cartel in 1984—seems unlikely to occur. The industry's export volume has expanded significantly since that time, and the number of refiners, smugglers, distributors, and financial managers has increased correspondingly. The viability of sanctions remains in question. Despite Gilberto Rodríguez's claimed power of assembly, the industry may be too decentralized for a relatively small number of leading traffickers to guarantee the shutdown of a significant percentage of cocaine export capacity. The cartels' middle managers and less affluent traffickers may resist any surrender deal. Possibilities of recidivism and outright cheating by traffickers have to be taken into account. Finally, as long as the demand for cocaine remains high, other suppliers eventually will enter the market to satisfy that demand.

Drug negotiations cannot take the place of traditional law enforcement measures that put pressure on narcotics industries, such as drug raids and dragnets, seizures of traffickers' wealth, and aerial spraying of illicit crops. Traffickers will not voluntarily furnish important pieces of the cocaine trafficking puzzle. Furthermore, stronger criminal justice systems in the Andean countries—credible laws, courts, and police investigations—obviously would improve the prospects for using bargaining strategies in the fight against cocaine trafficking empires—perhaps the most powerful and dangerous criminal enterprises that the world has ever known.

Part III

The Effects of Cocaine on the Andes

5

Coca and the Alternatives

The drug lords we have been analyzing up to this point are only part of the cocaine business. To produce cocaine requires coca leaf. Hundreds of thousands of farmers and their families throughout the Andes depend upon the income from growing coca leaves. The coca farmers present a quite different problem from the drug lords. The major traffickers are a murderous lot who deserve little sympathy. The farmers, on the other hand, are simple folk eking a living; they do not see and do not fully understand the evil effects of the drug produced from the crop. The U.S. government says the drug lords should be pursued with the full force of the law. The Andean governments sometimes prosecute or extradite traffickers, but often prefer negotiations or tacit accommodation. But no one proposes jailing the farmers for growing a generally illegal crop. To understand what can be done to wean farmers away from growing coca, we must consider how and why they grow coca instead of other crops.

Coca is a hardy and adaptable perennial shrub with several subspecies. It flourishes on steep slopes and in infertile acidic soils, that is, in conditions that restrict the growth of other crops. Coca can grow almost anywhere in tropical South America and in tropical regions of the world generally. It is currently grown almost exclusively in the Andean countries of Peru, Bolivia, and Colombia, generally at an elevation below 7,000 feet. Much of the land now planted in coca is simply unsuitable for legal agriculture. After planting, the bush must grow twelve to eighteen months before the first crop of leaves can be picked and three to four years before full production is reached, when the bush is three to five feet high. A bush can produce for ten to twenty-five years, depending on how well it is cared for.

Peru is the largest producer, according to U.S. government surveys, accounting in 1995 for 59 percent of the land area devoted to coca and 57 percent of the Andean output of coca leaves. Colombia and Bolivia account respectively for 24 percent and 33 percent of the land area and 13 percent and 27 percent of the leaf output. The two most important coca-producing regions in South America are Peru's Upper Huallaga Valley and the tropical provinces of Cochabamba Department, collectively called the Chapare, in Bolivia. Together these areas produce approximately 70 percent of South America's supply of coca leaves. In Colombia, more than 80 percent of both the coca area and coca leaf production is concentrated in three adjoining departments—Guaviare, Meta, and Caquetá—in the southeastern portion of the country.[1]

Actually, these numbers give a false sense of precision, for we do not have hard numbers about coca or the cocaine industry. While the bible for analysts is the State Department's annual *International Narcotics Control Strategy Report,* or INCSR, its authors admit to the problems in coming up with any data about an illegal activity in developing countries that do not have particularly precise data about most parts of their economy. To give an idea of the scale of the uncertainty, consider that in 1991 the INCSR increased its estimate of coca yields; overnight the U.S. government estimate of Andean coca leaf output rose 49 percent. Or consider the estimates about the area planted to coca, which the INCSR says is "the most reliable information we have on illicit drugs." The aerial photographs taken from 1985 through 1988 by a Peruvian government agency under contract to the Special Project for Control and Coca Crop Reduction in the Upper Huallaga (CORAH) were interpreted by a United Nations Development Program (UNDP) study to show 44,700 hectares of coca in one part of the Upper Huallaga Valley; the U.S. Narcotics Assistance Unit said these same photographs showed 60,000 to 70,000 hectares of coca.[2]

THE COCA-GROWING COMMUNITIES IN PERU AND BOLIVIA

A typical farm family in the main coca regions of Peru (the Upper Huallaga) or Bolivia (the Chapare) may grow one to two hectares of cocaine as well as five to seven hectares of food crops, including possibly some other cash crops. The farmers want some diversity in their crop mix, because they need to be sure they can survive if there are problems in the coca business, such as a temporary crackdown by police. Depending on coca prices and on the sophistication of the technology employed, a farmer in the Upper Huallaga Valley can earn perhaps $2,000 a year, according to Iban de Rementeria, a long-time Valley-watcher, or somewhat more, according to the price and cost data from UNDP and the U.S. Agency for International Development (USAID). Farmers in the Chapare may make somewhat less.

In both Bolivia and Peru, most coca farmers are migrants to the tropical regions from the Andean highlands, not long-settled farmers who have decided to switch into more-profitable coca from less-profitable legal crops. Most of those who work in the coca fields left the highlands specifically to produce coca.

Bolivia

Until the 1970s, Bolivian coca was concentrated in the Yungas region, where coca has been grown for centuries for chewing. The coca for processing into cocaine comes primarily from the Chapare region. Chapare coca is produced mainly by those who moved to the region after the coca boom started in the mid-1970s. With the influx of migrants, the Chapare's population swelled from perhaps 100,000 in 1976 to as high as 350,000 in the years from 1985 to 1988.[3] At the height of the boom, the recent migrants provided at least three-fourths of total labor. According to an in-depth study of where the labor came from to produce the coca, "Without this migratory labor, there could have been no coca boom."[4] It would be erroneous to say that coca invaded a peaceful farming community or that local farmers had long grown coca. To a large extent, coca created the towns and villages in the Chapare out of the isolated communities that had been there before.

The migrants went there, despite their dislike for the region, because job opportunities were poor elsewhere. The migrants complain bitterly about the weather, which is hotter and more humid than in their home communities. Serious acculturation problems sometimes ensue for these people in their move from the nearly treeless highlands to the dense tropical forests. In an interview, one longtime development worker in the area described how he tackled settlers' fears of the forest by teaching them about which trees to use for what purpose—it could take him a week to get the new arrivals to distinguish between palm trees and leafy trees, because they simply were unused to trees. The small bands of settlers who moved to the Chapare before coca typically had no experience with tropical farming and in some cases were miners who had never farmed. The head of the Chapare livestock cooperative had never touched a cow until the year he started raising them.[5] One reason the settlers stick with coca, once they have learned the very simple skills needed to raise that hardy bush, is that they are simply unfamiliar with how to raise anything else.

These migrants feel no commitment to the coca-growing region. For example, the 1994 Bolivian government Agricultural Survey showed that only 60 percent of the farmers spend ten or more months of every year on their farm. (See table 5.1.) The difference between a farmer who spends nine months on the farm and one who spends twelve months is fundamental, because the former cannot raise any kind of animal—not chickens, not cattle, and certainly not dairy cows. The survey also found that 58 percent of the farmers owned land outside of the Chapare—42 percent in the upland areas of the same department and 16 percent in other parts of Bolivia (presumably the highlands). Given that these people are in a low-income bracket and cannot be expected to have investment property, the land elsewhere may well be their original residences, which they have not yet fully left. The most detailed sociological study of the area found that 95 percent of the migrants retained homes in their areas of origin.[6]

There is quite a turnover among the farming community. While the overall population has declined from its peak around 1985, quite a few people still arrive each year. According to the 1994 Agricultural Survey, 42 percent of the region's farmers had arrived in the area since 1985; presumably, a higher percentage of the farm laborers had moved in since that date.

TABLE 5.1
BOLIVIA: CHAPARE FARMERS' COMMITMENT TO THE COCA ZONE, 1993/94

A. Farmers by Years in Charge of the Farm

	0–10	10–14	15 +	TOTAL
Number	14,139	11,263	8,112	33,514
Percent	42%	34%	24%	100%

B. Farmers by Months During the Year in Which Worked on Farm

	0–6	6–9	10–12	TOTAL
Number	5,008	8,468	20,038	33,514
Percent	15%	25%	60%	100%

C. Farmers by Land Ownership, Besides Their Land in Tropical Cochabamba

	Outside Cochabamba	Elsewhere in Cochabamba	None	TOTAL
Number	5,270	14,150	14,094	33,514
Percent	16%	42%	42%	100%

Source: 1994 Agricultural Survey, Government of Bolivia.

Peru

As in Bolivia, the 1970s and 1980s Peruvian coca boom was concentrated in a region of migrants, far removed from the zone where coca has been grown for centuries for chewing. Nevertheless, there are many differences between the Bolivian Chapare and the Peruvian Upper Huallaga.

Government settlement programs dating back to the early 1960s brought a small community of settlers—colonialists, as they are called—to the Huallaga Valley from the overpopulated Andean highlands. Substantial numbers of migrants also were attracted by employment opportunities in road construction and by the region's potential for producing tropical tree crops such as palm oil, coffee, and cacao. The 1969 land reform provided the migration with an indirect boost. Although it had few direct effects on the jungle regions like the Huallaga Valley, the law reduced the demand for seasonal agriculture labor on the Peruvian coast, which hurt the highland residents. Some moved to the Huallaga. Because travel to which the area is too difficult to permit easy seasonal movement, the migrants generally cut their ties to their regions of origin.[7]

The valley underwent a vicious cycle of cocainization in the 1980s. Guerrilla movements were attracted to the coca income and to coca farmers' grievances against the government, which sporadically repressed the crop. As the guerrilla movements and cocaine traffickers established themselves, government agents in the area were placed in danger. With less government presence, the infrastructure started to decay, and the costs of transporting legal crops to major markets became prohibitive. Therefore, cultivation of legal crops decreased; the most precipitous change was the fall-off in maize from 69,400 hectares planted in 1987-1988 to only 19,890 hectares planted in 1990-1991. Farmers then became more dependent on coca income.

During the 1980s, the population of the Huallaga Valley grew 4.8 percent per year, the same rate as the Greater Lima Metropolitan area. In contrast, the average annual population growth rate for the other rural regions in Peru was 0.8 percent during that time. In 1991, approximately 658,000 people lived in the Huallaga Valley.

By the late 1980s, three developments were causing a crisis in the coca economy of the Upper Huallaga. First, the government had established a police base at Santa Lucia from which U.S.-funded helicopters struck at coca processing facilities. Second, a variant of the long-present *fusarium oxysporum* fungus developed that targeted coca specifically, and it spread quickly. Finally, the security situation became intolerable under the influence of the fanatical Maoist Shining

Path (*Sendero Luminoso*) guerrillas. Thousands of farmers migrated. According to USAID, "The once booming narcotown of Tocache is currently in a major economic recession."[8] As the National Narcotics Intelligence Consumers Committee's *NNICC Report 1993* put it, "Farmers moved out of the [Upper Huallaga Valley] [in 1993] in part seeking less tumultuous areas, but they also abandoned plots due to soil depletion, fear of plant disease, and a 'gold-rush' mentality of new [coca-producing] areas."[9]

Farmers moved into areas where land was readily available, primarily to the east. Some went directly east into the Aguaytia Valley; others went northeast into the Central Huallaga; still others went southeast into the Apurímac Valley. Those regions generally lack economical access to the legal market, making coca the most attractive crop. By 1995, coca production affected eleven departments in Peru, including the traditional pre-boom coca areas, the Huallaga Valley, and the new areas, with a population of 5.7 million, or just under one-quarter of the national total.

LEGAL MARKETS FOR COCA

The vast majority of Andean coca leaf production is destined for conversion to illegal cocaine. In Colombia, coca plays little social role and has no legal status. A legal market, however, does exist for coca leaves in Peru and Bolivia, where they have been chewed and used medicinally and ritually since pre-Inca times.

There are several components to the legal coca market. Most of the legal leaf is consumed by households; in general, it is chewed (coca is both a stimulant and an appetite suppressant) or used as a remedy for stomach ailments and other illnesses. Some leaf is exported. The beverage producer Coca-Cola uses small quantities from which it extracts flavoring coca after leaching out the cocaine and other alkaloids. Some is converted to legal cocaine for pharmaceutical markets abroad. In the United States cocaine is still used in eye drops and nose drops and is widely administered during rhinoplasty, or "nose jobs"; however, new generations of synthetic drugs have largely supplanted its traditional role as an anesthetic. Also, coca has some limited use as a food additive, and commercially packaged coca tea is a popular brew in Andean highland regions.

Just how much coca is a part of Andean Indian tradition is a matter of some controversy.[10] Pro-coca and leftist nationalist forces in the Andes make much of coca's role in precolonial religion and daily life. On the other hand, there is a long history of domestic opposition to coca chewing, such as Peru's 1961 commitment to eliminate the practice by 1986.

Pro-coca groups argue that "industrialization" of coca—conversion to foods, medicines, and household products—could absorb much of the "excess" leaf now destined for illegal markets. Much publicity is given to the efforts to expand noncocaine markets. Some trial production of such products as coca crackers, coca toothpaste, and coca wine (which is said not to leave a hangover) has already occurred in the Andes. The Bolivian government on occasion promotes foreign sales of coca leaf tea, which are hampered by the small amount of active alkaloids in the tea.

Industrialization advocates probably have exaggerated the potential legal market for coca. The 1961 Single Convention on Narcotics Drugs remains a significant barrier to legalization.[11] Even if industrial countries were to permit free imports of coca leaf tea and similar products—which now are subject to varying and inconsistent restrictions—it is difficult to see how such products could become a significant source of income for Andean farmers. Furthermore, the economic consequences of industrialization might be different from those envisioned by its promoters. A significant expansion of legal production would precipitate a bidding war between traffickers and legal entrepreneurs for available supplies of both coca leaf and agricultural labor. Both leaf prices and wages in the illegal sector would rise, possibly resulting in an expansion of the amount of coca under cultivation—hardly a desirable outcome.

The legal coca sector functions quite differently in Peru than in Bolivia. In Peru, a state enterprise, ENACO, administers the purchase of coca from land registered before 1978.[12] The legal area is 16 percent of the total coca area as estimated by the U.S. government. ENACO, an inefficient enterprise, purchases only a small portion of the coca leaf produced on the registered land; the farmers sell the rest to traffickers. In Bolivia, many small merchants trade legal coca, buying the coca leaf in village markets supervised by counternarcotics police. The permanent legal coca area is largely in the Yungas region. Coca is legal in the Chapare region only on a transitional basis until it is fully phased out in accordance with the program set forth in law 1008 of 1986. In 1994 the domestic market absorbed 15 percent of Bolivia's coca leaf production. Small amounts are exported legally, as for coca leaf tea.

THE ECONOMICS OF COCA PRODUCTION

The economics of coca production changed greatly between the late 1970s and the mid-1990s. Although the prices paid for the leaf dropped, lower per-ton costs as farming technique improved partly offset this. Coca production now appears solidly profitable, but not fabulously so, once the higher risks are factored in.

To follow the development in coca economics, we need to analyze the price and the costs. That is no easy matter, given that much of the industry's activities are illegal. The information we have is all highly approximate. Not much significance should be attached to a change of a few percentage points in any variable. The analysis can only give the broad picture, not the fine details.

Coca Leaf Prices

From the limited information available, coca leaf prices appear to have followed a rather different trend in Peru and Bolivia. (No data are available for Colombia.) It is hard to account for the movements in price except by reference to counternarcotics politics in the two countries.

In Peru, prices from 1989 through 1995 fluctuated around $1.50 per kilogram except during two six-month periods when prices were much higher (about $3.00 per kilogram) and two six-month periods when prices were much lower (about $0.50 per kilogram). (See figure 5.1.) According to Peruvian analysts consulted in Lima, counternarcotics politics explains the changes. The prices were low in 1989-1990 because the Colombian government cracked down on dealers after the assassination of a presidential candidate. During the crackdown, few planes went to the Huallaga looking for coca, and the price dropped. The high prices during late 1992 occurred during a time of unsettled security. The Shining Path guerrilla movement was at its peak, both in the valley and throughout Peru, until its leader was captured in September. With the government weak and preoccupied, counternarcotics operations were not as effective as at other times.

A dramatic illustration of counternarcotics' effect on coca prices came in 1994-1995. After April 1994, Peru was unable to stop planes carrying drugs because the U.S. government shut its radars and ceased sharing information about drug flights; as discussed in chapter nine, the U.S. Department of Justice ruled that such assistance was illegal because Peru's threats to shoot down drug flights contravened international law. Then during the Peru-Ecuador border confrontation in December 1994 to February 1995, the Peruvian Air Force did little interdiction. Drug flights reached an historic high of more than fifty a month in early 1995.[13] With so many planes going to the Huallaga, the demand for coca was high, and the price rose sharply. But soon after the radars were turned back on, the Peruvian Air Force counternarcotics operations resumed, drug flights fell sharply, down to six a month in late 1995. With so few flights, the traffickers were not interested in buying as much coca. The price of coca leaf fell ninety percent from November 1994 to July 1995. It remained stuck at that low level through the end of the year, though by early 1996, it appeared to have recovered its historic average of $1.50 per kilogram.

In Bolivia, the coca price also fell during late 1989 and early 1990, presumably also due to the crackdown on dealers in Colombia. Abstracting from that price dip, the average price in Bolivia was on a slow downward trend from 1989 through 1991, starting out at $1.50 to $2.00 per kilogram and ending up around $1.00 per kilogram. (See figure 5.2.) Since 1991-1992, the price has not declined, fluctuating more or less around $1.25 per kilogram. More vigorous law enforcement seems responsible for the price decline, with $1.00 per kilogram being as low as the price could get.

The decline in price also may be illusory due to unreliable data. The Bolivian data are better than those from Peru and Colombia, be-

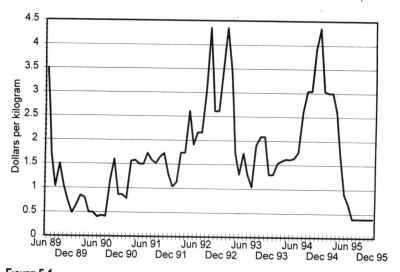

FIGURE 5.1

PERU: COCA LEAF PRICE.

Source: Tito Hernández, UNDP, Lima, personal communication to authors.

cause Bolivia has a large legal coca trade, with markets of considerable size in a number of towns. (Colombia has no legal market and Peru's state-run monopoly buys only small amounts for legal purposes.) However, the market prices may not be accurate. Traffickers may avoid the markets (and the police who watch them), and the leaf sold there is often the chewing variety rather than the type used for processing into cocaine. Bolivian planning minister Samuel Doria Medina has published an estimate of the prices paid for leaf to be processed; those prices vary from about half to about three-quarters of the market prices.

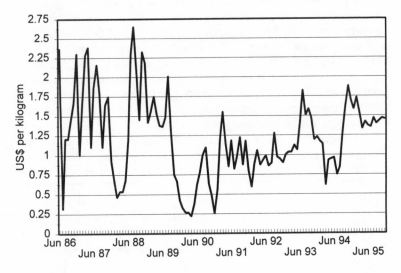

FIGURE 5.2
BOLIVIA: COCA LEAF PRICE: JUNE 1986–DECEMBER 1995.
Source: USAID La Paz.

The coca leaf price in Peru has been substantially higher than that in Bolivia, because Peru's economy is somewhat more developed than Bolivia's and the costs of labor are correspondingly higher. (Labor accounts for most of the cost of producing leaves.) An alternative explanation is that it is more expensive to fly coca products from Bolivia to the marketing centers in Colombia than to fly them from Peru. Small planes have to be used to minimize the risk of detection, and their range is limited, requiring either a refueling stop (with all the associated costs, such as bribes) or carrying a much smaller cargo load.

Coca Production Costs

The cost of producing coca depends on the technique used and the farmers' skill, both of which differ substantially from farmer to farmer. There are no credible estimates of what constitutes an "average farmer." The estimates used by the Andean governments and different U.S. government agencies vary by as much as 5,000 percent on technical coefficients; there is no agreement on the average amount of labor required for each stage of the crop, on the physical amounts of inputs needed, or on crop yields. A detailed 1993 investigation by the DEA in

Bolivia, involving visits to ninety Chapare fields, found different classes of farmers, including a low-yield class harvesting less than 350 kilograms per hectare per annum and a high-yield class harvesting 900 kilograms or more.[14] The DEA ascribed the differences to farmer skill, including "understory weed growth, plant canopy trimming, and the use of chemical fertilizers, herbicides and insecticides."

Table 5.2
PERU: Variable Cost of Production of Coca, March 1991

	Low Technology		High Technology	
	Quantity Per Hectare	Dollars Per Kilogram	Quantity Per Hectare	Dollars Per Kilogram
Dry leaf output (kilograms)	667	$1.56	2,070	$1.56
A. Labor (days)	69	.47	368	.81
Harvest	56	.38	173	.38
Weeding, other	13	.09	195	.43
B. Materials				.32
C. Unforeseen (10%)		.05		.11
TOTAL		.51		1.23
PROFIT		1.05		.33

Note: Excludes fixed costs, especially the cost of recovering initial investment.

Source: United Nations Development Program, Regional Development and Agroindustrial Promotion Project AD/PER/86/459.

Perhaps the most sophisticated model of coca production costs is from the UNDCP/UNDP project in Peru, which for years has produced monthly data on production costs. It tracks three different production technologies and examines the cost at several different stages in the life cycle of a coca bush. Table 5.2 shows the variability of costs depending on the production technology. In fact, however, the data understate the differences, because they do not include the cost of repaying the initial investment, which is larger for the high-technology producers than for the low-technology ones. The main conclusion that can be reached is that care should be taken before making any sweeping statement about the profitability of coca production, because profits depend greatly on production technique. For instance, when prices rise, more intensive cultivation (more fertilizer, more frequent weeding, etc.) becomes profitable; when prices fall, farmers can still make a profit if they use a simpler production method.

U.S. law enforcement and development officials have sought to identify a single break-even price for coca—a definitive income threshold below which farmers will abandon coca cultivation. There are several difficulties with this concept. First of all, the literature on coca cultivation records wide disparities in per-unit production costs. Farmers use different mixes of inputs and cultivate their fields with varying efficiency.

Second, farmers are likely to change their production strategy depending on prevailing prices. At low prices, farmers may opt to concentrate on harvesting the leaves, devoting little or no labor time to tending the plant (weeding or fertilizing) and applying few inputs, such as fertilizer and insecticides.

Third, a major complication in any analysis of coca production costs is that farmers make use of family labor when they need to cut costs. If leaf prices are high, farmers will hire more pickers; if the price drops, they will press into service their wives and children. This provides a flexibility that is not necessarily available with other crops, for which the prices and production techniques do not justify using hired labor.

Finally, what influences farmers' production decisions is the anticipated future price of leaves, not the current price. For example, in 1990—when coca prices plummeted to record low levels—Bolivian

⌖ TABLE 5.3
INCOME PER DAY OF LABOR PRODUCING COCAINE (IN DOLLARS, EXCEPT AS NOTED)

	Peru September 1994	Bolivia 1992
Sales per hectare	4,500	2,256
Harvest in kilos	2,070	2,625
Price per kilo	2.17	.86
Costs per hectare	1,919	303
Harvest cost	736	
Materials cost	600	134
Capital cost	334	169
Provision for other costs	249	
Net income per hectare	2,581	1,953
Days of farmer labor per hectare	169	277
Net income per day	15.27	7.05
For reference:		
Day labor wage rate	9.09	6.75
Initial investment	1,481	751

Note: The UNDP data for Peru assume wage labor, paid by the kilo, is used for harvest. If the harvesters earn the day labor wage rate, then 81 days of labor are needed per hectare.
Sources: UNDP data for Tocache, Peru; USAID data for Chapare, Bolivia; and authors' assumption about interest rate (20 percent) and period over which to amortize the investment (12 years).

farmers planted approximately 3,000 new hectares. In the following year, when average coca prices had rebounded to almost double their 1990 level ($0.95 per kilogram compared to $0.55 per kilogram), farmers planted only 2,700 new hectares. In effect, in 1990 farmers predicted that prices would stabilize at a higher level, which they did. In 1991 farmers were less confident about a future rise in price (with good reason, as things turned out) so they planted less coca. In sum, the concept of a break-even price, at which income equals cost, has many problems.

Another, more fruitful way to look at the issue of the profitability of coca production is to ask how much can the farmer earn for each day's labor in the coca fields. The answer depends greatly on the assumptions used to make the estimate, such as what production techniques are used or how the initial investment is financed. On the basis of assumptions we judge most realistic, coca turns out to earn the farmer a good income per day's labor. In Peru in 1994, the income from coca was $15 per day, compared to daily wages for simple laborers in the Huallaga Valley of $9 per day. In Bolivia in 1992, the income from coca was $7 per day, which was still above the $6.75 paid to the coca leaf stompers. (See table 5.3.) That is, the farmers made more than those who had to do the nasty work of stomping barefoot on the leaf/chemical mixture in the backyard pits in which leaf is turned into paste.

COCA AND ALTERNATIVE CROPS

Contrary to a widely held belief, net income from coca is not always higher than that from legal crops. For instance, in the Upper Huallaga Valley, returns from local citrus, bananas, and agriculture have compared favorably with those from coca, according to data from the Special Upper Huallaga Valley Project (PEAH), which was set up by USAID. In Bolivia, a 1992 USAID study found that a variety of nontraditional crops could compete successfully with coca at prevailing leaf prices, as shown in table 5.4. Calculations of costs and income are always approximate, so not too much importance should be attributed to small differences in the estimated net income per hectare or per day of labor. Coca, bananas, and citrus are all in the same rough range, while pineapples earn more, for those who can afford the higher investment they require and the longer wait until the investment pays off. The accuracy of these calculations seems to be borne out by the behavior of farmers, who recently have been producing more pineapples and bananas rather than more coca.

Alternatives to coca are less promising in Colombia. UNDCP data on net income from various crops show that the only crop anywhere near coca is opium poppy. (See table 5.5.) In 1993, in the town of Argelia in the UNDCP project area in Cauca-Nariño, UNDCP extension workers were approached by local farmers wanting seeds to plant opium poppy as a substitute crop for coca. Replacing coca bushes with opium poppies is not quite what the U.S. and Colombian governments hope for when they speak of alternative crops.

TABLE 5.4
BOLIVIA: COCA COMPARED TO LEGAL CROPS, 1992
(DOLLARS PER HECTARE, EXCEPT AS NOTED)

	Coca	Bananas	Pine-apple	Citrus	Black Pepper
Investment cost	1,120	887	5,068	908	4,575
Net income	1,480	1,023	3,764	1,731	1,647
Days of farmer labor	277	155	224	261	182
Net income per day	5.34	6.60	16.80	6.63	9.05
Note: Net income without capital cost	1,772	1,320	5,722	1,917	2,678

Source: Clark Joel, Alternative Development of the Chapare, June 1992, Tables 1 and 26 and authors' assumption of a 20 percent interest rate. Net income is before labor costs.

Recent Trends

Analysts can argue until doomsday about whether coca is or is not more profitable than legal economic activity. However, the agronomist and the economist do not know all the realities facing the small farmer. A much better indicator of the profitability of coca farming relative to other crops is to look at what farmers are actually doing. Here there is a puzzle for those who would claim that coca is several times more profitable than other crops.

If coca is so much more profitable, then we would expect the area planted with coca to expand rapidly. After all, there is a lot of land available and a lot of underemployed labor looking for better work. Indeed, the area planted with coca rose rapidly when coca prices were booming in the decade from the late 1970s through the late 1980s. From 1980 through 1989, throughout the Andes the area planted with coca went up from about 100,000 hectares to 216,000 hectares. But since 1989 this area has remained more or less stable, according to the U.S. government. As shown in figure 5.3, in 1995 the area planted with coca in the Andes was 214,800 hectares, contrasted to 211,300 in 1989. According to U.S. government estimates, leaf production fell at about the same rate as the area cultivated, with increasing yields in Bolivia offset by the effects of a fungus attack in Peru. Coca leaf output, which had been 298,000 tons in 1989, fell to 291,000 tons in 1994.

Have farmers decided that coca is not such an attractive crop, and are they therefore turning to alternatives, such that the coca area is slowly shrinking as old bushes stop producing and are not replaced by new plantings? That is certainly what the INCSR data suggest. However, the data for recent years may understate the area and volume of coca in Colombia.

TABLE 5.5
PER HECTARE YIELDS IN COLOMBIA; UNDCP PROJECT AREAS EARLY 1993

Crop	Gross Income	Costs	Net Income	Percent Profit
Sugar Cane	$1,185	$ 931	$ 254	21
Coffee	$1,385	$1,077	$ 308	22
Bananas	$ 369	$ 277	$ 92	25
Maize	$ 288	$ 264	$ 19	7
Yucca	$ 492	$ 385	$ 107	22
Cacao	$ 184	$ 154	$ 30	16
Vegetables	$ 31	$ 28	$ 3	10
Coca (cocaine base)	$4,462	$2,676	$1,784	40
Opium Poppy (gum)[1]	$7,388	$2,767	$4,615	62

[1] Conversion of opium gum or latex to morphine base may have increased gross yields to $14,000 per hectare.
Source: UNDCP, Bogotá and Popayán

Regarding Colombia, the INCSR data show an increased (net) area planted with coca in 1994, at 50,900 hectares compared to 37,100 in 1993. Other data, however, suggest a sharply higher area and yield in Colombia. Sergio Uribe and Sara Mestre argue that the 1994 coca area was 80,829 hectares rather than the 45,000 shown in the INCSR, which they say underestimates the areas planted on the Pacific slopes, in Solano municipality, and along the Caguan River.[15] In a subsequent publication, Uribe estimated a range of 65,000 to 83,000 hectares. A January 19, 1995, telegram from the U.S. Embassy in Bogotá cites a recent report that coca cultivators are "attaining high yields by employing modern agribusiness fertilization methods." The telegram recommends basing estimates on an assumed yield of 1 ton per hectare rather than the 795 kilograms per hectare ultimately adopted in the 1995 INCSR. Uribe, however, estimates average yields of approximately 4 tons of dry leaf per hectare, and some farmers interviewed said that yields on some of the large farms were as high as 10 tons per hectare. Uribe believes that large commercial farms were coming to dominate the Colombian coca scene. In other words, the INCSR may dramati-

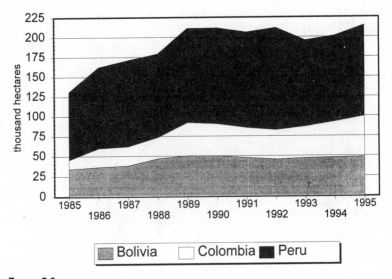

FIGURE 5.3
AREA PLANTED TO COCA (NET, AFTER ERADICATION).
Source: U.S. Department of State, *International Narcotics Control Strategy Report* (Washington, DC: Government Printing Office), various years.

cally understate Colombian coca production, which could be nearly as large as Peruvian production.

In Peru as in Colombia, it is not clear what has been happening to the coca area. The respected firm Cuánto, the UNDP, and the Peruvian Ministry of Agriculture all have estimated the area planted to coca. Their estimates track closely with those of the U.S. government during the 1980s. But, as shown in figure 5.4, they diverge for the 1990s. While the U.S. government's data show the area as stable or declining since 1989, the other sources suggest a steady rise through the mid-1990s. A region-by-region breakdown of the data shows that the differences lie in the new coca regions outside the Huallaga Valley, especially in the drainage of the Tambo/Ene/Apurímac River, which changes its name as it flows downstream. In 1993, Hugo Huillca, general coordinator of the Coca Growers Federation of the Apurimac Valley, indicated that production there had increased 60 percent in two years, to 35,000 hectares.[16] Experts interviewed in Lima in November 1994 all provided anecdotal evidence that farmers were moving to this region from the Huallaga.[17] However, in 1995-1996 the coca area fell, according to local experts, because of the lower coca prices since mid-1995.[18] Perhaps the decline in area in

1995-1996 balances off most of the increase in the new regions in the mid-1990s, so that the total coca area in Peru in 1996 is only somewhat larger than in 1990. That is really only a guess; the picture is quite confused.

Regarding Bolivia, there can be little doubt that the area planted to coca has stabilized or declined since the 1990s peak of 50,300 hectares. Unlike Colombia and Peru, the Bolivian coca-growing area is relatively peaceful, which makes possible ground surveys and farmer interviews. The decline in the area planted to coca matches well with other developments easily observable in the Chapare. The most obvious is the drop in population mentioned earlier. The longer-resident farmers, who moved to the Chapare before 1970, generally have eradicated much (though not all) of their coca and are expanding the area planted in legal crops.

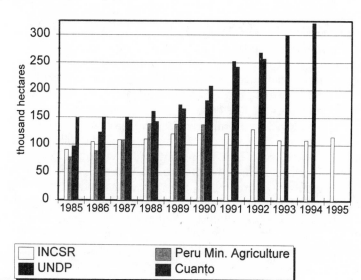

FIGURE 5.4

PERU: AREA PLANTED WITH COCA.

Sources: U.S. Department of State, *International Narcotics Strategy Report* (Washington, D.C.: Government Printing Office), various years; UNDP: Tito Hernández, "El Enfoque competitivo en el Marco del Control de Cultivos Ilícitos: Estrategias y Logros del Program UNDCP-OSP/ PNUD en las Regiónes del Huallaga, Pachitea y Ucuyali" (Lima: UNDCP, October 1994); Ministry of Agriculture: Instituto Nacional de Estadistica e Informatica, *Compendio de Estadisticas de Produccion y Consumo de Droga* (Lima: Direccion Nacional de Estadisticas Basicas, February 1994; Cuanto: Richard Webb and Graciela Fernandez Baca de Valdez, *Peru en Numeros 1994* (Lima: Cuanto, 1994).

However, the facts that less land is planted to coca and there are fewer workers in the Chapare have not translated into lower coca output, partly because bushes planted earlier have now reached their most productive phase. Also, a shift toward more advanced production techniques, using more chemical inputs and less labor, has increased yields.

In short, coca production is no longer on the steep upward track of the 1980s. In Bolivia, production is stagnant as farmers concentrate on other crops. The evidence about Peru is mixed: Coca is in decline in the Upper Huallaga Valley, and observers disagree about to what extent that is offset by the expansion of production in new areas. In Colombia, coca is in full bloom, with area and output rising. To understand the reasons why coca is still attractive in some areas but other crops are becoming more attractive elsewhere, we need to look at the barriers to and the incentives for shifting to legal crops.

BARRIERS TO SHIFTING TO LEGAL CROPS

Many barriers stand in the way of switching from coca to legal crops, such as fragile ecologies with dubious potential for legal cultivation, isolation from major markets, severe political and law and order problems, and the ease of growing and selling coca. Let us examine each of these problems in more detail.

The ecological problems with switching from coca to other crops are considerable. Excessive rainfall; extremely acidic soils; soils with toxic concentrations of iron, aluminum, and manganese; steep slopes that limit mechanization—such are the agricultural conditions in many jungle regions of South America. Coca flourishes in these conditions; other crops do poorly or cannot be grown at all. Vast areas of the Chapare and the Upper Huallaga Valley that are cultivated in coca should, ecologically speaking, remain in coca or revert to forest. To be sure, coca also grows in fertile soils, and in such cases substitution-in-place is possible. Yet "substitution" for many Andean farmers now cultivating coca means migrating to more fertile zones within a region or leaving the region altogether. At best, only 10 percent of the Upper Huallaga Valley and 5 percent of the Chapare (each of which comprises an estimated 2 million hectares) are suitable for legal farming, according to USAID and Andean officials. The development of the Upper Huallaga already has caused substantial environmental degradation.[19] The Chapare's prospects seem especially problematical. Kenneth Eubanks, a contractor for USAID, noted in a 1991 report on the Chapare that because of soil conditions in most of the region, "suitable alternative crops with acceptable marketing margins will be difficult if not impossible to identify." Also, in areas of excessive rainfall "productivity will decline over time . . . and unit production costs will increase accordingly."[20] James Jones, an anthropologist specializing in the Chapare, came to a similar conclusion: "Some areas of the Chapare, because of their ecological fragility, should have neither roads nor agriculture. So why build roads there? Why try to develop these areas?"[21]

Geographical remoteness is another problem in the coca-growing regions. Until 1994, the trip from Lima to Tingo Maria, just inside the Upper Huallaga Valley, took at least fourteen hours; rain, frost, or (most frequently) guerrilla sabotage often increased the travel time severalfold. To reach UNDCP projects in Guaviare and Putumayo in Colombia requires, respectively, fifteen to twenty-five hours and twenty-five hours of travel time from Bogotá. The Chapare is closer to local markets—normally two hours driving time to Cochabamba and four hours to Santa Cruz—but poor weather conditions and landslides frequently obstruct travel, and the trip to the large Buenos Aires market takes two days.

TABLE 5.6
PER HECTARE COSTS AND RETURNS FROM CULTIVATING MAIZE:
RIÓ CAGUÁN, MID-1995

Activity	Cost or Return (in pesos)
Preparation of land	80,000
Seeds	5,000
Sowing	54,000
Harvest	11,000
Shipping and Handling	80,000
Total Cost	254,000
Sale	168,000
Loss	86,000

Note: One $ US: 900 pesos.
Source: "La Sin Salida de los Cultivos Licitos," Cromos, June 26, 1995, p. 31.

The principal consequence of remoteness is high transport costs, averaging 60 percent of the value of products from the Upper Huallaga Valley and 80 to 85 percent of the value of Chapare products.[22] Because of these high transport costs, certain crops can be sold only on the local market; a larger harvest would require shipment to markets far enough away as to make the transport uneconomical. From 1987 to 1993, two-thirds of legal agriculture in the Upper Huallaga was producing foodstuffs for the local market. Since most of those in the Upper Huallaga who were buying food rather than growing their own were working in the cocaine industry, the farmers had a market for their food only because of the cocaine industry; if the cocaine industry went away, so would most of the market for food.[23] In Colombia's remote coca zones, transport problems, soil constraints, and other factors add up to an extremely inhospitable environment for legal cash crops. Table 5.6 shows the per-hectare loss suffered by a farmer growing maize in the Río Caguán region of Caquetá Department. The cost of cultivating, harvesting, and shipping maize is 1.5 times the sales price for that crop.

Finally, there is the law and order problem. In the Upper Huallaga Valley, Shining Path guerrillas, anxious to drive a wedge between coca farmers and the Peruvian government, opposed legitimate agricultural development. The Shining Path's rhetoric depicted agro-industrial enterprises as outposts of "Yankee imperialism" or "bureaucratic capitalism." Shortly after the Palmas del Espina palm oil plantation and processing complex started up in the Huallaga Valley, it sustained $1.5 million in damage in a Shining Path raid.[24] Over the next decade the owner, the Peruvian firm Grupo Romero, had to spend $1 million a year on security to protect its $55 million investment, which is by far the largest in the valley. During its heyday in the early 1990s, Shining Path destroyed roads and bridges that would be needed to take legal crops to market and discouraged peasants from engaging in legal agriculture. Shining Path reportedly allowed peasants in areas that it controls to cultivate only enough legal crops for subsistence; the group's aim was to make coca the only cash crop for peasants.

Shining Path's opposition to substitution was based in part on the large revenues it earned from the cocaine traffic in the valley. Scholars had long agreed that Shining Path drew substantial financing from the drug trade, but concrete evidence was lacking. As discussed in chapter 7, that evidence has been piling up since the capture of the group's leader, Abimael Guzman Reynoso, in September 1992.

In Colombia, the main guerrilla groups—the Army of National Liberation (ELN) and the Revolutionary Armed Forces of Colombia (FARC)—have adopted a more benign stance toward crop substitution and rural development. (FARC's rhetoric actually supports cultivation of legal crops in place of coca.) Yet FARC in 1991 collected an estimated $80 to $85 million each year from the coca trade and $25 to $30 million from opium, two-thirds of its total estimated revenues in that year.[25] Presumably FARC would not be in favor of crop substitution on a massive scale. A further source of opposition to substitution in coca regions is the traffickers themselves, who may try to "bribe" farmers by maintaining artificially high prices, or they may compel farmers to remain in the coca business. Farmers, in fact, may be obligated to grow coca to repay trafficking organizations' initial investments in their enterprises. As Bruce Bagley of the North-South Center notes:

> Trafficker networks typically establish close ties with coca growers in specific regions after providing them with seed, tools, suppliers credits and other forms of assistance that obligate the farmers to sell their crops exclusively to the trafficking group that sponsored them. The traffickers' brutal enforcement techniques and their patron-client relations give them considerable social and political control in coca growing regions and greatly limit the Colombian state's ability to execute alternative development projects in these areas.[26]

Despite its problems, coca as a crop has features that make it attractive. One is the ease of marketing. As a farmer in the Upper Huallaga Valley told a PEAH official, "Buyers go to the farms to get the coca. If I plant any other crop I must get it to market and spend money transporting it. This does not happen with coca."[27] The problem is not just the cost of transport, it is also the risk of whether there will be a market at all. The history of achiote (a local food crop) as a substitute crop in Peru illustrates this difficulty. At one time, some USAID workers convinced peasants in the Upper Huallaga Valley that achiote could be more profitable than coca. However, when the farmers planted achiote in large quantity, the price dropped and some could not be sold at all. Farmers who had relied on the crop found themselves with much less income than they had expected. A similar problem conceivably could be encountered with specialty crops such as macadamia nuts. Although prices may now be favorable, demand may be limited; increasing sales may require sharply lower prices. To be sure, USAID's strategy stresses diversified development, as opposed to reliance on a single crop, but still, the risk of oversupplying the market is considerable. A further problem is that certain particularly promising crops—such as passion fruit and papaya in the Chapare—cannot be exported in fresh form. Farmers will not even consider growing such crops unless processing facilities are introduced into the region, a development that could take years.

When the farmers develop more confidence that markets exist, they can shift quickly. In the Chapare, farmers were skeptical in the early 1990s that they would be able to sell the bananas and pineapples USAID was encouraging them to grow. Markets in Lima and Buenos Aires have in fact emerged as a result of much USAID efforts; from building roads to financing packing plants to seeking out wholesalers in destination markets. As farmers saw how much pineapples could earn, they became so eager to plant the crop that, in 1993-1994, the price of starter plants rose so high that pineapple farmers could make as much from the starter plants as from the fruit.[28]

Another advantage of coca is that it can be harvested less than two years after planting and that it generates cash quickly enough to repay the investment within four years. Most of the alternative crops are tree crops for which the cash flow becomes positive only after three or more years. In such cases, farmers must trust that the markets for these crops will remain favorable. That is quite a leap of faith. Most alternative crops have not been grown commercially in the Chapare before, while in the Upper Huallaga Valley, the alternative crops brought extremely low prices in the early 1990s, when world market prices for cacao and coffee were at record lows. While farmers may be hesitant to count on the alternative crops to provide the basic family income, they may be willing to diversify production—experimenting with non-traditional crops while continuing to cultivate coca.

Finally, coca offers many opportunities to increase income through use of better technology. There is evidence that coca farmers are implementing agronomic improvements that make the industry more profitable. As mentioned earlier, yields in Colombia may have increased to 4 tons per hectare from 1 ton per hectare in the early 1990s. Some Bolivian coca farmers speak about yields as high as four tons per hectare, whereas in the early 1990s, two tons per hectare was cited as a good yield.[29] Another way to increase profitability is to reduce the time from planting to first harvest. If the interval from seedling transplant to first harvest is on the order of fifteen months, then the internal rate of return (roughly, the rate of profit) is about 100 percent, whereas if the period is reduced to nine months, the internal rate of return rises to about 300 percent, according to the rate of return model developed by Clark Joel for USAID La Paz. In addition, coca farmers seem to be adding to their income by diversifying downstream into processing. The old pattern in Bolivia was for paste to be made in Chapare, base in clandestine labs elsewhere in Bolivia, and hydrochloride in Colombia. Yet "in 1993, virtually all processors in the Chapare produced base directly, skipping the intermediation production of coca paste."[30] In the Upper Huallaga Valley, according to a September 1992 World Bank report, "While farmers sold drug coca leaf to traffickers up to the mid-1980s, more than two-thirds of them now carry out the production of basic coca paste."[31]

Production of paste and base offers several advantages. While leaves spoil quickly in the jungle humidity, the refined product can be stored longer—an important factor because periodic police crackdowns sometimes cause temporary suspensions in the trade. Paste and base production also can be sources of profit in themselves. In the past, paste and especially base production were more remunerative than growing leaf. According to World Bank data from Peru and USAID data from Bolivia for the early 1990s, farmers could more than double their income by processing their own crop.[32] USAID data for 1994 in Bolivia suggest that farmers could earn a profit of $3,300 by processing leaves into base, about 40 percent more than they could earn by cultivating leaf alone.

Depending on price developments, downstream integration into base makes coca-growing more attractive to farmers. Of course, legitimate agricultural products can be processed too; but the economies of scale are different. While a moderate-sized coca farm can support a paste or base laboratory, a huge citrus grove or pineapple plantation or multiple smaller farms would be required to support a juice canning factory. But perhaps more important than the economic effects of farmer coca processing are the law enforcement and political effects. As farmers start running macerating pits or base labs, the distinction between farmers and traffickers is becoming increasingly blurred. That complicates the government strategy of driving a wedge between the farmers and the traffickers. Maintaining the polite fiction that coca farmers are law-abiding citizens and that the police are only after the traffickers becomes more difficult.

WHY FARMERS MAY SWITCH TO LEGAL CROPS

The most important incentives for crop substitution may come not from economic assistance to coca-growing areas but from factors that affect the intrinsic attractiveness of coca growing and from developments in the national economy as a whole.

The most powerful incentive for crop substitution is lower coca prices. In Bolivia, leaf prices were on a long-term downward trend for between 1986 and 1991, with many peaks and valleys around the trend line, and then stabilizing between 1992 and 1994. That is, the price stabilized in nominal dollars; the effects of inflation have eaten away some of the value. The lower coca leaf prices have not yet translated into lower coca production, partly because bushes planted during the boom will continue to produce for at least a decade. Also, as mentioned, farmers have raised yields through use of improved technology and techniques. While the failure of lower prices to reduce output is disappointing, if the prices had stayed at their 1986 levels in real terms—which would have meant a 1994 price of $5 per kilogram rather than $1—coca would have expanded on to many new plots in the Chapare and gained a foothold to the north as well.

In Colombia, unlike Bolivia, no true market exists for coca leaf. Cocaine base prices declined in mid-1995 but rebounded by the end of the year. In Peru, coca prices have been volatile. In the words of the State Department, the steep decline in coca prices in mid-late 1995 "created the precise economic circumstances required for the alternative development concept to work in Peru."[33]

Another possible incentive to switching to legal crops is higher coca production costs. In Peru, producers were hit in 1992-1993 by the removal of subsidies on kerosene, which is used in converting leaves to basic coca paste. More important has been the effect of law enforcement. Controls over precursor chemicals have forced use of less efficient substitutes or investment in recycling equipment. Destruction of processing sites—most of them simple farmer-run outfits, not the sophisticated facility that the misleading term "lab" implies—and seizure of the coca products found at the sites raise costs as well.

In Peru, production costs have risen sharply because of losses due to the *fusarium oxysporum* fungus. The fungus first appeared in 1987-1988 and now causes a 40 to 60 percent crop loss.[34] Fusarium spreads through soil-borne spores that are specifically adapted to a particular plant species. Monoculture creates excellent conditions for this fungus to get established and then spread. At least two genotypes have become specific to coca, although the mayor of Uchiza (the worst-hit area) says that since 1991, the fungus also has affected legal crops (to a lesser extent than coca).[35] Fusarium is particularly difficult to eradicate; it can be expected to remain in the area for years. The spread of this fungus, which was particularly rapid in the early 1990s, has been an important reason for the population movements out of the valley.

A third incentive to substitute legal crops is to avoid the consequences of illegality or quasi-legality. Farmers grow illicit crops in a high-risk environment. Police can confiscate their leaves, paste, or base. Coca farmers have no contractual rights or access to the courts, nor do they have much recourse against police abuses. Conflict with traffickers over selling prices for leaves or paste are as likely to be resolved violently as peacefully. Narcotraffickers do not hesitate to kill those farmers whom they think are cheating them or exposing them to attack by other narcotraffickers, the police, or the army. And in Peru and Colombia, guerrilla groups add another layer of violence, as they compel farmers to work for them or to provide them money or supplies.

Tito Hernández, the technical director for the UNDCP project in the Upper Huallaga, describes farmers' reactions to the violence of coca cultivation:

> Associated with the illegal cultivation of coca is violence from narcotraffickers, to establish their control over the coca farmers; by subversives, to appropriate part of the farmers' surplus and of the narcotrafficking income; and by the state, to fight against the former two. Among the coca farmers who had to suffer this triple violence, there developed a firm conviction and desire to substitute other crops for coca. . . . That is to say, the farmers who remained in these areas searched for legal activities that were competitive not only in economic terms but principally in terms of social peace.[36]

In the mid-1990s, the Huallaga Valley has had a fourth and related reason for the development of the legal economy: the return of greater security. Adequate security is a prerequisite for legal economic development. Coca production, like other illegal activities, thrives where the state is weak, because there is less risk of seizure or of punishment. Legal production, on the other hand, suffers: Investment is a gamble because there is no assurance that agreements will be honored, and costs at each stage are increased by the need to provide private security. In other words, where the state is weak, illegal activity will grow at the expense of legal activity.

It would be premature to say that terrorism has ended in the Peruvian drug-producing areas, although the government has smashed to bits the smaller of the two terrorist groups, the MRTA (Tupac Amaru Revolutionary Movement). Nevertheless, the terrorism problem has been reduced to the point that normal economic activity has become much more practical. An important symbol was the August 1993 inauguration by President Alberto Fujimori of a bridge across the Huallaga Valley; the very fact that he could visit the valley was no minor event.[37] One-third of the bridge had been built in 1985 before construction was suspended for eight years until the terrorists and traffickers could be chased away, with active aid from the local mayor. USAID, which financed completion of the bridge, estimated that it would make economical legal crops on 40,000 hectares of land.

A final factor that has worked to reduce coca cultivation has been the improvement in the national economy in Peru and Bolivia. As discussed in the next chapter, illegal coca really took root in those two countries during a period of national economic crisis, which has now ended. Peru has had a spectacular recovery since 1993—its economy grew 9 percent per year in 1993-1995. In 1994, Peru grew faster than any other country in the world, according to the World Bank. Bolivia's recovery began much earlier—in 1987—but has proceeded only slowly, with growth averaging 2.8 percent annually from 1987 through 1990 and 4.3 percent from 1991 through 1995. The day laborers who pick most of the coca and who stomp it in the pits, and even some farmers, have emigrated from coca zones altogether—to promising agricultural regions or to industrial jobs in the cities.

ALTERNATIVE DEVELOPMENT AND CROP SUBSTITUTION PROGRAMS

Crop substitution programs identify legal crops that replace the income from illegal narcotic-producing crops; they also provide farmers with materials and technical assistance for growing the legal crops. The best review to date of crop substitution programs, by USAID in 1986, concluded:

> The crop substitution strategy . . . has been unsuccessful in introducing substitute crops and in controlling illicit cultivation, at least in the limited span of a typical development initiative. Viable substitute crops are difficult to identify given the generally unfavorable climatic conditions and poorly developed infrastructures that characterize most remote poppy- and coca-growing areas. In many instances, there are not alternative crops that can be grown profitably.[38]

Consistent with the recommendations by the evaluation team, USAID shifted from narrow crop substitution to "area development," which means providing physical and social infrastructure as well as agricultural input and services. Variations of an area development strategy now guide all major crop substitution efforts, including those of USAID and UNDCP. Such a strategy consists of a chain of at least five interrelated elements considered necessary to lure farmers away from cultivating drug crops: (1) introducing replacement crops; (2) developing markets for legal produce; (3) industrialization; (4) providing social infrastructure, and (5) organizational development.

The first of these—corresponding to crop substitution in the narrowest sense—is to identify and introduce replacement crops that promise a reasonable income and that can thrive in regions where drug crops are cultivated. Agricultural research and extension activities are, of course, basic to this phase of the substitution process. A substitution project may seek both to increase the profitability of traditional agriculture in such regions (for example, coffee in the Upper Huallaga Valley) and to introduce high-value nontraditional crops (such as black pepper in the Chapare). Substitution does not necessarily occur on lands formerly planted in coca—lands that often are ecologically unsuited to most legal farming; decisions by farmers to abandon illegal cultivation and to expand planting of legal crops on more fertile lands elsewhere within the same project area accomplishes the same purpose.

A second aspect involves the development of markets for legal agricultural products. Here increasing producers' access to buyers and exporters is the central objective. Transport costs from the isolated areas that grow coca or opium are typically so high that the only profitable economic activities are those that have a high value per pound, typically the case with illegal products. USAID or United Nations (UN) initiatives that facilitate marketing include building or upgrading farm-to-market roads and bridges, constructing packing sheds and storage facilities, and providing trucks to haul produce to major markets at a fraction of the price charged by commercial truckers. In Bolivia, identifying potential domestic and foreign markets for nontraditional crops being cultivated in the Chapare—pineapples, export-grade bananas, and passion fruit—is an important part of USAID's market development strategy.

A third important link in the substitution chain is "industrialization"—introduction of processing facilities that improve the salability and increase the value-to-weight ratio of alternative cash crops. Technologies required range from elementary (fans for drying coffee beans), to medium (dehydration facilities for yucca or machinery for extracting raw sugar from cane), to sophisticated (juice-making and canning plants). Processing is a necessity for certain crops—yucca, papaya, passion fruit, and palm hearts—that have little or no shelf life; for some bulky products—citrus fruits, for example—industrialization in a sine qua non for competing successfully in international markets. USAID and UNDCP development experts stress the importance of value-added processing. However, so far little investment in processing capacity has occurred in coca-growing regions—a situation that doubtless limits farmers' enthusiasm for expanding cultivation of legal crops. Those facilities that have been built have had a considerable impact: the price paid for Chapare bananas rose in 1994 from 7 bolivianos per *chipa* (10 stalks, or about 720 bananas) to 18 bolivianos when they were packed in boxes that kept them from being mangled en route to La Paz.

A fourth aspect of area development involves providing social infrastructure—facilities or services designed to improve the quality of life in the zones that produce narcotics crops. U.S. and UN programs have delivered a variety of amenities to residents of such zones, including schools, roads, clinics, potable water systems, and auditoriums. While such benefits contribute only indirectly (if at all) to the actual process of crop substitution, politically they may serve to limit farmers' resistance to coca or poppy reduction programs. USAID and UNDCP administrators see quality of life as a bargaining issue. As one UN development expert in Colombia observed, "We have to improve farmers' standard of living as a quid pro quo for the reduced income that they receive from substituting other crops for coca."[39]

A fifth aspect can be described as organizational development. This entails promoting cooperatives of farmers that can aggregate product for sale to processors, intermediaries, or consumers and that can deliver government services to scattered peasant households. The UNDCP projects in Colombia have had to build such organizations virtually from scratch. The purposes here are largely economic—to strengthen farmers' bargaining power vis-à-vis buyers, to improve their technical skills and hence to increase their ability to cultivate profitable legal crops. Also, producers' associations are said to foster self-respect and a stronger sense of connection to the legal economic and political order. UNDCP's activities in Colombia—most of which are centered in areas controlled or dominated by guerrilla groups—may help to reclaim these isolated and forgotten communities for the government; certainly, this is a political selling point for such programs.

The impact of cooperative organizations in Bolivia has been exactly the opposite of their impact in Colombia. In Bolivia, the farmers in the Chapare coca-growing region organized themselves into syndicates. As we will discuss in chapter 9, the syndicates are powerful groups, led by a charismatic leader. The syndicates promote the growing of coca: they demonstrate against counternarcotics activities, they pressure the government to abandon its restrictions on coca-growing, and they have at times threatened farmers who substitute legal crops for coca. The Bolivian syndicates are a major obstacle to the success of the USAID-promoted alternative development programs and to reducing dependence on coca. The lesson from comparing the experiences in Bolivia and Colombia appears to be that the degree to which farmers can be organized to support legal economic activities is crucial to the success of alternative development.

Though conceptually an improvement over crop substitution in the restricted sense of the term, area development approaches have yet to be applied successfully in practice. To be sure, successes have been recorded within the confines of project areas. Yet such results usually are obscured by the expansion (indeed the explosion) of drug crop cultivation in neighboring areas and in other parts of the country.

From USAID's perspective, area development approaches represent an inadequate response to the challenges posed by deeply entrenched narcotics industries such as cocaine. The argument for a more widely gauged development strategy was well expressed in a recent review of USAID's narcotics programs, which concluded that "AID's extensive experience with crop substitution in both Latin America and Asia has clearly demonstrated that economic assistance to illicit growing areas alone is not effective. Both illicit labs and illicit crop production are dynamic and mobile. Alternative economic opportunities depend on sound economic policies to generate demand for diversified economic growth and job creation nationwide."[40]

Under this broader rubric, a "substitute crop" could be a mango plantation on the Peruvian coast, a soybean plantation in Santa Cruz, or even a factory in Lima or Cochabamba producing goods for the international market. Alternative development means improving economic opportunities in impoverished regions such as the Peruvian high plain or the high valleys of Cochabamba that are important sources of migration to coca-growing zones. The concept could imply developing commercial agriculture or agribusiness in agriculturally promising regions—Bolivia's eastern plains, for example—in order to attract farmers and processors away from the coca economy.

In other words, USAID's current Andean strategy is to promote economic development throughout the coca-producing countries, not just to substitute legal crops for coca in remote jungle locations. USAID still regards crop substitution and work in coca-producing areas as components of its alternative development strategy, but most of its money and attention now goes to other aspects, such as establishing a sound economic environment for growth. Overall, counternarcotics development focuses on creating alternative high-income employment so that those now growing coca will turn to these alternatives—farming in other regions, working in the urban informal sector or in industry, or farming new crops in the coca regions.

EXPERIENCES WITH
ALTERNATIVE DEVELOPMENT

The largest crop substitution program in the Andes has been USAID's activities in Bolivia. USAID began in 1975 with the $1.9 million Agricultural Development in the Coca Zones Project.[41] It followed up in 1983 with the Chapare Regional Development Program (CRDP). The project got going slowly, with continuing personnel problems and clashes until mid-1989.[42] Opposition by pro-coca organizations severely limited the work in the Chapare until 1990, when the price of coca plummeted and farmers became very interested in alternative crops. About $38 million was spent by the time CRDP was replaced in 1992 with the more ambitious Cochabamba Regional Development Project (CORDEP), which will spend $80 million between 1991 and 1997.[43] Whereas CRDP had focused on the individual farmer, CORDEP places much more emphasis on the marketing chain. By late 1995 it had financed twenty-six collection, selection, and packing centers for bananas and pineapples as well as twelve processing plants for various products.

Thanks to CRDP and CORDEP, pineapples and improved varieties of bananas and citrus are now being produced on a substantial scale in the Chapare. [44] USAID has nurtured the farmer mutual aid associations for these crops, with the significant side benefit of weaning farmers away from the pro-coca associations that dominate political life in the region. More important has been the $36 million spent from 1983 through 1993 on roads. Not only have truckers' transport charges dropped, but so have losses and damage to fruit in shipment. Thanks to better transport, better fruit varieties, and better packing, the farmers' income from oranges rose from 2 to 3 bolivianos per hundred in 1992 to 8 bolivianos for the local oranges or 15 bolivianos for the improved valencia variety in 1994.[45] When the last section of the road to Argentina is paved in 1998, Chapare products should become competitive on the Buenos Aires market, which is large enough to absorb all its output.

While USAID has dominated crop substitution in Bolivia, UNDCP has had some poorly conceived projects. In the Yungas, for example, UNDCP financed a coffee processing facility that competed with a private operation. In the Chapare it built a milk processing plant that was too large, located rather far from the areas where dairy cattle could be raised, and had inadequate refrigeration facilities to store milk.[46]

In Peru, the UNDCP is a more important actor. It has had a promising if small substitution program operating in the Upper Huallaga

Valley since 1986.[47] UNDCP works the *Cooperativa Agroindustrial Naranjillo* (the Small Orange Agroindustrial Cooperative). The cooperative members have planted 7,800 hectares of new, legal crops since 1987. How much of this new cultivation is due directly to UNDCP assistance, of course, is difficult to determine.

USAID's alternative development program in Peru was the Upper Huallaga Area Development Program, which spent about $30 million from 1981 until 1993. From the beginning, the program, which was run through PEAH (an agency created for this purpose), was plagued with security problems, which grew progressively worse for a decade, as guerrillas overran the project area. The project also was hampered by its association in farmers' minds with the U.S.-financed Peruvian eradication agency (CORAH). The USAID project had no perceptible impact on the coca situation in the Upper Huallaga.

USAID funded $5 million in alternative development in Peru in 1994. Rather than counternarcotics activities, USAID priorities in Peru for its $130 million annual program were health, democracy promotion, and microenterprises. In 1995 USAID's alternative development program consisted of a newly approved twelve-year project, with an average projected spending of $2.6 million a year.

Some successes have been achieved with the small funds that were available in 1994. For instance, with $120,000, CEDRO, a nongovernmental organization, was able to buy seed with which Huallaga Valley farmers could begin growing cotton, which they then sold for $2.5 million. The reasons for the success of this particular project, after years of failure with similar projects, were not hard to find. Conditions in the Huallaga Valley had become much more conducive to alternative development. The security situation was much better; the fungus had made coca less attractive; and some of those attracted by the coca boom had emigrated, leaving behind the old-time farmers who had never been as enthusiastic about coca as the recent arrivals.

At the same time that USAID was scaling back its funding for alternative development, others were stepping up their activities in the Huallaga Valley and other coca-growing areas, with the declining guerrilla threat after the 1992 arrest of the Shining Path's leader.[48] Nongovernmental organizations like Doctors Without Borders became active. The Japanese and Dutch governments and the European Union are planning aid activities. The German government is designing a three-year, $40 million integrated rural development project in the Lower Huallaga, and in 1995 it financed a UNDCP-run crop substitution program for the Apurímac Valley. These projects are financed by grants, because Peru borrows only for projects that directly generate enough income to repay the loans, a criteria that crop substitution programs do not meet. However, while Peru has refused to borrow for social programs in the coca areas, it has financed them from its own resources. Despite its acute financial crisis, the Peruvian government paid for 90 percent of PEAH's costs in 1993-1995.[49] In fact, PEAH's activities expanded despite the fact that the USAID program ended in 1993. Furthermore, the Peruvian military instituted a program of civil works—road work especially—to win the hearts and minds of locals. And Peru did borrow for economically attractive infrastructure projects benefitting the coca areas. The $200 million road rehabilitation programs of the World Bank and the Inter-American Development Bank (IDB) financed road work that cut the Lima–valley travel time from fourteen hours to nine. Those two banks are considering an additional $300 million in transport improvement loans which may also include rehabilitating roads in the coca-growing regions.

As of 1995, the UNDCP was the principal agency managing alternative development projects in Colombia.[50] According to UNDCP officials, more than 3,000 hectares of coca have been eliminated in the Cauca-Nariño project area, amounting to approximately 60 percent of the area's total coca cultivation. This was accomplished at a cost of $9 million, or less than $3,000 per hectare. Several other agencies have planned projects, the largest being a $300 million program announced by the Colombian government in part in response to demonstrations by coca farmers. As of mid-1995 it was unclear whether these plans have enough political impetus actually to be executed. Putting up the cash is much more difficult than making an announcement.

POLITICAL ARGUMENTS FOR ALTERNATIVE DEVELOPMENT

UNDCP's effort has had, and is likely to have, little impact on the Colombian coca scene because most coca is grown on large (15 hectares or more) trafficker-financed plantations in areas that are both geographically remote and, even for the UN, politically impenetrable. However, alternative development has advantages that go beyond its economic effects. The alternative development programs make excellent political sense for two reasons: they undercut the support for guerrillas, and they increase the degree of counternarcotics cooperation from Andean peoples and governments.

Guerrillas can do well only in areas where the state is weak. (Not that they thrive in every such area—government feebleness is a necessary but not sufficient condition.) In coca-growing areas, farmers naturally are going to be suspicious of the government, especially when the arm of the government they see most often is the police and the army. The police may tolerate the coca fields, even though they are technically illegal, but they pursue the traffickers on whom the farmers depend, and they destroy the maceration pits and labs in which farmers or their neighbors process the leaves into coca paste or base. As analyzed in chapter 7, that means guerrillas have a natural opportunity to form relationships with farmers (whereas there is an in-built tension between guerrillas and traffickers).

Alternative development projects can help counteract the potential alliance between guerrillas and coca farmers. Such projects bring into the coca region an active presence of government agencies devoted to helping farmers and to raising their income. The UNDCP has chosen to work in politically contested regions in which the influence of Marxist guerilla organizations is strong, and their projects in both Colombia and Peru have much to offer on this counterguerrilla front. The projects have taught farmers organizational and technical skills, reduced the isolation of rural communities, and possibly changed farmers' attitudes toward the state.

Such achievements must be weighed in the balance when contemplating the net effects of crop substitution programs—winning hearts and minds is no small factor in the fight against narcotics. Alternative development programs can influence the attitudes not only of coca farmers but also of the public as a whole. In urban as well as rural areas, Andean public opinion is influenced by the image, true or not, of poor farmers who grow coca because that is the only way to feed their families. That image undercuts support for counternarcotics programs, about which Andean opinion is torn. Alternative development projects offer a way to convince national public opinion that counternarcotics is not antipoor or antipeople.

Precisely because they need to show that they care about their constituents, Peruvian and Bolivian politicians have insisted that alternative development has to be a major component of counternarcotics programs. This was a sticking point at the February 1992 San Antonio Summit on narcotics between the heads of government of the United States, Bolivia, Colombia, Ecuador, Mexico, Peru, and the Venezuelan foreign minister. In what a U.S. diplomat called "an in-your-face outburst," Peruvian president Fujimori rejected closer cooperation against traffickers unless more was done to help farmers, saying "No government may fight against an entire population."[51] By the end of the summit, President Bush said, "One thing I learned out of all this was the need to work more cooperatively in alternative cropping." A pleased President Fujimori summed up the summit: "Up to now, there has been great emphasis on the subject of interdiction. But today, similar emphasis has been placed on alternative development." The Bolivian government also has repeatedly shown that its interest in cooperating with counternarcotics efforts is directly tied to the amount of aid that such cooperation brings. Andean governments will not allow the DEA to operate actively on their soil unless they can simultaneously show to their people that they are doing something to alleviate the social problems that are seen, rightly or wrongly, as driving farmers to raise coca.

WILL FARMERS SWITCH FROM COCA?

Coca is and will remain an attractive crop for some Andean farmers. The coca bush fits well with the region: It grows easily under conditions hostile to many other crops, it is easier to market than bulky and easy-to-spoil or bruise tropical fruit, and it can be grown by migrants without much knowledge about how to farm in tropical areas.

At the same time, farmers are not wedded to coca. In the zones that provide coca for narcotrafficking, there is no mystical traditional attachment to the crop. Indeed, the farmers are not attached to living in the coca zones, and many move willingly when conditions elsewhere appear more attractive. The issue is purely what crops, over the long term, bring the best income and the least risk of violence. A number of legal crops offer reasonable prospects of competing with coca, especially as the international community finances better roads into the isolated coca-growing areas.

Crop substitution away from coca has not occurred in the Andes on any substantial scale for a sustained period of time. Whether this might take place and, most important for U.S. interests, what effect it might have on the cocaine supply are the subjects of chapter 9.

However, before we can analyze the effects of counternarcotics efforts in Latin America, we need to discuss the relation of the cocaine industry to Colombian society. Whereas the principal element of the industry in Peru and Bolivia is the farmers discussed in this chapter, the situation in Colombia is quite different. There, due to the large profits from trafficking, the cocaine industry has penetrated into many aspects of life, including national politics.

6

Cocaine and Colombian Society

THE ECONOMY

Types of Investments

Much of the cocaine money that flows back to the countries of origin is spent on operating expenses, such as payments to farmers, refiners, and shippers, and on bribes to officials. A portion also is devoted to personal luxury consumption—traffickers' tastes range from gold chains, yachts, to Ming porcelain and antique automobiles. However, a considerable share of repatriate earnings is channeled into investments. Some such expenditures, so-called direct-use investments, relate to capital improvements in the cocaine industry itself; these include outlays for such items as large cargo aircraft, semisubmersible vessels, and state-of-the-art communications and encryption devices. Other investments are channeled into more or less legal economic activities, although legal businesses sometimes serve as covers or justifications for illegal ones.

Traffickers' legal investments fall into three main categories. The first includes business activities that serve both legitimate and illegal purposes—so-called dual-use investments. Dual-use patterns are pervasive in South America. For example, trafficker-owned pharmaceutical laboratories, retail drugstores, and battery factories sell legitimate products but also serve as legal fronts for diversion of chemicals (such as sulfuric acid or ether) to cocaine manufacture. Examples of such fronts in Colombia include the Rodríguez Orejuela brothers' Laboratorios Kressfor and Laboratorios Blaimar and their Drogas la Rebaja drugstore chain. (The commercial success of such operations was real enough. The Rodríguez discount drug chain reportedly accounted for 45 percent of the Colombian market for pharmaceutical products in the mid-1980s.) Trafficker-linked agribusiness enterprises facilitate exports of cocaine; the drug is concealed in containers of legal products such as shrimp, fruit pulp, or cut flowers. Traffickers' airline companies or transport firms serve obvious smuggling objectives; an example was the Ochoa family's fifty-five–aircraft *Pilotos Ejecutivos* (executive pilots) company, which played a major role in the family's multiton shipments of cocaine to the United States in the 1980s. Ownership of banks, financial institutions, and travel agencies provides cover for transfers and laundering of narcotic proceeds. The Cali Rodríguez brothers' large shareholding stake in the Banco de Trabajadores of Colombia and the First Inter-American Bank of Panama in the 1980s exemplified the dual-use pattern. Traffickers' extensive purchases of haciendas and ranches in Colombia's remote hinterland serve more than legal economic objectives; some ranches are training grounds for paramilitary armies (this was especially the case in the Middle Magdalena Valley in the late 1980s), and some house trafficking infrastructure, such as laboratories, airstrips, and storage sites. Finally, some narco-investment patterns relate to trafficking organizations' intelligence and counterintelligence requirements. For example, trafficker-owned taxi companies and security companies in Cali provide drug kingpins there with information on movement of Colombian and foreign counternarcotics personnel.

Another category of investments includes those designed to increase traffickers' influence or "system penetration and control" (to borrow a phrase from University of New Mexico political scientist Peter Lupsha). Such investments take a variety of forms; they include civic action projects designed to win popular support in poor communities; trafficker-sponsored improvements such as housing projects, water wells, sports facilities, and satellite TV dishes fall into this category. A famous example was Pablo Escobar's "Medellín without Slums" project in the early 1980s, which built some 450 to 500 housing units for marginalized urban dwellers. Pablo Escobar's personal zoo, "Napoles," in the Middle Magdalena Valley—open to the public free of charge—also reflected the trafficker's desire for prestige and influence. Peter Lupsha reports that in the Peruvian jungle town of Boca Manu, Colombian traffickers financed the introduction of satellite television and "provided monies to repair local roads, docking facilities, the school and the medical clinic." Also, according to Lupsha, traffickers made direct cash payments to police, teachers, politicians, and other notables to gain community approval and to turn Boca Manu into a major collection and transshipment point for cocaine base.[1] Traffickers have sought to influence opinion by investing in the media; enterprises such as the Rodríguez brothers' Grupo Radial Colombiano (a chain of radio stations) and the Escobar family's *Medellín Cívico* (a local city newspaper) were designed partly to convey traffickers' personal political agendas. Traffickers' sponsorship of paramilitary groups and assassin teams in Colombia also represent attempts to project influence. For instance, in the mid- and late 1980s, the Medellín cartel's financing, training, and equipping of a paramilitary forces to combat Marxist guerrillas and their civilian supporters formed part of a general political strategy; the aim was to limit Bogotá's influence in areas where traffickers owned property and operated laboratories. During this period traffickers almost succeeded in transforming the Middle Magdalena Valley into an independent narcorepublic with its headquarters at Puerto Boyacá, the so-called antisubversion capital of Colombia.

Finally, traffickers' investments may be essentially indistinguishable from ordinary legal investments—they may be designed simply to enhance traffickers self-image as legitimate businessmen. Investments in shopping centers, wineries, construction firms, hotels, sports clubs, modernized poultry farms and cattle ranches, and rice mills might fit this category. Colombian examples include the Rodríguez brothers' investments in Cali Hotels S.A., the Grajales brothers' Casa Grajales convenience store chain, and Gilberto Rodríguez's soccer team, the Club America de Cali.

Patterns and Trends

Drug money has a pervasive influence in the Colombian economy. For example, according to the Colombian Institute of Agrarian Reform and the Colombian Farmers' Association, ownership of agricultural land by drug dealers directly or through intermediaries increased from 1 million hectares in the late 1980s to an estimated 3 to 4 million hectares in 1993-1994. Today traffickers own or control 8 to 11 percent of Colombia's agriculturally usable land in at least 400 of its 1,060 municipalities; they are an acknowledged powerful force in the economic life of the countryside. Furthermore, with the ascendancy of the so-called Cali cartel—the trafficking coalition based in Valle de Cauca department—drug dealers' penetration of legal business spheres has reached significant new levels. Earlier generations of traffickers, such as the leader of the Medellín cartel of the 1980s (then the dominant trafficking group in Colombia), were relatively unsophisticated economic actors who were more concerned with laundering (legalizing) drug earnings than with realizing adequate returns on their investments. Some expenditures clearly were designed to enhance traffickers' status or their personal prestige. Conspicuous examples of such propensities were José Gonzalo Rodríguez Gacha's accumulation of 140 country estates, collectively worth an estimated $100 million (some were lavishly furnished with such items as pillows stuffed with ostrich feathers, gold-plated bathroom fixtures, and imported Italian toilet paper stamped with likenesses of Botticelli's *The Birth of Venus*)[2] and Pablo Escobar's famous zoological park at Hacienda Napoles in Puerto Triunfo in the Middle Magdalena Valley, for many years a convenient tourist stop along the main Medellín–Bogotá highway. Medellín traffickers also made large outlays to finance and equip rightist paramilitary armies in the 1980s. The Cali traffickers have not been so obvious; indeed, they have cultivated an image of business respectability and are investing in a wide range of economic activities. According to a recent report by Colombia's Department of Administrative Security (DAS), Cali drug money has "infiltrated the construction industry, drug store chains, radio stations, automobile dealerships, department stores, factories, banks, sports clubs and investment firms." As noted, drug money is said to finance 30 to 40 percent of the building construction in Cali. Buenaventura and San Andres, both embarkation points for Colombian cocaine, also host extensive Cali investments. Cali holdings also include taxi companies, bus companies, and agribusiness enterprises such as cut flowers, wineries, tropical fruit production, and poultry farms.[3] "In what sectors of the economy has the Cali cartel not invested?" remarked Gabriel de Vega Pinzon, the then head of Colombia's National Drug Directorate in a December 1994 interview.

The different orientations of Cali and Medellín traffickers vis-à-vis the legal economy deserve a word of explanation. The Medellín drug lords often are stereotyped as archetype criminal predators, whose economic behavior is appropriate to the "primitive accumulation" phase of the cocaine business in Colombia. However, the behavior also reflected Medellín's tumultuous and confrontational relations with the Colombian state in the 1980s and early 1990s. Cali, by contrast, has eschewed political adventurism; indeed, the cartel's strategy clearly was to maintain a low profile, to minimize the appearance of illegality, to coexist comfortably with the political authority, and even to help the government track down its Medellín rivals. The fruits of this political strategy are that, until recently, successive Colombian administrations have showed relatively little enthusiasm for persecuting the Cali godfathers; they even have held multiple meetings with their lawyers (and on three occasions with leading Cali traffickers directly) to negotiate surrender procedures and sentence-reduction terms. The Cali traffickers thus probably perceived the law enforcement environment as more benign (or less malevolent) than did their Medellín counterparts—hence, they were relatively more willing to acquire a serious stake in the Colombian economy.

NARCOPOLITICS

Corruption

Drug trafficking also has exercised a wide impact on political and administrative systems in Colombia and other Latin American countries. Cocaine money finances extensive protection and intelligence networks, including accomplices and informants in key national institutions such as the military, the various police forces, the court system, the government bureaucracy, the legislature, the church, the news media, the national telephone system, and (in Colombia) the national fingerprint registry. Corrupt officials in key government ministries (justice, foreign affairs, defense, government) furnish the cocaine lords with strategic intelligence on major antidrug plans and initiatives. On an operational level, traffickers pay the military and police to overlook cocaine refineries and drug smuggling. Informants supply advance information on exact plans for raids, checkpoints, and attacks on traffickers' bastions. The financial inducements to cooperate with the drug lords are enormous by Colombian standards; for instance, a police captain on the Cali cartel's payroll may earn $2,000 or more a month and a police general $5,000; the official monthly salaries received in their ranks are, respectively, $700 and $1,700.

The cartel's ability to control and manipulate sources of intelligence information is almost legendary: Taxi drivers inform on the movements of visitors to Cali. The cartel has access to passenger lists at the Cali airport and to hotel guest lists in the city. Cartel operatives have extensively infiltrated local units of National Police, the DAS, and the prosecutor general's office. There are persistent rumors that Colombian nationals working in foreign embassies in Bogotá supply information to traffickers. The Medellín cartel also infiltrated the command and control systems of Colombian security agencies. Escobar's organization regularly used disinformation to frustrate government search efforts. For instance, in the early 1990s, the Medellín Search Bloc received eighty to one hundred telephone calls each day on Escobar's whereabouts, most of which were deliberately designed to mislead the searchers.[4] For years Medellín and Cali traffickers have tapped into the national telephone system and even into the more secure communications systems of high government officials. For example, Monica de Grieff, who served as justice minister for several months in 1989, received several direct telephone calls from Medellín kingpin José Gonzalo Rodríguez Gacha at her home and at her office. "Don't bother to change your number, señora" the trafficker said once. "It will take you longer to get your new number than it will take me to find out what it is."[5]

In the Medellín cartel's heydey, narcopolitics was associated with extreme violence. The now-dominant Cali traffickers, however, have advanced their objectives via bribes, economic penetration, and legal manipulation rather than with assassinations and bombings.[6] Indeed, corruption has reached extraordinary proportions in Colombia both locally and nationally. In 1994 police and judicial investigations in Cali discovered evidence of traffickers' payoffs to twelve retired army officers (communication and security specialists "decorated for their outstanding service to the army"), a majority of the Cali city police force, almost the entire contingent of the Cali airport police, employees of the El Valle telephone system, the Cali regional prosecutor, 6 of 22 Cali city councillors, and Manuel Francisco Becerro, a Valle de Cauca political boss and former Colombian comptroller general who worked in Samper's 1994 presidential campaign. (Becerro, was arrested in early 1996 for allegedly having received more than $300,000 from the Cali cartel to help finance Samper's election).

Yet these local scandals were soon overshadowed by revelations that the nation's governing institutions had been compromised. An investigation by the prosecutor general's office (which began in mid-1984 and was ongoing as of February 1996) found that drug money had infiltrated the highest echelons of Colombia's political system, including the presidency and the Congress. By early 1996, Colombia's comptroller general, David Turbay, and attorney general, Orlando Vásquez Velásquez, and some twenty members of Congress, including the president of the Lower House of Congress,

Alvaro Benedetti, were under formal investigation for alleged ties to drug traffickers. (By May 1996, Velásquez and Benedetti were under arrest.) President Ernesto Samper's erstwhile defense minister and 1994 campaign manager, Fernando Botero, was in jail, accused of soliciting cartel funds in the 1994 election, and the president himself had been formally charged in connection with Cali drug-fund contributions to his campaign. Four members of Congress, Senators Alberto Santofimio, María Izquierdo, and Gustavo Espinosa and Representative Rodrigo Garavito (respectively, from the departments of Tolima, Boyacá, Valle de Cauca, and Caldas), and a prominent Liberal Party politician, Eduardo Mestre, who had served as a senator and as Colombia's ambassador to the United Nations, were arrested for illegal enrichment—taking bribes, promotional assistance, and other favors from traffickers. Mestre, according to police reports, had received payments of 5 million pesos ($6,000) per month from "paper companies" owned by the Cali cartel.[7] Additionally, testimony by a former Cali cartel accountant, Guillermo Pallomari, under a plea bargain agreement with the DEA (Pallomari had travelled to the United States under mysterious circumstances, apparently with DEA protection, in August 1995), provided further revelations of drug corruption within Colombia's political establishment. According to an October 1995 *Cambio-16* article, Pallomari's statement, backed by canceled checks and other documents, implicated thirty-five mayors as well as eighty representatives and thirty senators—35 percent of the entire Colombian congress; the politicians, he said, had received more than $7 million from Cali traffickers between the end of 1991 and mid-1994.[8]

The evolution of the scandal that affected the presidency is worth recounting in detail. Samper's problems began in June 1994 with the revelations of the now-famous "narcocassettes"—recordings of telephone conversations between the Rodríguez brothers and a Colombian journalist, Alberto Giraldo, concerning a possible donation of 3 billion pesos (approximately $3.7 million) to Samper's campaign. (Andres Pastrana, the losing candidate in the election, obtained the tapes, which were reportedly made in a DEA surveillance operation, and then released them to the media.) The tapes referred to a meeting between Santiago Medina, Samper's campaign treasurer, and Gilberto Rodríguez.[9] Clearly, something was amiss in Samper's camp. Many Colombian and U.S. observers, among them José Toft, the DEA representative in Colombia at the time, believed that the Cali cartel had heavily bankrolled Samper's election bid. Toft, who resigned from the

DEA in September 1984, articulated widely held beliefs about the state of Colombian politics in a comment to a Colombian TV news station on September 29, 1994: "I cannot think of a single political or judicial institution that has not been penetrated by the narcotraffickers—I know that people don't like to hear the term 'narco-democracy' but the truth is it's very real and it's here."[10]

Indeed, subsequent events suggested that infusion of drug money had played an important and possibly decisive role in the Samper campaign. In July 1995 former campaign treasurer Medina was arrested following revelations that he had accepted a check for 40 million pesos from a Cali front company, Agricola La Estrella, in June 1994. In subsequent "secret" testimony to the Colombian prosecutor general's office (which was published in August in *El Tiempo*), Medina claimed that the Samper campaign received 5 billion pesos (approximately $6 million) from top leaders of the Cali cartel. The funds, said Medina, had been solicited by Colombia's defense minister, Fernando Botero—the son of the painter of the same name—who had been the general manager of the campaign. Moreover, according to Medina, the scheme had the full approval of Samper himself. Botero, one of Samper's closest aides, resigned in early August as a result of these allegations; later that month he turned himself in to Colombian authorities after a warrant was issued for his arrest.

Medina's accusations may be legitimate. For example, he notes that the money was donated in installments of 1 billion and 4 billion pesos, corresponding to the first and second rounds of the campaign. (Neither Samper nor his rival, Andres Pastrana, had received a popular majority in the first round; as a result, the candidates faced off in a runoff election.) Botero, according to Medina, gave Cali drug lord Miguel Rodríguez Orejuela a signed receipt for the second tranche of 4 billion pesos; Rodríguez jokingly commented on receiving the document that "this is the smallest but also the most expensive Botero [alluding to the painter] that exists in the world."[11] (In testimony before Colombian prosecutors in Charlotte, North Carolina in late 1995, cartel accountant Guillermo Pallomari corroborated Medina's claim that 5 billion pesos from the cartel had reached the Samper campaign. The funds, said Pallomari, were shipped to the campaign headquarters in Bogotá in packages of 500,000 pesos.)[12] It is very likely that Cali drug money provided the margin of victory in the 1994 election. The contest was unprecedentedly close—Samper led Pastrana by only 18,000 votes, or 0.3 percent of the electorate, in the first round. The margin increased to more than 156,000 votes in the runoff. Medina himself noted that the Samper campaign was broke and desperate after the first round of voting. The Cali funds could have been used to pay for additional publicity, to fund speeches and rallies in support of the candidate, and even to buy votes.

The drug money scandal threatens to weaken the Samper administration and possibly to undermine the political class in Colombia generally. In light of this fact, the Cali cartel may have done more damage to Colombia's political order than did its Medellín counterpart. Whether the government can ride out the scandal is uncertain. In mid-December, Samper received a vote of confidence from the Commission on Accusations of the Chamber of Representatives (the lower house of Congress); the Commission voted 14 to 1 that there were insufficient grounds to open a formal investigation of the president. Following the decision, Samper expressed the belief that "the executive and government's credibility were restored."[13] Yet such optimism proved premature. By early 1996 clear signs appeared that Samper's administration was unraveling. For example, in January Fernando Botero testified that Samper not only knew about the inflows of Cali drug money into the campaign rounds but that he was seriously implicated in these events.[14] Similarly Santiago Medina stated, "The president not only knew, he was the organizer. He was the prime mover of the fund-raising effort."[15] An editorial in *El Tiempo* urged "President Samper must go. It defies all logic that Samper believes that he can continue governing the country."[16] A Gallup poll taken on January 25 and 26 showed that Samper's approval rating had plummeted— from 70 percent in December 1994 to 40 percent in January 1996. The same poll indicated that a majority of Colombians, 54 percent, thought Samper should step down from the presidency either temporarily or permanently.[17]

Accentuating the impression of corruption and incompetence in the Samper government was the successful escape of José Santa Cruz from La Picota, a maximum security prison in Bogotá, in mid-January. Apparently the Cali leader slipped out of the facility accompanied by a visitor who had displayed fake credentials from the prosecutor general's office and who had come to "interrogate" the prisoner. Chief prosecutor Vladivioso called the escape "a product of the corruption that is besieging the country and the Colombian judicial system."[18] (Santa Cruz was subsequently killed in a firefight with police in early March 1996.)

In February 1996, the prosecutor general's office formally accused Samper of illegal enrichment, electoral fraud, and concealment (*encubrimiento*) of the origin of campaign funds, thus forcing Samper's case to go again before the Commission on Accusations of the Chamber of Representatives. The Commission exonerated Samper by a 10 to 3 vote in May and the full Chamber now debates the case. Technically, both the Chamber and the Senate must decide on impeachment and the Supreme Court must pass sentence for crimes committed in office before the president is required to resign his office (although he must step down temporarily pending a verdict). Of course, domestic and external political pressures could force Samper to leave office long before this process culminates in either impeachment or sentencing.

The United States clearly is fed up with the Samper administration. In March 1996 President Clinton, citing pervasive narcocorruption in the Colombian government, formally decertified Colombia as a partner in the fight against drugs. (See discussion of the certification process and its significance in chapter 4.) The move will directly cost Colombia some $14 million in U.S. aid; also it will affect hundreds of millions of dollars in Export-Import bank financing for U.S. exports to Colombia and exposes that country to possible trade sanctions and the discontinuation of international loans.[19]

The irony in these distressing events is that Samper has been a fairly effective president from a narcotics control perspective. He has demonstrated significant resolve vis-à-vis the cartel by incarcerating six of seven major Cali kingpins between June and August 1995—a remarkable achievement by any standard—and by pushing through tough anticorruption laws. Furthermore, Samper has tackled the politically difficult task of eradicating Colombia's coca crop, spraying many thousands of hectares with herbicides during 1995; a point to be discussed in later chapters. The Samper administration can claim that even if drug money did sway the campaign results, the government should be judged on its actions. Samper himself has shown no inclination to resign from the presidency. Moreover, though he has admitted that Cali drug money may have covertly entered his campaign, he has dismissed the entire corruption scandal as a cartel-led conspiracy to undermine the nation's institutions and to weaken the government's effort to fight drug trafficking. While he may have a point, the revelations still have compromised his administration's ability to govern.

While the veracity of Medina's, Pallomari's, and Botero's allegations is difficult to establish, traffickers have long attempted to influence Colombian presidential politics. For example, Ernesto Samper was present at a meeting in the International Hotel in Medellín in 1982, at which a local business group ·headed by Pablo Escobar contributed 20 million pesos, approximately $310,000, in the (unsuccessful) reelection campaign of Alfonso Lopez Michelson. Samper was Lopez's campaign manager at the time. The 20 million pesos represented almost one-third of the total funds (65 million pesos) contributed to the Lopez campaign in that year. What impact might this contribution have had on Colombian politics had Lopez been elected in 1982 instead of Belisario Betancur?[20] Alberto Giraldo—the intermediary in the scheme to funnel money to the Samper campaign—revealed in his personal diary (which somehow reached the offices of *El Tiempo*) that Gilberto Rodríguez also had donated more than 50 million pesos, or $780,000, to Betancur's successful election effort in that year.[21] Furthermore, a April 1995 *Semana* article cited testimony by a U.S. government informant that Samper had received $1 million from Cali dons Miguel Rodríguez and José Santa Cruz in a 1989 meeting in Cali to discuss ways of ending extradition. At the time, Samper was seeking the Liberal Party's nomination for president. (He was unsuccessful and Cesar Gaviria was nominated and then elected president in 1990.)[22]

Displacing the State

In modern narcotics enterprises, criminal authority tends to grow at the expense of legitimate state authority. Narcocorruption, of course, diminishes the legitimacy of governing institutions. Yet traffickers not only buy government officials, politicians, and electoral outcomes, they also increasingly displace the state in the performance of key social and political functions. In Latin America, this encroachment has occurred in such areas as social welfare, counterinsurgency, and (ironically) maintenance of law and order. For example, in Mexico, Colombia, Bolivia, and elsewhere, traffickers have cultivated a kind of Robin Hood image by devoting vast sums to community development projects or by giving money and gifts to the poor. Such activities have cemented drug capos' bases of political support among marginalized social groups—that is, among populations that governments or legitimate nongovernment organizations are unable to reach with services. In Colombia, narcowelfare projects are associated more with Medellín kingpins than with the leaders of Cali; the difference may reflect Cali's preference for lower-profile spending. (No Barrio Gilberto Rodríguez comparable to Medellín's Barrio Pablo Escobar exists in Cali, but Cali money may reach the slums via legal front companies and charitable networks.) Also, weak government penetration of rural areas, ongoing rural insurgency problems, and drug lords' acquisition of landed estates in the 1980s created new political opportunities and functions for narcotics dealers. The result was the emergence of paramilitary organizations financed by trafficking interests that supplanted an impotent Colombian state in providing local security against predatory guerrilla groups. By the mid-1980s, drug dealers in the Middle Magdalena Valley were committing substantial funds to an umbrella organization called ACDEGAM (*Asociación Campesina De Agricultores y Ganaderos del Magdalena Medio*) that provided training and equipment for local "self-defense groups" and that also sponsored various educational, health, public welfare, and road-building activities.[23] Though curbed somewhat in the Colombian government's 1989-1990 crackdown on the Medellín cartel, narcobacked paramilitaries continue to operate in the Middle Magdalena Valley, Córdoba, Uraba, and other guerrilla-infested regions. (Of course, paramilitaries' activities in rooting out and exterminating guerrilla sympathizers represent a serious and ongoing human rights problem for Colombia.) Admittedly, legitimate private groups—coffee growers' associations, cattlemen's groups, and foreign oil companies, for example—that operate in Colombia's hinterland also perform public welfare and security protection functions; however, the narcotraffickers' intrusion into these activities has particularly ominous overtones for the Colombian political process.

With respect to law-and-order issues, traffickers tend to adopt a "support your local police" attitude regarding defense of property rights and maintenance of basic community services. (Police identified as spearheading government crackdowns or working for rival trafficking organizations, on the other hand, stand a good chance of being murdered.) The social cleansing groups supported by the Cali cartel were a perverted and socially regressive example of narcofunded law enforcement, but another less perverted example was the cartel's assistance in the Colombian government's ultimately successful manhunt against Pablo Escobar and some of his lieutenants; a contribution that recently has been acknowledged by Colombia's prosecutor general, Alfonso Valdivieso. According to the Cali regional prosecutor's office, the Cali group hired Japanese communication experts to track Escobar's movements in the months prior to the trafficker's demise. Gilberto Rodríguez himself supplied information from wiretaps of Escobar's telephone conversations and from an extensive network of informants within the Medellín cartel. One Cali informant based in Cartagena, Enrique Velásquez (known as "El Navegante," the Navigator), worked as a transportation manager for both Escobar and Rodríguez Gacha. El Navegante told his Cali contacts about a visit by Rodríguez Gacha to a *finca* (a country estate) near Cartagena to take charge personally of an important cocaine shipment to the United States. The Cali leaders passed the information to the authorities. In mid-December El Navegante established direct contact with members of Colombia's elite police force; information he provided about Rodríguez's movements along the Caribbean coast may have been instrumental in the police operation that discovered and killed the trafficker in Tolu later that month. Moreover, Valdivieso's predecessor, Gustavo de Grieff, cited a persistent report that the Medellín Search Bloc had received a $10 million payment from Cali traffickers shortly after Escobar was killed; the money allegedly was distributed among the Bloc's ranking members. "Apparently, the Bloque [the Medellín Search Bloc] was an instrument of Escobar's enemies, not of the government," commented de Grieff. Such scattered examples point to the ability of traffickers— who command enormous power and resources—to piratize government functions or to acquire them by default. (Not surprisingly, in their ongoing surrender negotiations with the Colombian government, the Cali traffickers have used their contributions to the anti-Escobar campaign as a point of leverage in their own campaign to obtain lenient treatment such as reduced sentences or house arrest.)[24] Such informal collaboration left a bad legacy: It weakened the government's bargaining position in negotiations with the Cali leaders during 1994, and generally diminished Colombia's commitment to fighting the Cali organization, which by the end of 1993 controlled most of the cocaine business in the country.

7

Relations with Guerrillas

Perhaps because of the cocaine industry's multifront challenges to the Andean governments, Washington has expressed concern about a connection between the cocaine industry and Marxist guerrilla groups. Indeed, the Reagan administration analyzed the drug problem within the framework of the East-West conflict. Administration officials spoke publicly and privately about a "deadly connection" and an "unholy alliance" between cocaine kings and guerrillas. A 1985 U.S. government report on Soviet influence in Latin America warned of an "alliance between drug smugglers and arms dealers in support of terrorists and guerrillas."[1] The idea of a narcoguerrilla alliance played very well in Washington, Bogotá, and Lima. In general, governments found it expedient to depict cocaine traffickers as hostile to the political order—working outside of the system—and the narcoguerrilla label served that purpose admirably.

By the late 1980s, however, the concept of a political tie or "alliance" between drug dealers and guerrillas had lost considerable credibility. Evidence suggested that the two groups were not natural allies and that their relations were essentially opportunistic. Furthermore, in Colombia, narcoguerrilla interaction was characterized as much by conflict as by collaboration: Indeed, the upper echelon of the cocaine business emerged in the mid-1980s as a determined foe of revolutionary movements. In Peru, by contrast, a symbiotic relationship developed between the cocaine trade and the Shining Path (*Sendero*

Luminoso) terrorists. The narcotraffickers and terrorists were in conflict, with Shining Path exacting payments that formed the heart of the movement's finances, but the two groups also cooperated in the face of the forces of law and order.

Significant emphasis has been placed on the financial nexus between the cocaine trade and insurgent groups. Here governments have legitimate strategic concerns. In Colombia, some thirty-seven guerrilla fronts comprising more than 4,000 insurgents, most of them members of the FARC, are engaged in taxing and protecting the narcotics trade. Guerrillas levy taxes on cocaine base laboratories and on shipments of base out of growing-processing zones; they also tax incoming shipments of chemicals used in the conversion of coca leaves to base. Table 7.1 summarizes the taxes imposed at different stages of the cocaine business.

TABLE 7.1
GUERRILLA TAXES ON COLOMBIAN COCAINE AND HEROIN INDUSTRY 1994-1995

Activity	Tax Amount
Cultivation	10,000 pesos per hectare per month
Processing	5,000 pesos per kilo produced
Export from trafficking zone	20,000 to 30,000 pesos per kilo shipped
Operation of laboratory	Up to 12 million pesos per month
Use of airstrip	10 million pesos per month
Import chemicals into zone	1,000 pesos per liter
Import gasoline into zone	1,000 pesos per 55-gallon drum

Source: Adapted from Sergio Uribe. Centro de Estudios Internacionales. Bogotá 1995, and Miller Rubio, "National Police Report Examine Drug Trade," *El Tiempo,* December 19, 1994.

In 1992, according to *Semana* magazine, the FARC reportedly earned approximately $118 million from the coca and opium trade, which amounted to an estimated 70 percent of the movement's total revenues in that year. (The rest of FARC's income derived from kidnapping, extortion, and gold mining, in that order of importance.) In Peru in the late 1980s, the Shining Path earned $20 to $30 million yearly from taxing the cocaine processors and shippers in the Upper Huallaga Valley.[2] In the early 1990s the group reportedly was able to pay its militants as much as $500 per month, five times Peru's per capita monthly income at that time. With access to such resources, guerrilla movements can fester indefinitely. Contribution to insurgency thus represents an important indirect cost of narcotics industries and a reason why governments should take steps to eradicate them. The narcoguerrilla nexus probably is stronger in the upstream phases of the industry (cultivation and low-level processing) than in the downstream phases (refining and distribution). Guerrillas in Peru provide political guidance and armed protection for coca-growing peasants who must contend with government eradication programs and exploitation by drug dealers. In Peru, Shining Path attempted to establish a high floor price for coca leaves in those areas under its control. In Colombia, the two main guerrilla groups, FARC and ELN, administer vast coca cultivation zones in several Colombian departments—Meta, Vichada, Vaupes, Guaviare, Caquetá, Putumayo, and Magdalena. Guerrillas act as a kind of surrogate government in these zones; their protective function extends to supporting (or organizing) episodes of peasant resistance against the Colombian governmet's anticoca policies.

Yet the relationship between the guerrilla movement and the principal trafficking coalitions has been uneasy at best. Financial power is unbalanced; the annual income of the cocaine business, calculated at $6 billion to $10 billion, is forty to seventy times greater than that of the FARC. Traffickers thus are in a position to make large outlays to protect cocaine HCL laboratories and shipping routes (although, as argued below, they may find it cheaper to pay off the guerrillas). Moreover, both Medellín and (to a lesser extent) Cali organizations have a history of sponsoring violence against the revolutionary left.[3]

PERU

In Peru, the cocaine business has been a vital source of finance for guerrillas. The main guerrilla groups operating in the Upper Huallaga Valley have been the Shining Path and the MRTA (Tupac Amaru Revolutionary Movement). As mentioned, evidence of a narcoguerrilla connection has become especially apparent since the capture of Shining Path leader Abimael Guzman Reynoso (known as President Gonzalo) in September 1992.[4] Peruvian forces have been able to round up many of the terrorists and to seize some of their records. For instance, an "Economic Balance of the Shining Path," dated March 1991, was seized in August 1993 in the Tingo Maria area.[5] In its daily detailed information on income and expenses, it showed charges of $3,000 to $7,000 per flight for drug planes leaving the Valley. After the arrest in Colombia and extradition to Peru of that country's most important drug trafficker, Demetrio Limoniel Chavez Penaherrera (known as Vaticano), Chavez and captured terrorists he dealt with confirmed that he had supplied Shining Path arms and had paid $5,000 per flight plus $3.00 per kilogram of paste (or $6.00 for base) transported in the aircraft. A May 1994 article in the Peruvian newspaper *Expreso* reports that Peru's other main guerrilla force, the

Tupac Amaru, received $225,000 per week for cocaine base shipped to Colombia from Villa Rica, an important entrepot and collection center in Pasco department for Peruvian coca products.[6]

Since Guzman's capture, the Shining Path has become a mere shadow of itself. Many of its members have turned themselves in or been arrested. The group has split, with one part abandoning armed struggle, in line with the orders of the jailed leader. But the "Red Path" faction under Oscar Alberto Ramírez (known as President Feliciano) has continued terroristic activities, with financing coming primarily from the drug trade. According to arrested drug traffickers and former Shining Path members, Ramírez had collected $200 million by early 1994.[7] Weapons and communications gear captured in battles against Ramírez's gang in November 1994 came from the drug trafficking group of Waldo Vargas (known as The Minister).

The drug traffickers financed Shining Path not due to any political alliance, but because they were too weak to resist effectively the guerrillas' exactions. Peruvian trafficking groups are relatively weak, disorganized, and dependent on Colombian groups for leadership, technical advice, and armed support. Relatively little of Peru's cocaine production, perhaps 10 to 20 percent, is processed into cocaine hydrochloride. Nearly all Peruvian cocaine base and hydrochloride is sold to Colombians who fly in payments and fly out product. That is, Peruvians do not obtain the value added in transporting cocaine to overseas markets. In addition, Colombians appear to control several cocaine trafficking organizations in Peru. According to *Expreso,* of twenty-one trafficking "firms" operating in the Upper Huallaga Valley in 1991, eleven were owned by Colombians, three by Peruvians, and the rest by nationals of both countries. Peruvian traffickers have increased their control of the cocaine business since that time but as U.S. political scientist Peter Lupsha notes: The Colombians "view themselves as the superiors and dominant partners in the Peruvian case."[8]

Possibly because of the Colombians' domination in the area, Peru never developed exporters' associations—cartels—or a self-conscious bourgeois narcoclass comparable to those in Colombia. Similarly, Peruvian dealers did not develop an effective common strategy against the Shining Path or MRTA. Considerable evidence documents turf disputes between Peruvian (and Colombian) traffickers and the Shining Path guerrillas. However, Shining Path made inroads into the cocaine paste and base industry in the Upper Huallaga Valley by exploiting both conflicts among Peruvian traffickers and their sense of nationalism (their hostility toward the Colombian overlords). Some Peruvian dealers cut deals with Shining Path, providing money to the guerrillas in return for the exclusive right to operate in a particular territory. Some traffickers even recruited armed guerrillas to help them subjugate rival groups. From the late 1980s to the decline of the Shining Path in the mid-1990s, the trafficker-Shining Path balance of power in much of the Upper Huallaga clearly favored the Shining Path, and, as noted, the movement was able to extract significant resources from the drug trade. Buyers for the Colombian cartels sometimes even negotiated prices for coca paste and cocaine base directly with guerrilla representatives.[9]

Guerrillas and traffickers did share one common strategic goal, namely, the reduction of law enforcement in the Huallaga Valley. That brought them together to oppose coca eradication. The United States had funded a coca eradication program in the Upper Huallaga Valley that eliminated approximately 18,000 hectares of coca between 1983 and 1989. Shining Path successfully exploited the eradication issue to gain adherents among the local peasantry. In a sense, then, a narcoguerrilla alliance existed in the valley. The Peruvian military, however, which was sent to the valley in 1985 to curb the growing insurgency problems, concluded that a modicum of popular support was necessary to combat the guerrillas. This meant less, not more, repression of the coca trade. Military commanders needed intelligence from local residents to distinguish friends and enemies and to locate and assess the strength of guerrilla forces. But just who were "the people" in the Upper Huallaga? According to the U.S. Agency for International Development (USAID), in the late 1980s some 65 to 75 percent of the rural economically active population was engaged in coca cultivation, and between 85 and 95 percent of the valley's income was derived from exports of coca products.[10] Eradication campaigns, attacks on paste producers, and other programs that affect large numbers of people thus carry a strategic downside.

Brigadier General Alberto Arciniega Huby, who was in charge of the Huallaga Valley emergency zone from April to December 1989, observed, "If we repress 50,000 coca farmers, we create 50,000 recruits or collaborators for Sendero."[11] The Peruvian military thus has tended to be unsympathetic to crop eradication campaigns and has suppressed, restricted, or prohibited such efforts. As soon as General Arciniega assumed command, he made clear that his priority was the elimination of the Shining Path, for which task he had to win the support of coca farmers.[12] He therefore did little to support police actions against coca. Indeed, during his first week in office, he prevented the reestablishment of the Uchiza police post that Shining Path had destroyed, because the local population said the police were harassing them. During his seven months in office, Arciniega displaced the guerrillas and built up support among the local population. Shining Path suffered grievous military reverses, most notably a disaster in July 1989 when it lost 110 fighters in one week in successive engagements with the Peruvian military in the Upper Huallaga Valley towns of Madre Mía, Nuevo Progreso and Tulumayo. Arciniega was so popular that 30,000 people turned out in Uchiza to celebrate Armed Forces Day.

The general was dismissed in December 1989 under pressure from the United States, which claimed he was in the pay of the narcotraffickers. The allegation of personal corruption seems unlikely, given that now Arciniega lives a life of relative poverty in exile, but there is no doubt that he put counternarcotics in second place. He did supplement the meager resources he was allocated by Lima during this time of extreme economic crisis with money raised through informal taxes on the local population—which means from those involved in the coca trade. While some of the money flowing from the cocaine industry to the military was purely and simply corruption, some paid for aspects of the Peruvian war effort (boots, uniforms, food) and for public works that benefited villagers.

During the 1990s, there have been many episodes—at times a general pattern has appeared—of military cooperation with drug traffickers. Sometimes that cooperation has been part of a strategic doctrine of building a broad united front against Shining Path, including coca growers and at least low-level drug traffickers. At other times the cooperation has been straightforward corruption, with the military reportedly offering protection to traffickers in return for money and intelligence information. Such protection includes keeping the Peruvian antidrug police and the DEA away from trafficking zones or informing traffickers about impending raids on airstrips or laboratories.

The cocaine trade has provided a source of funds for the military, the guerrillas, the police, and the local government. A source at the Institute of Liberty and Democracy in Lima reports that for one shipment of cocaine flown out of the Uchiza municipal airport in mid-late 1991, traffickers paid bribes totaling $13,800: $1,200 to the police guard at the airports, $3,000 to the local military command, $2,800 to the town of Uchiza (for civic improvements), $4,800 to the Peruvian antinarcotics police at Santa Lucia (a nearby staging area for interdiction missions), and $2,000 to Shining Path.[13] In late 1994 the Army Inspector General's office revealed that it was investigating fifty-eight officers and noncommissioned officers for protecting drug flights, selling cocaine, and selling weapons to traffickers.[14]

The guerrillas' relationship to drug trafficking acquired a new wrinkle in late 1995. As discussed in Chapter Five, more vigorous disruption of flights to Colombia caused a crisis in Peru's coca economy. Coca leaf and paste prices fell by three-fourths, and farmers often could not find anyone to buy their product. Farmers' income dropped off so steeply that families went hungry: USAID started an emergency feeding program for the hardest hit.[15] The Shining Path has taken advantage of the farmers' resentment at their new poverty. It has regained sufficient support in the Upper Huallaga Valley and once again has become an important force, though it is not as strong as it was in the early 1990s.[16]

COLOMBIA

In one important respect, the situation in Colombia made the army there more ready than in Peru to take on the guerrillas and the traffickers at the same time. The Colombian military's counterinsurgency strategy does not emphasize building alliances with drug farmers and small processors. As guerrillas have entrenched themselves in coca- and opium-growing regions and cemented ties with growers, the government's opportunities for winning "hearts and minds" are limited. Massive eradication of illegal crops, therefore, is the only answer. A January 15, 1995, article in *El Tiempo* outlines the strategic perspective in the following terms:

> The decision of the government to undertake a thorough offensive to eradicate coca, opium and marijuana plantations can put the country in the path of peace, even while increasing conflict in the short term.
>
> If anything can persuade the guerrillas to negotiate a definitive and stable peace with the government, it is a substantial and prolonged reduction in the high revenues that they receive regularly from the traffic which permits them to maintain and equip an expanding armed force.
>
> The drug traffic may effectively create a major division within the guerrilla movement between those who stay in the business and do not incorporate themselves into civilian life and those who decide to lay down their arms. . . .
>
> In other words, no solution to the problem of armed insurgency in Colombia today is possible while the drug traffic continues to grow. . . .[17]

At the same time, the relationship between the Colombian drug lords and the guerrilla movement has been characterized by much hostility, at least since the mid-1980s. Fundamentally, the issue was that the wealthiest traffickers associated themselves with the defense of private property and hence found common cause with the Colombian elite against the extreme left. As Pablo Escobar once remarked, "Call me a narcotrafficker if you want. But to present one as a member of the guerrillas is unacceptable because it hurts my personal dignity. I am a man of investments, and this reason could not be allied with guerrillas who fight against private property."[18]

An important catalyst in trafficker-guerrilla hostilities was the decision of the Medellín cocaine leadership to invest much of its newfound wealth in farms, ranches, and land and estates in Colombia's relatively unprotected hinterland. Like other landowners, traffickers become vulnerable to extortion by the FARC and other guerrilla predators. Consequently, Medellín kingpins developed close ties with the traditional rural power structure and cooperated actively with local elites against the common insurgency threat. During the mid- and late 1980s, Colombian traffickers sat on the cutting edge of the dirty war being waged between the property-owning classes and the revolutionary leftist groups—a struggle that had substantial implications for the future economic and political development of the nation's rural areas.

From a strategic standpoint, no clearer evidence of narco-guerrilla confrontation can be cited than the Colombian paramilitary movement of the 1980s. Armed self-defense organizations had operated in Colombia for some time, seeking to protect local communities against extortion, kidnapping, and other guerrilla practices. However, the self-defense movement suffered from a lack of equipment, training, and resources, so local landlords often had no alternative but to pay taxes to guerrillas.

This situation changed as Colombian cocaine barons invested some of their profits in vast tracts of land—reportedly at least 1 million hectares in the mid-to late 1980s in Córdoba, Antioquia, Meta, and other Colombia departments. For example, in the Middle Magdalena Valley town of Puerto Boyacá, which became the epicenter of the paramilitary movement in Colombia, drug trafficking purchases raised the price of a hectare of land from $100,000 in the early 1980s to $1 million in 1989.[19] Many of the recently purchased tracts of land lay in *zonas rojas*—red zones, where predatory guerrillas maintained a strong presence. Some traffickers' *fincas* (ranches) and farms housed cocaine laboratories; others were purely legitimate operations. Regardless, the new landed narcogentry found itself face to face with Colombia's guerrillas.

This historically significant process precipitated the revival and overhaul of the local self-defense forces or created such forces where none previously existed. Cocaine barons or their representatives assumed the leadership of, and most of the financial responsibility for, such forces, which served as an instrument for combatting guerrilla influence. The paramilitary movement also offered cocaine traffickers a way to acquire a modicum of social legitimacy. By supporting such paramilitary activities, cocaine dealers have cemented their ties with established groups in Colombian society, especially with the landowning classes and right-wing military factions.

The narco-backed self-defense movement has been instrumental in dislodging Communist guerrillas from certain regions of Colombia. As one Colombian official put it, "The truth is, where there are paramilitary with money from narco-trafficking, there are no guerrillas. The paramilitary forces are well-trained, well-paid, and bloodthirsty, and the guerrillas respect that."[20]

The Middle Magdalena Paramilitaries

Perhaps the clearest paramilitary success story was in the Central Colombian region of the Middle Magdalena Valley—an area of roughly 600,000 hectares that encompassed six provinces and forty-two towns—where various guerrilla forces had maintained a strong presence since the early 1960s. (After 1965 the FARC became the dominant guerrilla force in the valley.) Over the years, the guerrillas had progressively tightened their economic hold on cattlemen and ranchers. When some larger landowners fled the region, the FARC began to exact tribute from small peasant owners, thus undercutting much of the movement's original political base. By the early 1980s, the situation had become desperate. As one landowner recalled in a 1983 *El Tiempo* interview:

> Twenty-three years ago the guerrillas began to ask us for various things—a hat, shoes, some shirts, a chicken or a cow. Then came ever-increasing demands for "voluntary" quotas for 20,000 or 50,000 pesos which we paid to be left alone. Then there were times when we brought guerrillas to Bogotá to give them medical treatment. But the guerrillas returned our kindness by kidnapping many cattlemen. . . . Finally we held a public meeting in Puerto Boyacá and proposed to pay the guerrillas a tax for each head of cattle if they would let us work in peace. Yet the offer was refused and the kidnappings got worse.[21]

In response, the besieged landowners and local army units organized self-defense militias to fend off the FARC battalion and to create a measure of security in the region. In 1983 an umbrella organization—the Farmers and Cattlemen's Association of the Middle Magdalena Valley (ACDEGAM)—was set up to coordinate the counterinsurgency effort in the region. Now the landowners' contribution financed the militia units, not the FARC; yet the new arrangement seemed a far superior economic proposition. As one ranch owner remarked, "If I had to pay 20 million [pesos] for a kidnapping now I pay one million to defend myself and save 19 million."[22] Also, by the late 1980s, resident cocaine bosses were paying the lion's share of the expenses of paramilitary forces; the contributions of the nontrafficking landlords were minuscule.

Initially poorly equipped, poorly trained, and poorly funded, the self-defense forces performed badly against the FARC. Indeed, major FARC offensive in 1985 combined with sudden collapse in meat prices, bankrupted many cattlemen in the region and almost wiped out the militias. As the decade went on, however, the balance of power in the valley shifted radically in favor of the anti-Communist forces. The most important factor was the influx of narcowealth into the valley. By the end of the decade, according to a Colombian army report, traffickers' controlled (mostly through intermediaries) some 40 percent of the land in the Middle Magdalena.[23] The drug lords, of course, could pay for more elaborate, more aggressive, and better equipped counterinsurgency operations than could simple cattlemen and farmers. Moreover, the Colombian army also enthusiastically promoted the growth of the paramilitaries, partly out of fear that President Belisario Betancur's "peace and democratic opening" policy (announced in 1983) would severely undercut the military's counterinsurgency mission in the valley and elsewhere; the policy aimed at negotiations with and eventual amnesty for guerrillas. The army supplied the paramilitaries with weapons (including a range of sophisticated automatic weapons such as AK-47s, M-16s, and Galil 762s) and collaborated with them in operations against guerrillas and suspected Communists.[24]

By the late 1980s the self-defense units had metamorphosed into an armed force with powerful offensive capabilities. The army's Bárbula battalion, based in the valley, furnished automatic weapons to rightist paramilitary forces that were funded by traffickers or landlords. According to Colombian journalist Maria Duzan, drug lord Gonzalo Rodríguez Gacha maintained direct radio contact with the military command center at the Bárbula battalion.[25] ACDEGAM, the umbrella organization for the militias, hosted "military training schools, instructions, modern armament, a motor park with jeeps, trucks and motorcycles, and sophisticated radio communications equipment for mobilizing military and security personnel throughout the region."[26] Training courses were staffed by FARC deserters, retired military officers, and U.S. and Israeli advisors. In one school, *El Cincuenta,* paramilitary trainees studied techniques of camouflage, intelligence and counterintelligence, use of arms and explosives, concealment of one's true identity, and assault against population centers.[27] Quite clearly, the original self-defense mission of the militias (now virtually paramilitary armies) had become subverted. Moreover, the strategic reach of the paramilitaries extended well beyond the Middle Magdalena. In 1988 and 1989, paramilitary graduates of the Middle Magdalena training school massacred presumed guerrilla collaborators and other "leftists" in the towns of La Mejor Esquina in Cordoba Department, in Segovia in northeastern Antioquia, and at two banana plantations—La Negra and Honduras—in the Uraba region of Antioquia. Nearly one hundred people, some of them women and children, perished in these attacks. Two Colombian army officers and an army sergeant reportedly collaborated in the Uraba incidents, furnishing descriptions of the intended victims, paying the assassins' hotel bills in Medellín, and arranging for the killers' transportation to Uraba.

Furthermore, by the mid- and late 1980s, the counterinsurgency movement in the valley had acquired distinct political and even separatist overtones. ACDEGAM itself was a network of "patriotic" and anti-Communist schools. The militias distributed pamphlets claiming that Colombian police and judicial institutions were infiltrated by Communist militants. One militia hymn "To Our Patron the Virgin of Carmen" read: "Liberate Colombia dear beloved Mother from the infamous Communist guerrillas. The campesino self-defense force is ready to serve thee, Immaculate One."[28] In early 1989, the secretary-general of ACDEGAM, Ivan Roberto Duque, announced the formation of a new political movement, the Movimiento de Restauración Nacional (MORENA), in the Middle Magdalena. MORENA was to be the political arm of the armed paramilitaries, just as the Patriotic Union (a far-left political party) often was considered the civilian face of the FARC. MORENA's stated aim was to gain 250,000 votes in the 1990 regional election to control the valley's forty-two mayoralty slots and eventually to field candidates throughout Colombia to appeal to "all good citizens who are against subversion."[29] The organization reportedly was the brainchild of Medellín kingpin José Gonzalo Rodríguez Gacha, a militant anti-Communist and long-standing antagonist of the FARC, who was also the largest landowner in the Middle Magdalena—in all of Colombia as well.

Two observations can be made regarding the situation in the Middle Magdalena and other guerrilla-infested regions during the mid- and late 1980s. One is that subversion was widely perceived as a more important threat to Colombia's political and social order than was drug trafficking. In Puerto Boyacá, a Middle Magdalena town describing itself as "the anti-subversion capital of Colombia," the entire local power structure—the mayor, the councillors, farmers, cattlemen, businessmen, and even representatives of Texaco (which maintained producing wells in the region)—supported or at least condoned the ACDEGAM counterinsurgency infrastructure that developed. A second point is that paramilitaries largely accomplished their economic and political objectives in many locations. As Maria Duzan noted in her 1994 book, *Death Beat,* "The guerrillas had been forced to retreat, not in battles with the regular army, but with these drug-financed militias." Moreover, as a result of pacification campaign in the Middle Magdalena Valley and other parts of Colombia, "landowners were able to return to their lands and the areas that had suffered a strong economic depression were receiving an influx of drug money that brought in a certain newfound prosperity."[30]

The drug-financed paramilitaries and the proto-fascist political movement associated with them suffered severe blows in the Colombian government's offenses against the Medellín cartel from 1989 to 1991. In August-September 1989, the military's XIV brigade based in the region raided forty-two residences of alleged drug bosses and confiscated fifteen large estates, six of which belonged to Rodríguez Gacha and two to Pablo Escobar.[31] Large quantities of cocaine and weapons were seized in the raids. MORENA disappeared following the death of its alleged patron, Rodríguez Gacha, in December 1989, and ACDEGAM probably no longer exists as such. (A vice-president of ACDEGAM and other militia leaders were brutally murdered in internecine struggles with Pablo Escobar and his associates in the early 1990s.) With the demise of the original Medellín cartel, the financial impetus and backing for the paramilitary have greatly diminished. Nevertheless, private violence is still alive and well in the Middle Magdalena. As of late 1994, at least eight separate paramilitary groups operated in there, according to the Colombian Army Command. Moreover, the rightist coalition that guarded the military activities in the 1980s still shows signs of life. In October 1994 *Semana* cited an intelligence report that "narcoparamilitaries" are plotting to create a separate administrative "department of the Middle Magdalena" and to "resurrect the dominance of Escobar and 'El Mexicano' (Rodríguez Gacha)." The point men for the alleged scheme include Nicholás Gomez, a priest who is running for mayor in the Caldas city of La Dorada; Jairo Correa Alzate, a former drug dealer and former confidant of Rodríguez Gacha; and Ivan Roberto Duque, the "veteran political leader of the paramilitaries" and former ACDEGAM chief.[32]

Columbian Developments in the Mid-1990s

Paramilitaries continue to flourish in Colombia today. In 1994 the army and the Department of Administrative Security identified 130-odd self-defense groups, paramilitary organization, and assassin teams operating in at least twenty Colombian departments. Undoubtedly, many such groups are financed by drug dealers, who now comprise by far the most powerful economic group in the country. Many of the factors that gave rise to the paramilitary groups of the 1980s—predatory guerrilla movements, a weak state, large narcolandowners—still operate today. (Indeed, according to recent estimates, *narcotraficantes* actually have increased their landholdings in Colombia by 200 or 300 percent since the late 1980s.) Still—the recent machinations in the Middle Magdalena notwithstanding—narcoparamilitaries no longer pose the organized threat to the Colombian democratic order that they did in the mid- and late 1980s. There are two major reasons for this. On the one hand, such groups lack powerful sponsors: The leader of the Cali trafficking coalition, which now controls a majority share of the Colombian cocaine business, shows little interest in uniting with rightist groups in establishing independent territorial enclaves to wipe out Communist guerrillas. Furthermore, with "international communism" largely a spent political force, guerrillas are abandoning their Communist ideals and behaving more like reformists—or common criminals. Under these circumstances, anti-Communist coalitions are likewise losing their ideological threat and momentum. In the heyday of the Medellín cartel, traffickers gained internal political status by posing as defenders of the status quo (or an idealized version of it) against a Marxist revolutionary threat. Such a political opportunity no longer exists in Colombia in the mid-1990s—at least not to the same extent. The modern generation of traffickers exercises enormous power in Colombia not by advancing rightist or populist agendas but by increasing its penetration of the legal economy and by manipulating legislators and government officials behind the scenes.

Two final observations: First, it is worth noting that while the guerrillas are active in coca-growing regions, their presence in the production of refined cocaine is not well documented. Some cocaine laboratories are located deep in the Amazon jungles along the Peru-Colombia-Brazil border, where virtually no guerrillas can be detected. Many other laboratories are located in regions such as Valle de Cauca or the Middle Magdalena Valley, where traffickers hold a preponderance of power. Still others, though situated in unsecured zones, are heavily fortified by traffickers. Maria Duzan cites the example of a Medellín cocaine hydrochloride laboratory La Azulita in Putumayo Department that was protected by one hundred militia patrolmen who had received paramilitary training in the Middle Magdalena Valley. In late 1987 guerrillas attacked the laboratory, but failed to dislodge the traffickers and lost fifty men in the process. However, guerrillas probably do tax some percentage of cocaine hydrochloride production. From the traffickers' perspective, the issue of how best to locate and protect cocaine refineries may come down to dollars and cents: In some cases, it may be cheaper to pay taxes to guerrillas than to fund elaborate guard systems and counterinsurgency projects or to buy protection from government officials or military officers in more settled areas of the country. The La Azulita complex originally had been a Cali-owned operation and had been "protected" by FARC guerrillas. But Cali lost it in a raid by Medellín armed militiamen who "killed six guerrillas and seized $10 million in cash and an adjacent airstrip."[33]

Second, the likelihood of symbiosis or convergence of objectives between traffickers and guerrillas seems greatest when traffickers are weak, disorganized, or under severe pressure from the authorities. Recall above the example of Peruvian traffickers who hired guerrilla "muscle" to consolidate their positions vis-à-vis rival trafficking groups. In Colombia during 1993, an intense government assault on the military arms of the Medellín cartel may have impelled Pablo Escobar to make tactical agreements with guerrillas to continue his war against the state. Reportedly Escobar hired ELN "urban commandos" on various occasions to place car bombs near government buildings[34]—that is, guerrillas substituted for the cartel's weakened capability to commit terrorist acts. Similarly, the Colombian crackdown on the Cali cartel might induce some Cali leaders to commandeer guerrilla support for a renewed narcoterrorist campaign against the government. In Colombia, where two important lawless groups, drug traffickers and guerrillas, share the same territory (if not the same political space), occasional alliances of convenience seem almost inevitable.

8

The Costs of the Cocaine Industry to Andean Society

Cocaine obviously brings a great many advantages to Andean economies. It is the largest single source of foreign exchange in Colombia, Bolivia, and Peru. It probably contributes more to gross national product than does any other single industry in Colombia, and it is among the top industries if not the largest in Bolivia and Peru. It employs directly some 500,000 workers throughout the region. Thanks to cocaine, a few of the largest traffickers are billionaires. And these are just some of the more obvious advantages; there are also second-order advantages, some of which are discussed herein.

The objective of this chapter is to illuminate the darker side, namely, the disadvantages that come from the cocaine industry. The principal disadvantages, political and social, are relatively straightforward. Some economic problems also result from the cocaine industry, those problems are more subtle and take longer to explain. The fact that the discussion of economic problems is longer than the discussion of political and social problems in no way implies that the main disadvantages from cocaine are economic.

It may seem paradoxical to say that cocaine can cause economic problems. Cocaine is profitable for both farmer and trafficker; otherwise it would not be produced. How then can cocaine harm the economy, if it is profitable—indeed, superprofitable—for the producers? Even the most conservative of economists recognize that sometimes that which is profitable can be bad for society. Cocaine is a good example of what economists call "market failure." That is, in some situations, markets encourage behavior that is unprofitable for society as a whole and discourage behavior that is better for development. Market failure occurs when there is a difference between the costs of an action for an individual—as with cocaine production—and the costs of that action for society. In the case of cocaine, market failure occurs because the small minority of the population involved in the cocaine industry does not bear many of the costs it imposes on society.

The technical term for this problem is negative externalities, which are costs that society has to bear but are outside (external to) the producer's obligation to pay. One example is a factory that pollutes the air. If a company has to choose between two ways of making a product, with one method that costs less but produces air pollution while another method costs more but does not pollute, the company will make more profit if it chooses the polluting method. That makes sense for the company but not necessarily for society, because the pollution causes health problems. It would be wrong to say that the polluting method is more economical: It is cheaper for the company itself, but it is more expensive for society as a whole.

This chapter focuses on problems that the cocaine industry causes; it does not evaluate the impact of that industry. In other words, it does not attempt to weigh the cost of the cocaine industry against the benefits in order to come up with an overall balance. Any such an effort would be suspect. Few hard data exist on many vital points. More important, it is not clear if there is any way to measure something as abstract as the cost of fear and intimidation from greater violence. That said, it is our gut feeling that cocaine has been mixed blessing for the Andean nations. It has increased income but at a political price, and it has brought benefits to some but has imposed costs on many others.

POLITICAL COSTS OF THE COCAINE INDUSTRY

A variety of political costs result from the cocaine industry; their burden cannot be quantified. Nonetheless, the costs are real. In general, cocaine inhibits liberty and undermines the rule of law in the fragile

Andean democracies through terrorism, intimidation, corruption, and by overwhelming the police and courts.

Terrorism

The relationship between terrorism and the cocaine trade varies among countries in the Andes. In Bolivia, for example, cocaine has not provided a major basis for guerrillas. There is essentially no terrorist movement in that country, and the coca business has had little connection with organized political violence (or at least violence more serious than tumultuous demonstrations and beating up of opponents). By contrast, in Peru the cocaine trade has been the main source of finance for the guerrilla groups, as discussed in chapter 7. It also has provided the groups with opportunities to organize disaffected farmers who viewed the government as an instrument of repression out to destroy their livelihood. The intimate connection between the cocaine trade and the guerrilla movement was an important factor in persuading the Fujimori government that coca and the cocaine business were threats to the security of the Peruvian state.

And in Colombia, as discussed in detail in chapter 7, the long-standing guerrilla movements feed off the cocaine business as they do off all other economic activities. As a result, drug traffickers have organized private militias to fight off guerrillas. The net effect of the cocaine business on Colombia's guerrilla problem is therefore unclear: Cocaine provides a rich source of pickings for the guerrillas' exactions, but the drug traffickers may have been more effective than the state in combatting the guerrillas in certain localities.

Intimidation

Censorship by the bullet or by the wallet has undermined public discussion of politics in the Andean nations. In Colombia, only bold politicians or leaders stand opposed to the drug lords who have murdered an attorney general, a Supreme Court judge, and a leading presidential candidate. *El Colombiano,* Medellín's largest newspaper, greeted the imprisonment of drug kingpin Pablo Escobar in his designer jail with the headline "A Step Toward Peace"; Bogotá's crusading antidrug *El Espectador,* by contrast, bravely described the Escobar deal under the title "Terror Won."[1]

Buying journalists is another technique those involved in the drug trade use to pervert public discussion of the issues. Journalists and officials interviewed in Bolivia in late 1994 told of some coca-growing groups' paying journalists by the inch of favorable copy and television reporters by the minute.

The most effective form of intimidation may be brandishing the power that comes with great wealth. According to Colombian economist Francisco Thoumi, Colombian traffickers may have accumulated a net worth of between $39 billion and $60 billion by 1989-1990, based on cocaine profits and investment earnings. Thoumi argues:

> The scale of narco-wealth is very threatening to the Colombian power structure, since it suggests that the narco-capitalists may well have a combined drug and capital income that is enormous relative to the size of the country's economy. . . . Narco-capitalists [have] as much capacity to invest in Colombia as the entire private sector of the country. . . . Narcobusiness income is so large in relation to some key economic variables in Colombia that narco-capital could easily alter the status quo of the economy. . . . The full impact of this wealth has yet to be felt. It could be truly dramatic, and narco-capitalists could eventually become the dominant economic group within Colombia.[2]

With their immense financial resources, the Colombian drug lords can challenge the authority of Latin American governments. As mentioned, they can be—and are—informed about every visitor to Cali, know about every phone call made to the government offices there, and watch the comings and goings of government employees. When traffickers know their every move, it is difficult for civil servants to face up to them. Of necessity, justice suffers.

Corruption

Corruption has been a long-standing practice in the Andean countries, and it may become more onerous where the cocaine industry thrives. Because the traffickers can pay vast sums for bribes, the practice of demanding bribes has become more prevalent and the size of the typical bribe has increased. As there are no data on corruption, there is no way to quantify this problem. But look at the list of some of those accused in 1994 and 1995 of having received payoffs. As discussed in chapter 6, in Colombia, the president and his closest advisors stand accused of accepting campaign funds from the Cali cartel. Several congressmen have been jailed on corruption charges. In early 1995, within two months of being given authority to dismiss summarily any policeman suspected of corruption, the commander of the Colombian National Police (General Rosso José Serrano) dismissed 220 officers, 400 noncommissioned officers, and 1,600 policemen.[3] In Bolivia, president Jaime Paz Zamora was prompted in 1991 to appoint a known drug dealer, Faustino Rico Toro, to head the Bolivian Special Narcotics Force due to traffickers' support of his 1989 campaign (although pressure from the United States subsequently forced the president to dismiss Rico Toro from that post and, in early 1995, the Bolivian Supreme Court authorized the extradition of Rico Toro to the United States on drug charges). The leader of Paz's political party (the Movement of the Revolutionary Left), Oscar Eid, was arrested on charges of protecting cocaine dealers in December 1994; in the same month, the Bolivian Congress mandated an investigation (which is still going on) of Paz's own ties to traffickers. Moreover a major scandal developed in late 1995 after Peru seized a DC-6 aircraft that had flown in from Bolivia with 4 tons of cocaine aboard. The DEA had tipped off the Bolivian antinarcotics police (FELCN) about the flight, but they had taken no action. As evidence mounted of payoffs by traffickers, a number of senior members of the FELCN were dismissed by the Interior Minister.

In Peru public scandals of drug corruption have centered more on the Peruvian armed forces than on the country's governing institutions. As of late 1995, one Peruvian general had been convicted by a court for protecting drug flights from the Upper Huallaga Valley to Colombia; two more generals and nine other officers were under arrest for accepting "contributions" from the Cachique Rivera drug gang; and scores of officers who served at one time in coca-producing emergency zones were being investigated by Peruvian courts for collaborating with drug dealers.

As the above revelations suggest, cocaine corruption extends far and wide in the Andes. Such revelations might be considered a sign of progress—at least corruption is being exposed instead of festering in secret. A number of officials and politicians now face prosecution and jail sentences. On the other hand, Colombia's corruption scandal, which tarnishes a significant segment of the ruling elite, could undermine the legitimacy of governing institutions and aggravate the country's internal political problems.

Weakened Legal and Judicial Institutions

Drug-sponsored violence has contributed to the high murder rate in Colombia, where homicide occurs eight times as frequently as in the United States. (In 1993, the rate was 85 per 100,000 inhabitants compared to 10 per 100,000.) The homicide rate in Colombia has always been high (it was 25 per 100,000 in 1975), but it more than tripled after the cocaine trade boomed. Despite the decline of the violent Medellín cartel, drug traffickers made the Medellín area into Murder City, with 5,577 murders in 1994 in a population of 1.7 million, more than five times the murder rate in any U.S. city.[4] In 1990-1991, over 400 Medellín policemen were killed in the line of duty, many assassinated by the traffickers' agents or killed during counternarcotics operations. Also in Colombia, 242 judges and court officials were killed from 1981 through 1991, according to the Judicial Workers Union. It is painfully evident that the courts cannot judge drug cases normally. Moreover, when tens of thousands of people in a region are living off an illegal activity, many may regard the police as their enemy, which deprives the police of the public trust they need to carry out their job. The problem is exacerbated by police abuses, such as corruption and persecution of a select few. Meanwhile, even though the police arrest and the judges convict only a fraction of those involved in the drug trade, their numbers clog the courts and overcrowd the jails.

Just as the legal system's human resources are overtaxed by drug enforcement, so too are its financial resources. Enforcing the drug laws requires increased expenditures for police, courts, prison systems, and the military. Estimates of Colombian annual expenditures on counternarcotics operations range from $500 million to $1 billion; the latter figure was frequently cited by Cesar Gaviria, Colombia's president from 1989 to 1994.

Further, in Colombia the drug lords have demonstrated the ability to shape national drug policy to their advantage. The policy on extradition to the United States is an important case in point. In 1987, following several high-profile murders of prominent Colombian extradition supporters, the Colombian Supreme Court nullified a U.S.-Colombian extradition treaty signed in 1979. And in 1991, in the wake of a wave of narcoterrorist attacks by the Medellín Extraditables, Colombia's Constituent Assembly outlawed extradition of Colombian citizens in the country's new constitution.

ECOLOGICAL PROBLEMS CAUSED BY THE COCAINE INDUSTRY

Cocaine can cause ecological problems, primarily by the dumping of vast amounts of chemicals. U.S. government studies indicate that, throughout the Andean region, cocaine processors dump 10 million liters of sulfuric acid, 16 million liters of ethyl ether, 8 million liters of acetone, and anywhere from 40 to 770 million liters of kerosene. [5] The processors simply pour on to the ground these dangerous chemicals, which quickly end up in the region's rivers. Buenaventura Marcelo of the Universidad Nacional Agraria in Peru estimates that the pollution is even worse than the U.S. government sources show.[6] He describes how the chemicals have killed off many species of fish, amphibians, aquatic reptiles, and aquatic plants in the Huallaga River in Peru. The Amazon, into which the Huallaga feeds, is seriously polluted many kilometers into Brazil.

In addition to the chemical pollution, planting of coca results in needless destruction of valuable forests. According to Marc Dourougeanni, chief of the Inter-American Development Bank's Environmental Protection Division, "One can safely deduce that since the coca boom began in the early 1970s, coca production has directly or indirectly caused the deforestation of 700,000 hectares of jungle in the [Peruvian] Amazon region."[7] To be sure, alternative development projects also would cut down trees, but the legal crops would be planted in the rich alluvial soils of the valley floors instead of the steep, erosion-prone hillsides preferred by coca farmers, both because coca grows better there and because they want to be far from roads along which police and military units travel. Also, because coca requires more rainfall than any of the alternative legal crops, it is grown in the wettest parts of the jungle, where the danger of erosion is greatest. Indeed, as Dourougeanni stated, even the first report, from 1947, of the Tingo Maria Experimental Station, located in the heart of the Upper Huallaga Valley, noted that coca was environmentally the worst crop possible in the high jungle of Peru."[8]

Hillside deforestation in the Huallaga Valley has increased water runoff, making flood problems worse, according to a study by the American Association for the Advancement of Science.[9] In November 1987, heavy rains in the Upper Huallaga Valley resulted in the worst flooding in Peru's history.

Furthermore, coca farmers use large amounts of herbicides and insecticides, including such dangerous products as Paraquat and 2, 4-D. As Joseph Antognini, research leader of the U.S. Department of Agriculture Tropical Plants Research Laboratory, explained, pesticides must be used particularly heavily for coca, compared to other crops, because it is highly vulnerable to infestations and because coca farmers have the cash to pay for chemicals that other farmers cannot afford. According to Antognini, coca farmers use more pesticides and insecticides each year than would be required to eradicate the crop entirely; indeed, some farmers use five times as much as would be applied in an eradication program.[10]

This fact is not general knowledge. The environmental protests that have taken place thus far have been against the government's use of pesticides to eradicate coca; for example, Greenpeace has protested against U.S. firms' selling pesticides. In fact, however, the environmental cost of spraying pesticides to eradicate coca bushes is far less than the cost of growing that coca and processing the leaves into cocaine hydrochloride.

SOCIAL PROBLEMS CAUSED BY THE COCAINE INDUSTRY

The illicit drug trade brings with it drug abuse and a host of other social problems. Available evidence, however, suggests that consumption of cocaine and other drugs is far less widespread in Latin America than in the United States. In Colombia, for instance, a 1992 study commissioned by Colombia's National Drug Council showed that 1.4 million people (4.1 percent of the population) had consumed some illegal drug at some time in their lives; in the United States, however, lifetime drug prevalence is 77 million, or 31 percent of the U.S. population.[11] Comparable figures for cocaine are 338,000 (1.0 percent of the population) in Colombia and 23.5 million (9.4 percent of the population) in the United States. Also, an estimated 343,000 Colombians have used basuco, a compound of cocaine base and tobacco. In Peru, according to the National Statistical Institute, lifetime prevalence as of 1995 is somewhat higher than Colombia—1.5 percent for cocaine and 2.9 percent for cocaine paste. Such numbers still are much lower than U.S. ones, however. In Bolivia, a study by the National Directorate of Drug Prevention, Treatment Rehabilitation and Social Reintegration found that only 1.2 percent of the Bolivian population had used, respectively, cocaine hydrochloride and cocaine paste or base at some time in their lives.[12]

The main societal costs of the drug trade have more to do with the working environment and the general quality of life in affected countries than with drug use. In Colombia, drugs have contributed to the high level of social violence, as mentioned above. In Colombia, for example, drugs are associated with the degradation of the judicial sector and with the increasing ineffectiveness of the court system is resolving civil disputes. The prevailing climate of violence and insecurity and the quick-profit mentality associated with drugs have channeled investment capital into short-term, speculative activities. The cocaine ethic also has diminished the moral basis of Colombian society, fraying family ties and neighborhood bonds, spawning corruption at all levels, and increasing the incidence of kidnappings and street crime. Such problems are eroding the morale of ordinary Colombians and are threatening the country's future. Furthermore, as Francisco Thoumi notes, the scale of narcowealth is threatening to the Colombian power structure. Thoumi estimates that accumulated traffickers' wealth from narcotics sales and capital investments had reached $39 to $60 billion by the end of the 1980s, or 85 to 130 percent of Colombia's 1990 gross domestic product. "Narco-business income is so large in relation to key economic variables in Colombia that narco-capital could easily alter the status quo of the society," notes Thoumi.[13]

ECONOMIC COSTS OF THE COCAINE INDUSTRY

Cocaine imposes some direct economic costs. An important direct cost associated with the drug trade is the cost of enforcing the drug laws, prosecuting drug kingpins, and implementing demand-reduction via treatment and prevention programs. In 1995 Colombia's national drug budget was more than 890 million pesos (roughly $990 million), or almost 2 percent of the nation's GDP.[14] Of this sum almost 90 percent is allocated to the Ministry of Defense, which also includes the National Police, for crop eradication and countertrafficking activities. Demand reduction, by contrast, represents a far larger share of U.S. antidrug spending (37 percent)—which is appropriate, considering the dimension of America's drug abuse problem. However, total U.S. federal drug control spending represents less than 0.3 percent of U.S. GDP—far less than in Colombia.

The costs of security measures to prevent Colombian businesses from being caught up in the narcotraffickers' web also are great. For example, the number of private security firms in Colombia's major cities jumped from 30 in 1968 to 551 in 1988.[15] In addition, businesses must take extra precautions to prevent the use of their export containers for drug smuggling, lest they run the risk that a shipment will be confiscated or at least delayed if drugs are found. Timely processing of shipments has been a major problem for the Colombian cut flower industry, one of the country's most dynamic. Patricia Correa, a private economist in Bogotá, explained, "There is a stigma attached to all Colombian products." To which Gustavo Gaviria, general manager of the Gavicafe companies, added, with exaggeration, "We spend so much time and money proving to the world that we are not all drug traffickers that we cannot attend to our own economic development."[16]

Displacement of Legal Industry

The direct economic costs of the cocaine industry, while real, are relatively small. More important are the ways in which cocaine income is gained at the expense of legal economic activity. First, resources used in the cocaine industry are unavailable for use elsewhere in the economy. Thus, each dollar received from cocaine is not an additional dollar added to national income. The income from the cocaine industry is really the difference between what can be earned from cocaine and what could be earned with the same inputs of capital and labor were there no cocaine industry. To the extent that the cocaine dollar comes at the expense of a reduction in legal income, cocaine looks less attractive than it would appear at first glance.

Second, and more important than competition for resources, has been what economists call "Dutch disease." The term describes the problems the Netherlands had in the 1960s when a boom in one industry (natural gas) caused such an inflow of foreign exchange that dollars became cheap relative to the local currency, reducing the competitiveness of local products both in foreign markets and domestically. The gain from the boom industry was largely if not completely wiped out by the loss of output from the other industries. In other words, what appeared to be a boom was actually mostly a shift from one industry to another. It is not clear if the economy benefited at all from this shift.

Indeed, the economy could be a net loser if the boom industry was one that would fade quickly while the industries that suffered had better long-term prospects. That may have been the case in the Netherlands, where the boom industry was based on a natural resource that could be depleted. The same may apply to the Andean nations; shifting drug tastes and accelerated enforcement efforts could make the cocaine industry into a temporary affair. Also, the resources from the boom industry may be used poorly. Many countries spend windfalls unwisely, rather than saving them during the boom to draw on later.

A large increase in foreign exchange earnings is no problem if that increase will be sustained; the Dutch disease is a problem to the extent that the new source of foreign exchange is temporary and unsustainable. Bolivia's former planning minister Samuel Doria Medina points out that coca fits this criteria well, as can be seen by the drop in income since 1989. Furthermore, the appreciation of the exchange rate undoubtedly hurts local production, but it increases the real income of consumers, for whom imports are cheaper. Andean consumers have benefited from the low price of imported goods, such as the electronics flooding into Colombia.

In Peru, the president of the Mine Engineers Society, Celso Sotomarino, complained, "The narcotraffickers oversupply the foreign exchange market, which keeps the price of the dollar low, and that is precisely the principal problem for the mining sector."[17] One study found that when the dollar became cheaper, Peruvians turned to consuming more imported foods and less domestic food. Each 10 percent decrease in the value of the dollar cut the price of potatoes, the main food grown in Peru's poverty-stricken mountain areas, by 4.8 percent. In Bolivia, the private economic firm Müller y Asociados argued, "It is clear that the coca economy has created the problem known as the 'Dutch Disease' in Bolivia. . . . Manufacturing industry suffered because of cheap imports. . . ."[18] The share of manufacturing in the economy fell from 15.0 percent in 1980 to 10.7 percent in 1989. A part of this decline is due to the effects of the coca/cocaine boom." In Colombia, manufacturing has suffered because of imports made cheap by the overvalued exchange rate and by widespread smuggling, perhaps for sale at a loss, as a way to launder narcodollars. Low-cost contraband imports have seriously hurt the textile industry, the centerpiece of Medellín's economy. A General Electric factory producing portable radios in the 1980s went out of business because its products could not compete with a flood of illegally imported radios.

Inefficient Investment to Launder and Protect Money

As just mentioned, cocaine income has been of dubious benefit in yet another way: Some of the money has been wasted in low-profit (or unprofitable) investments undertaken to hide the funds from the law.

At least in Colombia, a significant proportion of private firms have narcotrafficking investors. Some of this investment is normal economic activity. But traffickers also invest to launder money. Here is how Andres Benitez, economics editor of *El Mercurio* in Chile, described one such waste of money: "A while back there were people who came to Santiago and bought expensive houses which they paid for in dollars and almost immediately sold at a loss. They then deposited the cash from the sale at a bank, and the banks reported that the money came from the sale of the houses, which it did only indirectly. This tainted people on both sides of the deal."[19]

The purchase of homes at inflated prices is relatively harmless from an economic point of view. More serious are loss-making firms, run primarily to launder cocaine money, that have caused legal rivals to fail. In Bolivia in the 1980s, traffickers sold imported goods at less than they had paid for them in order to launder money, according to Planning Minister Doria Medina.[20] Joseph Finnin of the Colombian-American Trade Council notes that "Traffickers now import goods legally and sometimes sell them in Colombia at prices even lower than paid in the United States."

In a June 1995 interview, Finnin cited as an example of unfair narcocompetition the experience of a U.S. machine tool company's direct sales office in Colombia. A Colombian businessman linked to a major trafficking organization had devised a clever laundering scheme: He bought the company's machine tools in Miami and imported the tools into Colombia, invoicing them at 50 percent of the purchase price (and thus avoiding part of Colombia's value-added tax on imports). Then the businessman sold the equipment to Colombian buyers at 70 percent of the Miami sales price. Obviously, the company's legal outlet in Colombia lost sales as a result. Eventually, lawsuits and other pressures forced the Colombian competitor out of business, but similar laundering operations continue to plague the nation. "They are killing the legal distributor here," observes Finnin. Similarly, according to the DEA's Greg Passic, drug dealers or their henchmen buy Caterpillar tractors in the United States and transport them with false documentation into Colombia. As Passic notes, "They sell for less in Bogotá than in Miami."[21]

Also noteworthy are inefficient manufacturing enterprises financed by traffickers. Joseph Finnin mentioned examples of large operations—a snacks factory in the 1980s and a nylon stocking plant in the 1990s—that were equipped with the latest manufacturing and warehousing technology. The traffickers then proceeded to undersell legal competitors and to drive down profits in the respective business lines. Yet the operations were incompetently managed, apparently generating losses that were intolerable even for their trafficking sponsors. Ultimately, the factories were sold to legitimate businessmen, which perhaps can be considered a happy end to the story.

In other industries, the narcotraffickers' laundering activities drive up prices in ways that endanger legal investors. For example, drug money has funded a construction boom in Cali, including shopping centers, hotels, and luxury apartment buildings. Salomón Kalmanovitz, of Colombia's central bank, points out that urban property prices rose 50 to 60 percent a year from 1991 through 1994, while inflation averaged just 22 percent a year. He worries that the artificial coca-financed property boom could be followed by a collapse in property values. Such a collapse could well result from the Colombian government's wide-ranging crackdown on the Cali cartel (which resulted in seizures of many Cali-owned properties and businesses in early-mid 1995).

During a 1992 interview, Bolivia's planning minister, Doria Medina, expressed the hope that there could be important positive effects from investments financed by traffickers who have left the cocaine business.[22] While this is an intriguing possibility, ex-traffickers' investment goals may not be greatly different from that of active drug dealers. In any event, there is little evidence of the positive effects cited by Medina.

Less Economic Stimulus from Each Dollar of Growth

Cocaine has few linkages, as economists say. That is, the industry generates relatively little demand for local products, and cocaine cannot be used to feed into other industries. For Bolivia, Mario de Franco and Ricardo Godoy found, "each dollar of cocaine exported requires the purchase of $0.03 of goods and services from the non-cocaine economy; in contrast, commercial agriculture, mining, manufacturing, and construction require the purchase of, on average, $0.23 from the rest of the economy." That is a sevenfold difference.[23] Presumably the difference is even greater if a comparison were to be made between the cocaine industry and the legal sector excluding mining activities (such as tin and natural gas), which use many imported inputs.[24] A similar pattern can be seen in Colombia. Central Bank president Miguel Urrutia explained, "Textile production creates demand for cotton and labor in César and the other cotton-growing areas of the country. It also generates demand for farm machinery and transport and inputs for the clothing industry, which is now an important export sector. Drugs have no backward or forward linkages."[25]

On the other hand, cocaine base has high employment effects per dollar of sales, because it is so labor intensive. Also, coca leaf output has high foreign exchange effects because it uses few imported inputs. Consider the contrast between a dollar of coca sales and a dollar of tin sales, tin being the traditional foundation of Bolivia's modern economy. The tin generates less value added (it uses more inputs), it creates fewer jobs (it uses more equipment), and it generates less positive effect for the balance of payments (it uses more imported machinery and parts). But overall, legal industries are more positive than cocaine because they do more to stimulate production in the rest of the economy.

Loss of Control Over Economic Policy

The vast size and enormous revenues of the cocaine industry reduce governments' ability to control economic and financial policy. Huge inflows and outflows of narcotics earnings, resulting from government crackdowns, may destabilize the national currency, undermine foreign trade, and debilitate entire economic sectors.

Furthermore, the cocaine industry has contributed to dollarization, which means that the dollar rather than the national currency is used to carry out transactions. Because the cocaine business is overwhelmingly on a cash basis, it puts hundreds of millions in dollar bills into Andean economies, facilitating use of the dollar for everyday transactions. The more the dollar is used, the less the national currency is used. When the national currency is used only for small transactions, then the government loses the ability to influence the economy by managing monetary policy. For instance, dollarization means that the exchange rate has little effect on the economy, since so many transactions are carried out in dollars. Changes in the exchange rate, one of the most powerful policy tools in the arsenal of a central bank, have less effect in Andean nations than they would have if the local currency were more widely used.

Another problem caused by the cocaine industry has been that it has forced Andean governments to reimpose, for law enforcement purposes, regulations that had been lifted because they were strangling the economy. For instance, the United States complained, "New problems emerged for enforcement agencies . . . when, in an effort the United States encouraged to modernize the Colombian economy, banking practices were liberalized to allow Colombians to repatriate foreign-held funds and to hold dollar accounts. The DEA believes there has been a massive influx of narcodollars as well as legitimate funds."[26] Whether or not the DEA's worries were justified—the Colombian Finance Ministry maintains the DEA is wrong and the inflow was a response to improved policies—Colombia's cocaine industry makes the country vulnerable to suspicions.[27]

IN LIEU OF A CONCLUSION

If the drug trade were eliminated, the resources that are used to produce cocaine could be used in another activity. For that reason alone, the net benefit from cocaine is less than the gross income it generates. That said, the cocaine industry is probably a net economic boost to the Andean nations, despite the economic problems it creates. Using the sketchy data available, Franco and Godoy tried to build a model of the Bolivian economy that would predict what would happen if the cocaine industry were to expand, taking resources away from other activities. Their conclusion was: "Cocaine production confers unambiguous economic benefits to the nation. A 10 percent increase in cocaine production raises GDP by 2 percent and lowers unemployment by 6 percent. Real incomes grow for all social groups." [28] That conclusion was drawn from data at the height of the coca boom when prices were high; using today's data, the results might be more ambiguous in Bolivia and Peru, where the cocaine business consists mostly of growing coca leaves and their basic processing, which is not an extraordinarily profitable activity.

In Colombia, the center of the highly profitable cocaine trading and smuggling business, it is conceivable that cocaine is a large net contributor to the economy. However, it should be noted that Colombian economists disagree. As Thoumi put it, "It is not surprising that the majority of Colombian economists argue that the negative effects of the [narcotics] industry clearly surpass the positive, and that they do not consider the [narcotics] industry benefits the country."[29] Supporting Thoumi's view is a decline in rates in Colombian GDP growth after 1978, which apparently coincided with the rise of the Colombian cocaine industry. (From 1965 to 1978 growth averaged 5.6 percent annually; from 1978 to 1991 it averaged 3.5 percent.) Of course, such a phenomenon lends itself to multiple explanations, such as government mismanagement, the rise of guerrilla terrorism, or trends in the international economy; yet cocaine probably played some role in the decline.

At the same time, cocaine economically has been a double-edged sword. In certain respects it has played a positive role. The influence of hard currency associated with narcotics exports made possible more imports and less external debt. As argued earlier, coca and cocaine substituted for the failures of the formal economy in Peru and Bolivia, providing alternate employment, maintaining income levels, and stabilizing the national currency. Cocaine possibly contributed to these countries' economic problems; yet the industry's cushioning effects might have prevented serious outbreaks of societal violence in the 1980s. On a subnational level, cocaine money helped to prop up the economy of Medellín during the 1980s—boosting construction spending and stimulating demand for locally produced services. As a result of this increased activity, Medellín's unemployment rate declined almost 25 percent between the mid- and late 1980s.

In addition, in the 1990s the economic situation in Colombia has become ambiguous. Increased infusions of drug capital, increased Cali dominance of the drug trade, more rational investment patterns by drug dealers, and major reductions in drug-sponsored violence appear to correlate with improved economic performance. Consider Colombia's GDP growth: It was 2.3 percent in 1991, 3.5 percent in 1992, 5.3 percent in 1993, 5.7 percent in 1994, and 5.3 percent in 1995. Foreign investment in Colombia soared between 1991 and 1994, from $311.2 million to $1.7495 billion, reflecting increased investor confidence in the nation's economy. At the same time, Colombia's crackdown on the Cali cartel hierarchy during 1995 may have had negative economic repercussions, at least locally. Construction activity in Cali dropped 10.7 percent in the first four

months of 1995, and retail sales declined 3.2 percent in the first se-
mester of that year. Real estate prices dropped by one-third between
January and November. Cali's unemployment rate rose from 6.9 percent in December 1994 to 11.3 percent in June 1995—an increase
of 64 percent—compared to an average urban increase (for seven
major Colombian cities) of 16 percent.[30]

Nevertheless, Andean economies and societies would benefit in
the long run from the disappearance of the cocaine industry. Of course,
there would be problems of adjustment. In Peru and Bolivia, agriculture is important to specific regions, although cocaine's importance
on the national economies is declining. In Colombia, traffickers' huge
surplus earnings irrigate a substantial portion of the urban economies
of Medellín and Cali. Yet most people employed in the industry—
farmers, chemists, pilots, shippers, and others—could find jobs in
Colombia's large and diverse legal economy, albeit with some dimi-
nution in income and lifestyle. The main constraint on counternarcotics
policy in Colombia is the traffickers' ability to corrupt and intimidate
the Colombian political system at all levels, not the threat of a social
uprising by masses of producers.

Whether it contributes to national economic well-being or not,
cocaine has pernicious political, social, and environmental effects.
Without income from cocaine, the Shining Path guerrillas might never
have been able to finance their murderous activities on as large a
scale. Cocaine traffickers have perverted Colombian politics, distort-
ing public debate by using violence and money to silence opposition.
And throughout the Andes, the cocaine industry has undermined the
rule of law, which is the foundation of a civilized society.

Part IV

What Can Be Done?

9

Effects of Counternarcotics Efforts in Latin America on U.S. Cocaine Use

The principal goal of U.S. counternarcotics efforts in Latin America is, or at least should be, to reduce use of cocaine and other illegal drugs in the United States. Any assistance that the U.S. efforts provide to the Andean nations—economic development, improved law and order—should be seen primarily as means toward an end, not an end in itself. Washington has no reason to be apologetic about putting U.S. interests first. Nor is it convincing to argue that Congress should pass counternarcotics funding because it supports general foreign aid, such as promoting democracy and stability in the Andes.

How much effect U.S. counternarcotics efforts have on U.S. cocaine consumption is debatable. Officials working on the different programs vigorously dispute which are the most efficacious. Partisans of law enforcement disparage alternative development. Many development workers regard eradication as an aid to the coca industry, arguing that reduction in the area planted drives up the price. And then there are those who say that controlling drug supply is nowhere near as effective as treatment programs or public campaigns to reduce consumption.

Evidence on effectiveness is slim, while prejudged views are strongly held. A RAND Corporation study of the cost-effectiveness of different counternarcotics programs concluded that to get a 1 percent drop in U.S. cocaine consumption, it would be necessary to spend $34 million on treatment, $246 million on domestic law enforcement, $366 million on antismuggling efforts, or $738 million on antidrug programs in countries where cocaine is produced.[1] While these figures sound definite, our knowledge of the cocaine trade and of the reasons why people use the drug is so poor that putting too much trust in any one study would be inappropriate. Some people with experience in fighting drugs strongly defend international counternarcotics programs. For example, William Bennett, former director of the ONDCP, argues, "Interdiction and cocaine source country programs seem to have been the crucial cause of the only reductions in heavy or addictive cocaine use in the past decade."[2]

Unfortunately, strong arguments can be made against the effectiveness of each counternarcotics program. Treatment, for instance, is no panacea. In 1989, 3.9 million people needed treatment, and in the next six years, 8.2 million treatments were administered.[3] But, in 1996, 2.4 million people still needed treatment (and 1.4 million treatment slots were available). The problem in understanding these figures is that people go through treatment repeatedly. While some of those 8.2 million people were in treatment for the first time—old users or new users (that is, people who had not started yet in 1989)—many were repeaters, people who go through programs again and again. Thus, treatment does not reach as many people as it might seem. Addicts typically stop using drugs after some years whether they go through treatment or not. How much treatment programs speed up the process is not known. According to one long-term nationwide follow-up study, of those who dropped out of treatment, 44 percent had no relapses after six years, a rate not appreciably different from the rate for those who completed treatment.[4]

With the understanding that all counternarcotics programs are of limited effectiveness, let us examine the impact of U.S.-supported eradication, countertrafficking, and alternative development programs in Latin America.

THE EFFECTS OF SUPPLY ON CONSUMPTION

The main question about all three programs for controlling supply outside of the United States—eradication, interdiction, and alternative development—is whether controlling supply has any effect on consumption. The connection between supply and consumption seems obvious: the more drugs are around, the more will get used. Many people in the drug rehabilitation and law enforcement communities favor this theory. Economists, however, have a professional prejudice against this simple "supply creates demand" theory. When economists think about what determines demand, the first word that comes to mind is "price."

In the words of RAND's Jonathan Caulkins, we only have "scraps of empirical evidence" on the effect of price on the demand for illegal drugs. Price may make a difference as to whether new consumers start using an illegal drug, although fashion may matter most in determining initiation rates, and fashion is remarkably insensitive to price. Addicts would seem, on first consideration, to be insensitive to price, but perhaps there is an analogy to heavy alcohol drinkers, who are highly price sensitive. One way to understand the price sensitivity of addicts is that so much of their income goes into cocaine that, when the price rises, they have no alternative but to cut the amount they consume. Addicts who rely on illegal income may steal more when drug prices rise, but they may not be able to increase their take enough to compensate for the higher costs.

The limited evidence available about the effect of price on overall drug consumption is "not inconsistent" with the theory that demand for drugs behaves much the same as demand for tobacco and alcohol.[5] A 100 percent increase in the price of tobacco or alcohol reduces the quantity sold by 50 percent. That suggests that if the price of cocaine were to double, then all other factors being equal, the amount used in the United States would be cut from 300 tons to 150 tons, while if the price were to be cut in half, consumption would rise from 300 tons to 450 tons.

The work of Kevin Jack Riley provides an interesting variant on the theme that price affects demand.[6] He looked at the effect of a short-term disruption in the cocaine market, which drives up price and reduces availability for six to twenty-four months. As he explains, it is much easier to disrupt the cocaine trade for a short term than to permanently knock it for a loop. Over the long run, producers adapt to any new circumstances—the narcotics industry is highly dynamic. As an economist would put it, the drug dealers are risk-takers, so they will risk new techniques. Riley concluded that a shock eradication or interdiction program that disrupts the cocaine trade might drive up cocaine prices and reduce the availability enough to lead some cocaine users to abandon the drug. In this way, a shock interdiction program could have an effect on U.S. cocaine consumption for some years.

Economists ask whether counternarcotics programs in Latin America affect the price of drugs sold to the consumer on U.S. streets. The answer is that we do not know, because we do not know what determines the retail price of cocaine.

At first glance, it would seem that nothing that happens in Latin America could have much effect on the retail price of cocaine in the United States. Cocaine prices in Colombia have averaged 2 percent of the U.S. retail price: $2,650 per kilogram compared to $130,000 per kilogram in 1992.[7] So it would seem that doubling the cost of cocaine in Colombia would increase the retail price in the United States by only 2 percent, and that would reduce consumption by only 1 percent. Those who disparage U.S. counternarcotics efforts in Latin America frequently make this argument.[8]

However, while this view is intuitively appealing, it rests on less than solid foundations, as it assumes that any changes in costs are passed through dollar for dollar into the retail price—what one researcher calls the "Wheaties model" (if the price of wheat goes up, the price of Wheaties rises by the same amount as the costs go up).[9] A less colorful name for this is the additive view. In essence, with the additive view, if costs increase by $1, then the retail price goes up by $1.

The additive theory of price formation seems logical because it describes well enough what happens for most products. But not all products. Consider the book business (or movies or records). The author, the retailer, the distributor, and so on each get a certain percentage of the retail price. It would not be unusual for them to get more than 50 percent of the retail price. So if the publisher raises the price by X, the retail price goes up by 2X. That means that a $2 increase in what the publisher charges on a $20 book raises the retail price by $4, not by $2. In this case, the retail price is a multiple of the wholesale price, so we can call this the multiplicative theory of price formation. Briefly, in multiplicative theory, if costs go up by $1, then the price goes up by X times $1. The multiplicative theory of price formation seems to work well for risky products, such as illegal goods.

The multiplicative theory implies that raising the cocaine cost in Latin America can have a substantial effect on the price of cocaine to the U.S. consumer. To take the earlier example of the effect of a doubling of the cost of cocaine in Colombia: If prices are purely multiplicative, that would translate into a doubling of the price on U.S. streets, which could reduce consumption by 50 percent.

While they are cautious in their conclusions, Jonathan Caulkins and David Boyum both suggest that the multiplicative theory has some truth. "Caulkins analyzes some historical price series from the retail and low-level wholesale level which are more consistent with the multiplicative than the additive model, and Boyum analyzes data that cast doubt on the additive . . . model."[10] Caulkins and Boyum are too careful to state which theory is more accurate, but their work certainly suggests that it is inappropriate flatly to assert without evidence that one theory is obviously correct.

While the debate about how cocaine prices are formed may sound like an arcane dispute among economists, nothing could be further from the truth. In fact, what the economists have done is made explicit and clear a difference that is at the heart of any discussion about whether drug control efforts in Latin America affect U.S. drug use. As explained by Mark Kleiman, one of the most sober analysts of drug issues, "Nothing less than the value of a large part of federal government's drug law enforcement effort is at stake in this debate over whether the relationship of retail price to wholesale price is almost additive (with a small multiplicative term) or almost multiplicative (with a small additive term). . . . To date, the question remains open, with arguments and evidence on both sides."[11]

As Kleiman says, the key question is what of additive and multiplicative factors determine the price. There are many possible answers. For instance, some stages in the processing of cocaine may be additive and other stages may be multiplicative. We simply do not know.

THE EFFECT OF ERADICATION ON SUPPLY

Coca can be eradicated by being uprooted by hand—a tedious process—or by aerial spraying. Aerial spraying has been the subject of environmental controversy. In 1984, the Colombian government decided to start an aerial spraying program of coca, similar to its spraying of marijuana. It identified Garlon-4 as an effective herbicide, but the U.S. manufacturer refused to provide the product because it had recently lost a product liability lawsuit about the use of another of its products. Since 1986 Congress has allocated funds to research coca herbicides. Field tests in Peru had to be suspended in 1988 because the U.S. manufacturer refused to provide the herbicide Spike, fearing liability lawsuits in the U.S.[12] More recently, the U.S. government has researched in Panama the effects of aerial spraying of three herbicides: glyphosphate (commercial name: Roundup), tebuthiuron (Spike 40 P), and hexazinone (Pronone 5G). All three can be effective, but Roundup has to be applied carefully because too little may have no effect while too much can cause leaves to drop so rapidly that the plant survives to grow new leaves. According to the U.S. Department of Agriculture specialists, "no unfavorable environmental effects were observed from any of the three herbicides."[13]

The Clinton administration's drug control policy has "stressed the importance of eradication."[14] That sounds like such a commonsense approach to the coca problem because it directly reduces the area planted to coca. That is indeed its initial effect. But it also has many indirect effects, most of which undercut any progress made in controlling narcotics.

First, eradication in existing production areas may drive farmers farther from roads, thereby opening up new producing areas—a pattern that has been repeated numerous times in both Bolivia and Peru. According to the *International Narcotics Control Strategy Report* (INCSR), Bolivia eradicated 30,228 hectares of coca from 1989 through 1995, but the area cultivated rose by 100 hectares, which suggests that there were 30,328 hectares in new planting. That is equal to 62 percent of the 48,600 hectares of Bolivian coca at end of 1995. In the Upper Huallaga Valley, under a U.S.-supported eradicated program that operated from 1983 through early 1989, 17,000 hectares were forcibly eliminated.[15] Meanwhile, coca cultivation in the area increased by 72,500 hectares—implying that 89,500 hectares were planted.[16]

The problem facing eradicators is that there are millions of hectares suitable for coca growing in the Andes. Eradication in one area may simply lead farmers to shift to a new zone, as has been occurring in Peru with the shift in production from the Huallaga Valley to valleys farther east and south, such as the Apurímac-Ene.[17]

Second, eradication can encourage farmers to raise yields. According to the 1996 INCSR, between 1990 and 1995, the area cultivated in coca in Bolivia fell 3 percent while the harvestable leaf rose 10 percent. One way that this occurs is that eradication may destroy old plants at the end of their useful life. Programs that compensate farmers for eradication may cause them to dig up old, low-yield plants to get the cash with which to plant new, vigorous plants.

Third, eradication can be a coca price support program. Eradication is supposed to reduce the supply of coca, and the laws of economics predict that lower supply means higher price. That higher price can benefit the farm, depending on how the eradication is done. In a forced eradication program, the farmers lose the income from the fields eradicated but gain income from a higher price; the net effect depends on the balance between those two trends. However, in the Andes voluntary compensated coca eradication programs are more common than forced programs. The voluntary programs are similar to the crop acreage reduction programs that the U.S. government uses to raise the income of wheat farmers. It is not clear why Washington thinks that a crop reduction program raises the income of Midwest wheat farmers but lowers the income of Andean coca farmers. In fact, in both cases, the crop reduction program really is a price support program that can raise farmer income.

Fourth, eradication can undercut political support for counternarcotics efforts. In the 1980s Peruvian eradication programs helped the Shining Path guerrilla movement, which opposes both eradication and crop substitution, to establish a powerful political foothold among coca growers and other disaffected populations; this, in turn, contributed to the general deterioration of law and order in the valley in 1990. The sociopolitical effects of eradication depend greatly on whether the program relies on force or on compensation. Forcible eradication contaminates relationships between farmers and government, including agricultural extension agents. This impedes substitution of legal crops for coca, since farmers usually must be taught on how to grow new crops. Compensated eradication programs might be expected to be popular, since they offer farmers cash, but in practice they have more often been lightning rods for discontent against the government.

Besides all these negative effects, eradication also can have positive effects. For example, compensated voluntary eradication provides funds that can be used to finance planting legal crops; lack of financing is a major barrier to growing the tropical tree crops that may not bear first fruit for several years. Eradication—especially forcible eradication—may be associated with a more vigorous government presence in a region, which increases the risks for the traffickers.

Peru

The experience with eradication differs from country to country in the Andes. In Peru, eradication began in 1979, funded by the U.S. State Department's Bureau of International Narcotics Matters. The U.S. Agency for International Development (USAID) has never been involved in eradication, which is seen as a police function incompatible with its role as a development agency friendly to farmers. To run the eradication, a special agency was established in 1983 named CORAH (*Control y Reducción del Cultivo de la Coca en el Alto Huallaga*).[18] Between 1983 and 1989, CORAH eliminated 18,018 hectares, primarily in two waves (1984-1985 and 1988). Farmers were paid up to $1,000 per hectare eradicated and given a certificate that was to give them access to credit and technical assistance for legal crops. In practice, most farmers took the money and replanted coca on new fields.

The CORAH eradication program drew fierce domestic reaction. One of the grounds was environmental, fed by the refusal of the U.S. manufacturer Eli Lilly to supply the pesticide Spike for aerial spraying tests. Without access to the pesticide, CORAH had to use the labor-intensive technique of uprooting and burning plants. More serious was the terrorism problem: Eradication was driving farmers away from the government at a time it needed their support against the Shining Path guerrillas.[19] Within days after the first field test of Spike in March 1989, the Shining Path captured the Uchiza police post in the center of the Upper Huallaga after a bloody night-long battle. The interior minister resigned in disgrace, and a new commander was appointed for the Huallaga emergency zone. (The area was under military rule.) That new commander was General Alberto Ariciniega Huby who, as discussed earlier, made his priority the fight against Shining Path, not against coca growing. In 1989, the year during which Arciniega was in command, eradication of mature coca stopped and only 5,603 square meters of seed beds were eradicated. (The year before 184,073 square meters had been eradicated, and 244,105 square meters were eradicated the year after.)

Already essentially suspended since mid-1989, eradication of mature coca ended in 1990, after Alberto Fujimori became president. He forced into retirement Juan Zárate, the police general most closely identified with the program.[20] In October, Fujimori gave a major speech in which he explained why he in effect abandoned eradication:

> In no way are we opposed to an effective program to eradicate illegal coca crops. . . . But we wish to address repression in a larger context. . . . An effective program of repression that leaves the peasants without other alternatives would sharply increase the numbers of those in extreme poverty and could unchain a civil war of unsuspected proportions. . . .We will not repeat the errors of President Ngo Dinh Diem of Vietnam who, during the 1950s, pitted himself against the informal, common law order of the peasants. . . . We will not push peasants and their families into the arms of terrorists and drug traffickers.[21]

No mature coca was eradicated after 1989, as the focus of law enforcement activity shifted to interdiction rather than eradication. CORAH continued, concentrating on the eradication of seed beds, which it had begun in 1988. In the two-year period from 1994 to 1995, CORAH tore out 328,072 square meters of seed beds; that translates into the equivalent of 21,871 hectares of mature coca. The increased eradication of seed beds came under strong U.S. pressure. A sore point for the U.S. was CORAH's insistence that the INL-owned helicopters in the Huallaga Valley would be used to eliminate only the 15,000 square meter per month target (set in negotiations between the U.S. and Peru) and no more.[22]

Colombia

In Colombia, eradication has enjoyed more support than in either Bolivia or Peru. The government decided in 1983-1984 to use aerial spraying to eliminate both marijuana and coca. The program was successful for marijuana. Between 1984 and 1988, 27,000 hectares of marijuana were eradicated, essentially all by aerial spraying, which reduced the cultivated area to 2,400 hectares in 1988, at which it stabilized until 1992. (Since then, marijuana cultivation has come back, reaching 5,000 hectares in 1995.) For coca, spraying did not work for many years. First came the problems of securing a pesticide from reluctant U.S. manufacturers. Then there were political objections to coca eradication, which meant that it was carried out only on a small scale. In 1990 through 1993, total eradication was 3,624 hectares out of an initial area of 41,000 hectares. (Meanwhile, 2,324 hectares were newly planted, bringing the area planted in coca bushes at the end of 1993 to 39,700 hectares.)

Recently, Colombia has stepped up its eradication efforts. Soon after assuming office in 1994, Colombian president Ernesto Samper Pizano pledged that all illegal crops would be eradicated in two years.[23] The National Police began an aggressive program of spraying coca fields with Roundup in November 1994. More coca—4,910 hectares— was eradicated in that year than in the preceding four years, and the pace was further accelerated in early 1995. The Colombian National Police report that they sprayed 24,081 hectares in 1995, although the U.S. government only lists 8,750 hectares as eradicated in that year.[24] While the spraying effort was substantial, covering one-third of the country's coca fields, at the same time Colombia was experiencing an explosion in new plantings—24,860 hectares in 1994-1995 or nearly half the area in coca at the end of 1995, or four times more than had been planted in the preceding four years combined. Eradication was unable to keep the coca area from growing sharply, to 50,900 hectares at the end of 1995 compared to 39,700 hectares at the end of 1993.

Because of the drug trade's economic significance in many rural zones, government efforts to eradicate coca by force have met widespread resistance from farmers and other affected groups. In December 1994, for example, some 4,000 coca farmers and other community residents occupied the airport in San José del Guaviare, the capital of Guaviare Department, approximately 300 kilometers southeast of Bogotá. In January 1995 farmers in the southern border department of

Putumayo occupied seven Ecopetrol pumping stations, blocking the flow of oil and causing the state millions of dollars in lost revenues. Both actions were in response to the government's decision to conduct large-scale spraying operations against illicit coca plantations.

As in Peru five years earlier, there is concern that the vigorous eradication program may drive local farmers into the arms of leftist guerrillas. Journalist Robert Pombo warned in his column in *Semana,* "In the coca zones . . . subversion has found a definitely solid popular base. . . . With the coca growers, the FARC achieved the eternal dreams of the guerrillas, which is to share an enemy with the people: the state."[25] In December 1994 guerrillas trapped Colonel José Leonardo Gallego, director of the antinarcotics police, for two days in Miraflores. Colombian soldiers report intercepting a message from a guerilla commander offering a $200,000 bounty for every eradication plane or helicopter shot down; the first one fell to a FARC attack on February 16, 1995, killing three policemen. Guerrillas probably also were responsible for the September 1994 attack on the police helicopters carrying Defense Minister Fernando Botero Zea and U.S. ambassador Myles Frechette. (No one was injured.)

Government representatives negotiated an end to the San José protest by agreeing not to spray plantations of less than 3 hectares and by promising assistance for development and crop substitution programs in the region. A similar agreement was negotiated with Putumayo farmers in January, although the threshold for aerial spraying in that case was reduced to 2 hectares. However, in March 1995, according to the Andean Commission of Justice, Colombia was "indiscriminately fumigating small coca plantations, in particular, those between one and three hectares," thereby failing to fill the San José and Putumayo pacts.[26]

Bolivia

Bolivia embarked on an extensive program of compensated voluntary eradication after the passage of law 1008 in 1988. Under that law, the coca planted before 1988 was permitted under a program to eliminate it gradually in "transition" areas (in practice, the Chapare). Voluntary compensated eradication was to be complemented with forcible eradication of newly planted coca anywhere outside of the "traditional" coca zone (in practice, the Yungas region). In fact, however, there has been little forcible eradication of mature coca plants. Data from DIRECO, the Bolivian agency charged with monitoring eradication, show that 1,700 hectares of newly planted coca was eradicated from 1989 through 1994, mostly in the first half of that period. More active has been the program of forcible eradication of seed beds in the Chapare, which destroyed the equivalent of 8,260 hectares of coca from 1989 through 1994.

The heart of the eradication program has been the $2,000 per hectare eradication payment for coca fields planted before 1988 and voluntarily uprooted by farmers. From 1987 through 1994, 25,232 hectares were voluntarily uprooted, and $49.7 million was paid out. The program has some implementation problems—determining the age of bushes to verify that they were planted before 1988, registering the area eradicated to ensure that compensation has not been paid in past years, and making the cash payments on time. But none of these problems has been a major factor in determining the progress of the program. By contrast, the continued plantings of coca have thrown in doubt, the effectiveness of the program. USAID La Paz estimates that during the same period that the Bolivian government reports 25,232 hectares were eradicated, 37,380 hectares of coca were planted, for a net gain of 10,300 hectares.[27]

The voluntary compensated eradication program, adopted under strong pressure from the United States, has been intensely controversial. U.S. cash aid to the Bolivian government, called Economic Support Funds (ESF), was made conditional on progress in eradication; the various other targets, such as economic reform measures that were supposed to be met, never influenced release of the cash aid. Even though the Bolivian government had launched a courageous program of economic reform in 1985, ESF support was small until the eradication program got going. This fact indicates the hollowness of claims made by U.S. government officials that ESF supports Bolivian reforms. ESF funding has been carefully calibrated each year according to an agreed schedule of so much money for so many hectares eradicated. However, despite the U.S. Government claim that ESF does not finance compensation, in practice, the ESF provides enough to cover the compensation costs and to give extra cash to the Bolivian government as an incentive to carry out the politically unpopular eradication program. While essentially all the legal political parties supported the compensation program—indeed, opposition politician ex-Prime Minister Hugo Banzer recommended in March 1995 raising it to $3,000 per hectare—it is by no means clear if the voluntary compensated eradication program would continue if ESF financing were no longer available.

Syndicates in the Chapare region have waged a vigorous campaign against the program. Highly politicized grass-roots syndicates are a common feature of Bolivian society, having been created in conjunction with the 1952 revolution. (Similar organizations exist in Peru but are much weaker.) They are grouped into *centrales* and, higher, into federations. The Chapare syndicates, among the strongest in Bolivia, are organized partly on the basis of geography (farmers in one locality tend to belong to one syndicate), but also on the basis of what products are grown, where the farmers came from before moving to the Chapare, and what their political orientations are. The syndicates historically provided order to the newly formed communities when the Chapare was settled; for years they were the principal if not the only form of government in the area. In the early 1990s, when the area's population was 200,000 to 250,000, the five principal coca-growing syndicates claimed to have 37,193 members.[28]

The charismatic politician Eva Morales Ayma is executive secretary of the largest coca-producing federation (FETCTC). Morales has effectively mobilized opposition to the counternarcotics program, tapping into the strong leftist and antiAmerican strains in Bolivia, a country that to this day has a vigorous Trotskyist movement. Morales gets extensive favorable coverage in the Bolivian media, partly from ideologically sympathetic reporters and partly—according to Bolivian journalists and politicians interviewed in fall 1994—thanks to payments made to reporters. His movement's finances are unclear. It seems remarkably well funded for a peasant association; for example, the organization of its marches in 1994 must have required tens of thousands of dollars. In interviews, several Bolivian and USAID officials provided specific details of their allegations that Morales receives funds from European leftists and from narcotraffickers.

Coca-producing syndicates have strongly opposed the voluntary compensated eradication program, mixing their complaints about inadequate compensation with a defense of coca cultivation as an appropriate activity. Much of the opposition has occurred in meetings and demonstrations, such as the high-profile protest march in August 1994 that, after being forcibly dispersed by the narcotics police, regrouped and made its way to La Paz. The opposition also has been more direct. One reason farmers cited for not participating in the program was syndicate opposition. In interviews in the Chapare in December 1994, non–coca-growing farmers complained about physical violence (broken bones, burned fields) directed at those who were interested in legal agriculture.

Since beginning his five-year term in 1993, the attitude of Bolivian president Gonzalo Sanchez de Lozada toward the coca-growing federations and toward eradication in general has fluctuated. He scaled back the eradication programs sharply; the area eradicated in 1994 was about one-fifth that in 1992. In June 1994 he allowed the issuance of a master plan for the Cochabamba Tropics that makes no reference to eradication and implies that ending dependence on coca depends on massive amounts of public financing.[29] To resolve the September 1994 protest march led by Morales, Sanchez de Lozado agreed to a joint statement (also signed by the church's Episcopal Conference, the main urban union federation, the journalists' association, and other groups) that said nothing about eradication and was ambiguous about counternarcotics in general.[30] On the other hand, in November 1994 he launched a major campaign around the theme of the Zero Option. At a press conference he explained that his aim was the total elimination of coca in the Chapare: "The plan includes converting fields to other crops, relocating farmers to other regions of the country and establishing industrial plants in areas not suitable for farming."[31] Miguel Urioste, chief of the governing MBL (*Movimiento Bolivia Libre*), followed up with explanations about plans to "depopulate the Chapare" by offering free land elsewhere in the tropical zone. Vice President Victor Hugo Cardenas added, "The eradication of the coca growth in illegal areas cannot be questioned. They must be eradicated either voluntarily or by force."[32] Compensated eradication rose to 600 hectares a month, for a 1995 total of 5,493 hectares—five times that of 1994.[33] Coca grown in the national park bordering the Chapare was particularly targeted. A 256-person Ecological Police Unit was created to destroy illegal coca seedbeds. The government continues to talk about ending coca production in line with law 1008, despite vigorous attacks on the law by the opposition (It was slightly amended in February 1996 to resolve some technical and constitutional problems). Social Defense Secretary Victor Hugal Canelas proclaimed that by 2001, not a single coca plant would be left standing in the Chapare.[34]

One view about Sanchez de Lozada's actions is that he acts only when under foreign pressure. This view, favored by U.S. government officials, would explain the Zero Option plan as a way to make a good impression at the November 2-4 Consultative Group meeting of Bolivia's donors and as a response to the warning he received on October 28 from the State Department's counternarcotics chief, Robert Gelbard, that Bolivia could be declared uncooperative on drug matters, which would effectively end most U.S. aid to the country.

Another way to read Sanchez de Lozada's behavior is that he initially hoped a soft stance on counternarcotics would let him avoid the issue so that he could concentrate on his number-one priority: economic reforms such as privatization and reduction in the size of the government bureaucracy. That did not work, because Morales and his allies used the coca issue to rally leftist (anti-American, anti-free market) forces. When the president saw that the soft stance only emboldened the opposition in its attacks on his economic reforms, he decided to take a confrontational stance toward the Chapare coca growers and toward his leftist opponents in general. This view seems to fit the facts better than the theory that Sanchez de Lozada acted under U.S. pressure. It explains why he adopted a strong stand against his opponents in 1995, including arresting Morales for three weeks in April/May and putting the entire country under a state of emergency in response to a teachers' strike.

THE EFFECTS OF COUNTERTRAFFICKING PROGRAMS ON SUPPLY

U.S. policy is to lower the coca leaf price in order to promote farmers to abandon the crop but to raise the cocaine price to consumers in order to discourage consumption. These policies may seem to be inconsistent. However, the two targets can be made compatible by increasing the cost of getting from coca leaf to cocaine at the consumer level. That can be done by raising the cost of the chemicals used in processing, by destroying more of the processing labs, by severing or interfering with shipping routes, and by forcing smugglers to use more expensive and less effective techniques.

Compared to eradication, countertrafficking appears more promising. Its political impact is better. Countertrafficking hits at a smaller number of people than eradication: a few tens of thousands of local coca paste processors and thousands of trafficker agents, instead of several hundred thousand farmers. Not only are there fewer traffickers than farmers, but they have a less positive image. Coca leaf farmers are seen as the salt of the earth, while traffickers are seen as violent, unpleasant people—and in Bolivia and Peru, the traffickers are seen as foreigners. In addition, countertrafficking hits at cocaine, which is acknowledged throughout the Andes to be an evil product. Eradication, on the other hand, can be seen as targeting coca leaf, which is a widely accepted product (for tea or chewing). Local nationalists, ever sensitive to perceived slights from the United States, resent what they see as an uninformed foreign campaign against a local tradition.

Economically, interdiction in theory reduces local demand for coca leaves and therefore cuts the prices paid to the farmer. Price trends for coca leaf apparently testify to the success of interdiction. In July 1986 Operation Blast Furnace, a series of U.S. military raids against Bolivian cocaine laboratories, caused a massive collapse in coca leaf prices in that country. Prices declined from an average of $2.30 per kilogram in June 1986 to 30 cents per kilogram in July and remained depressed for several months before recovering at the end of the year. The Colombian government's offensive against the Medellín cartel that began in August 1989 produced a 60 percent drop in average leaf prices in Bolivia from 1989 to 1990 and a smaller but still substantial decline in Peru over that period. Correspondingly, wholesale prices in New York, the largest U.S. market, increased 40 percent on average from 1989 to 1990 and U.S.-wide purity levels dropped 8 percent—an indication that less cocaine was being shipped to the U.S. market. In Bolivia, the Colombian effort (augmented by intensified law enforcement in the Chapare) produced a record spate of voluntary compensated eradication—8,100 hectares in 1990.

Developments in late 1995 proved the power of interdiction. In Peru, prices of coca leaf and processed coca plummeted. The price of raw cocaine paste fell 89 percent from February to August 1995, while the price of washed paste fell 88 percent during the same time, reaching an all time low of $100 per kilogram in September, 1995. Over the same period, prices of leaf in Bolivia showed only a decline (10 percent). The difference in price developments between the two countries shows that the reason for the Peruvian price collapse was Lima's vigorous interndiction of fights between the Huallaga Valley and Colombia, as discussed later in this chapter. Bolivia was not affected in part because flights bypassed Peru, taking the more direct eastern route over Brazil. Bolivia has no air interdiction capability to speak of in the northern departments of Beni and Pando. Also, Bolivia converts a larger share of its cocaine base production to hydrochloride than does Peru and apparently is shipping some of this output by land and sea to non-Colombian buyers, principally Mexican and Brazilian traffickers.

The effects of the Cali crackdown and the Peruvian interdictions on the U.S. marketplace, however, still are far from certain. The *New York Times* reported a 50 percent increase in the New York wholesale price of cocaine between May and September, 1995.[35] However, an official in the White House Office of National Drug Control Policy interviewed in October said that there had been essentially no change in price, purity, or availability of cocaine in New York or any other major U.S. city since early 1995.

But countertrafficking has a variety of problems: First, it affects the short-term price, but it does not necessarily change the price the farmers expect to prevail over the long term. The farmers are a tradition-minded group, and they seem to think in terms of a "normal" price that they expect will reassert itself. Only when the price has been below "normal" for some time do the farmers adjust their expectations about what constitutes a normal price. Since law enforcement affects the price for only a short term, it is unlikely to have much effect on the area under coca cultivation.

Second, traffickers and farmers are creative at finding new ways around any restrictions. When flights into the Chapare are watched closely, traffickers take the product out by road to the neighboring Beni region; Upper Huallaga traffickers use boats to reach the Lower Huallaga. Faced with more vigorous flight interdiction between Peru and Colombia, traffickers moved substantial quantities by truck and boat to Brazil, along with smaller amounts trucked across Bolivia to Argentina, Chile, or Brazil. When controls are placed on the chemicals processors would like to use, traffickers use recycling technology (which can reduce the amounts needed up to fifteen times) or they substitute readily available chemicals that work almost as well.

Third, and most important, countertrafficking becomes a cost of doing business that the traffickers can adjust to. They can replace lost product, either by buying it back from corrupt police or by encouraging farmers to grow more coca leaf. According to the RAND cocaine model, "moderately successful seizure rates, in the 30-70 percent range, have little effect on the world cocaine market because market forces simply induce more workers to enter cocaine production to make up for the seizures." [36] While that simplistic model may overstate the case, there is something to it.

This combination of factors has produced a succession of troughs and highs in prices of coca products in the Andes. (See figure 9.1.) From this perspective even the low prices in Peru in the second half of 1995 were a blip in time. Yet price volatility is a serious problem for the farmers who have few savings to fall back on when prices are low and buyers are few.

In sum, the hope is that countertrafficking will lower coca leaf price while raising the price of cocaine. To the extent that countertrafficking has this effect, it packs a double punch—it encourages farmers to abandon growing coca leaf while it discourages cocaine consumption. However, the reality is that countertrafficking may just become part of the cost of doing business.

The Andean nations assign principal responsibility of carrying out countertrafficking to special police units. Interagency cooperation has become generally reasonable, whether with other national units (the rest of the police, the military), with neighboring countries, or with U.S. agencies. This cooperation among the Latin American countries along the smuggling flight path is a sharp break with history. The smugglers travel over the most remote regions of Colombia, Brazil, Ecuador, and Peru, in a region rife with border disputes. The 1995 Peruvian-Ecuadoran border conflict was the latest in a long series of episodes. The traffickers have taken full advantage of this situation by using routes that keep planes over no country's airspace for more than an hour, which means that no one country can use its national resources to detect the plane and then intercept it. The countries concerned are cooperating reasonably well with each other and with the United States to identify the planes while they are over one country and then to inform the authorities of the next country on the routes. This allows use of the most effective counternarcotics technique, which is to follow a plane until it lands—allowing identification of the clandestine strip, increasing the chances for seizing the traffickers on the ground as well as the pilot and plane, and eliminating the risk of shooting down an innocent plane.

The U.S. countertrafficking effort is divided up into little slices, each given to a different agency. Not including intelligence agencies, fourteen U.S. agencies claimed a role in international drug control programs in 1995, up from eight in 1981, and most of those do countertrafficking, including interdicting drugs while they are being transported.[37] The largest budgets go for the Coast Guard, the Customs Service, and the Department of Defense, but other agencies involved include the DEA, the State Department's Bureau of International Narcotics and Law Enforcement (INL, known until 1994 as INM, the Bureau of International Narcotics Matters), the Immigration and Naturalization Service, the Federal Aviation Administration, the Federal Bureau of Investigation, the U.S. Marshals, and several agencies in the Interior Department (the National Park Service, because 365 miles of the U.S.-Mexico border are under its jurisdiction). The division of responsibilities leads to some peculiar practices. Offhand, it would not seem appropriate to ask the State Department to run an air force, but bureaucratic politics led to the creation of an air wing for INL that now has more than fifty planes and helicopters the United States puts at the disposition of antidrug forces.

Several incidents put in doubt the U.S. cooperation with Andean nations. In September 1993, faced with a budget cut, the United States decided to stop funding the DEA-run helicopter base at Santa Lucia, which began operations in 1987. The DEA and the State Department maintained that the base had become ineffective because drug traffickers had moved their operations. The Peruvian reaction was summed up in the *Expreso* editorial headline: "U.S. Abandons the Field of Battle."[38] The withdrawal of the helicopters meant a substantial reduction in the state's presence in the area, removing an important practical and psychological barrier to narcotraffickers. While the base shut in late 1993, a new, smaller base opened in early 1994 in Pucallpa, east of the Huallaga in the new coca zone, demonstrating the continued U.S. commitment.

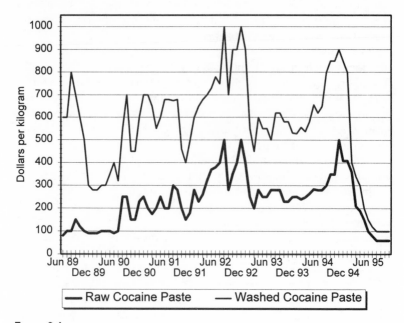

FIGURE 9.1
PERU: COCA PASTE PRICE.
Source: Personal communication with Tito Hernández, UNDP, Lima.

Another episode concerned the U.S.-operated mobile ground radar installations. Three such radars operated for four months in 1991-1992, under Operation Support Justice III. Beginning in early 1993, Operation Support Justice IV supported four radar installations: one in Peru, two in Colombia, and one in Ecuador. Evaluations about their effectiveness conflict. For example, the Peruvian media pointed out that the radar at Yurimaguas had been built in 1992, suffered from periodic breakdowns, and had an effective radius too small (300 miles) to cover the most actively used drug-trafficking routes.[39] The constant complaint was that the United States was not providing more and newer equipment. However, the shared intelligence was of no minor importance; U.S. officials argue that in 1993, the ground radars detected 600 flights and allowed Colombia to destroy twenty-seven planes on the ground as well as to raid more than 100 airstrips used by traffickers.[40]

The radars became a major embarrassment to the U.S. when the U.S. Defense Department decided to stop providing the Peruvian and Colombian governments with information from those installations and to block their nationals from U.S. surveillance flights.[41] On November 4, 1993, Peru shot down a plane, an event that caused the Defense Department to review its policies toward sharing intelligence. Due to a dispute between the Pentagon and the State Department, Lima and Bogotá received no warning and scant explanation of the May 1, 1994, intelligence cutoff. The State Department took strong exception to the Defense Department decision and thus refused to warn the countries concerned. While shootdowns are not the normal procedure in either Peru or Colombia—especially because the four Brazilian-made T-27 Tucano planes used by the Peruvian air force are no match for the much faster planes used by traffickers—the Defense Department, supported by the Justice Department, maintained that its hands were tied by the law. To provide intelligence that might be used to shoot down civilian planes would, they said, violate the 1944 Chicago Convention on Civil Aviation and could expose U.S. military personnel to prosecution for murder.

The decision to stop sharing intelligence drew outraged comments from members of the U.S. Congress and editorial writers. Representative Robert Torricelli (D-NJ), chairman of the Foreign Affairs Subcommittee on the Western Hemisphere, complained, "Rather than implying that the Colombian government's shoot down policy is risky and irresponsible, Washington should be applauding this policy."[42] The *Wall Street Journal* voiced a common suspicion that Washington's "impetus for the policy change seems to lie in the military's discomfort with anti-drug missions." Wrangling in Washington continued, despite rapid action by Congress, which approved legislation in August clarifying that intelligence sharing was legal. On December 8 President Clinton determined that U.S. cooperation could resume, although in practice it only restarted some months later because the Peruvian air force was preoccupied with the Ecuadorian border conflict that erupted in late 1994. Not surprisingly, Lima and Bogotá took the temporary intelligence cutoff as evidence that the U.S. commitment to counternarcotics had weakened.

The dispute over intelligence sharing was particularly unfortunate because it came just as the Peruvian government had decided to get serious about interdiction. Once the U.S. government sorted out the bureaucratic snafu, the U.S. and Peruvian military and law enforcement began to cooperate with unprecedented efficiency. Over 23 narcotics aircraft were forced down or destroyed on the ground, including 6 shot down.[43] The number of narcotics flights declined 47 percent in 1995 compared to 1994. On a month-to-month basis, the results were even more impressive: from a record high of over 50 flights in February 1995 to a record low of at most 6 in one month late in 1995. As discussed earlier, the result of the increased interdiction was an 89 percent drop in coca leaf prices and an 88 percent drop in washed coca paste prices.

As for the focus of activities in each country, Bolivia has concentrated on the destruction of the small-scale base labs—really, upgraded maceration pits—that are so common there. Of the 2,244 labs destroyed in 1995, 2,226 were base labs and 18 were cocaine labs. A special police unit, *Unidad Mobilaria de Patrullaje Rural* (UMOPAR), which works closely with the DEA, destroys the labs. Ethnic differences contribute to poor relations between the Chapare population and UMOPAR, whose agents the locals call Leopards (Leos for short): "Many, probably most, of the drug operatives are cambas, or lowlanders. Because of government 'Andeocentrism,' lowland isolation, and a keen sense of 'racial' purity (of being white rather than dark, or Indian) among lowlanders, they often hold kollas, or highlanders, in low regard . . . border[ing] on contempt. . . . UMOPAR . . . soldiers are overwhelmingly highlanders from the lower classes (where the dark, Indian features are the strongest)."[44]

Bolivia has been the most active Andean country at seizing drug trade assets. However, "the office of seized assets now controls upwards of $300 million in property, but is unable to provide an accurate inventory of the property under its control or to protect those assets from misappropriation." [45] A December 1995 decree allowed sale of the seized property, relieving the government of managing physical assets, but the proceeds of the sales will still remain tied up for years.

The Colombian countertrafficking program is part and parcel of its efforts against the cartels, which was discussed in chapter 2. The countertrafficking program, which is run by the National Police's Anti-Narcotics Division (DANTI), has been more successful in Colombia than in the rest of the Andes at seizing drugs, partly because a seizure from a smuggler or large lab (the norm in Colombia) typically is much larger than a seizure from a farmer (the Bolivian norm). Aggregating together the seizures of coca leaf, paste, base, and cocaine, and converting each into the equivalent amount of cocaine, Colombia has accounted for most of the Andean seizures. For the period from 1990 to 1995, seizures in Colombia amounted to 305 tons out of the total 402 tons for Bolivia, Colombia, and Peru combined. During that time the Colombian seizures averaged 51 tons per year, which was between 5 and 8 percent of the cocaine passing through the country. Colombia also has become active in targeting precursor chemicals. In March 1994 the National Police seized 1,754 tons of suchchemicals from eight offices of Holanda Chemicals International[46]—enough chemicals to produce 136 tons of cocaine.

In Peru, most of the countertrafficking activities are carried out by the 1,160 agents of the National Police's *Dirección Nacional Antidrogas* (DINANDRO). In 1995, after years of mediocre performance in seizing drugs, Peru seized the equivalent of 22 tons of cocaine—or 5 percent of what the U.S. government estimates as its maximum production—in coca leaf, base, paste and cocaine hydrochloride.[47] Peru has destroyed fewer labs and seized less than the other two countries, but it has had the most arrests. Furthermore, the arrests have been shifting away from consumers towards traffickers; according to DINANDRO data, traffickers accounted for 37 percent of those arrested in 1993 but 67 percent of those arrested in the first quarter of 1995.[48]

Like Colombia and Bolivia, Peru has the most advanced program to control chemical inputs, most of which are produced domestically. It also has a seldom-used program of seizure of assets from drug dealers. As in the other Andean nations, asset seizure fits poorly with the local legal tradition, in which asset forfeiture historically required demanding standards of proof that the assets came from illegal activity. It is also difficult to administer in face of the agents' temptation to keep the funds seized themselves to make up for shortfalls in agency financing or, more typically, to add to their low pay.

DINANDRO has difficulty securing funding for its operations.[49] Its personnel costs are inflated by the rotation of personnel from Lima to the drug areas, necessary because of the poor security situation in the Huallaga Valley. (Neither the agents nor their families would be safe there, and in any case they would not want to live in such a remote region.) DINANDRO has to use eight planes just to rotate personnel, in order to give each agent six days a month off in Lima. In January 1994 the $100 per month supplement to agents posted in the valley was cut off, which devastated morale and complicated problems of maintaining honesty. DINANDRO has continuing problems with access to helicopters— Peru's fleet of Soviet-built military helicopters is getting old and are gas-guzzlers, while there were diplomatic problems with using the State Department–run helicopters after an April 1994 episode in which President Fujimori was denied a ride (for safety reasons) when he made a surprise inspection visit to the valley.

Countertrafficking activities in the Andes increasingly must involve not only the producing countries but also the geographical giant neighbor to the east, Brazil. While there are no statistics on trafficking via Brazil, one indicator is the coca seizures in that country, which have gone up dramatically in recent years (admittedly in part because of one 7.3 ton seizure in June 1994). (See figure 9.2.) Brazil's large legal economy provides cover for coca exports. More directly, its thinly populated and lightly policed regions bordering the Andean nations, far removed from the center of Brazilian attention, provide areas in which to hide processing facilities and landing strips for refueling. When Peru became more effective at intercepting drug flights in 1995, Brazil became a more attractive route for the traffickers.[50] Reducing their reliance on flights directly from Peru, they moved perhaps a quarter of all Peruvian drug exports into Brazil by road and by river. Border controls are lax to nonexistent in the area where Brazil, Peru, and Colombia meet along the Amazon; the economies of the three neighboring border cities are effectively integrated. In November 1995, the Brazilian government was shocked to find a major clandestine drug landing strip in the border region. The federal police have be-

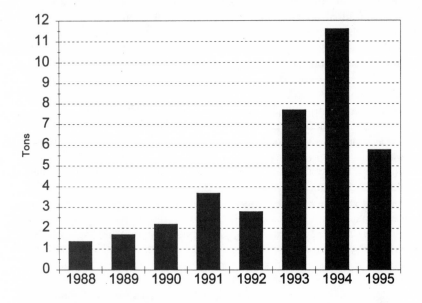

FIGURE 9.2

COCAINE SEIZURES IN BRAZIL.

Source: U.S. Department of State, International Narcotics Strategy Report 1996 (Washington, D.C.: Government Printing Office, 1996) and International Narcotics Strategy Report 1995 (Washington, D.C.: Government Printing Office, 1995).

come more active in searching for landing strips and in monitoring suspicious activities in the tri-nation border area.

Uprooting the traffickers now that they have become established in Brazil will be much more difficult than it would have been to keep them out in the first place. Brazil had plenty of warning that its Amazon basin could become a cocaine highway.[51] Brazil's response was to award a contract for a $1.4 billion surveillance system with fixed and airborne radars. That project has been held up by controversy over allegations that Raytheon, the U.S. firm awarded the contract, bribed officials to counter the bribes the CIA claims were offered by Thomson, the competing French firm.[52] The border zone is already monitored by U.S.-assisted radars on the Colombian side, but Brazilian nationalist suspicions impede cooperation.[53]

THE EFFECTS OF
ALTERNATIVE DEVELOPMENT ON SUPPLY

The most powerful effect of foreign-financed alternative development programs is that they increase the degree of cooperation from Andean governments in counternarcotics. The producers can form an important lobby opposing counternarcotics, as seen in Bolivia's Chapare region. By enabling farmers to raise their incomes—by merely allowing them to earn some extra income by diversifying into other activities while still growing coca—the programs may improve the image of the United States and of the national government, thereby reducing resistance to counternarcotics efforts. While the roads, schools, and other facilities provided by alternative development programs may have no effect on inducing farmers to abandon growing coca, they do induce nationalists and leftists to tolerate counternarcotics programs that they see as serving U.S. rather than Andean interests. In short, alternative development may be the price the United States has to pay to prevent Andean governments from turning a blind eye to the narcotics trade.

Theoretically, alternative development reduces supply by providing farmers with other sources of income. However, there are several significant problems with relying on alternative development to reduce coca leaf supply.

First, there is a danger that development work in the coca-producing regions may provide infrastructure that facilitates coca production and makes life attractive so that farmers move there and plant more coca. Take two examples. First, the development of schools and clinics in the Chapare may make it a less unattractive region in which to settle, thereby discouraging out-migration to the Santa Cruz area or to other regions that could absorb labor. Second, USAID and other agencies provide technical assistance, such as training on how to use fertilizer, which coca growers can use just as well as legal farmers. Certain types of assistance—road improvements, for example—arguably lower costs for legal farmers more than for coca farmers. (Roads and vehicles are essential to get legal crops to market; coca can be carried on farmers' backs.) Still, roads that facilitate transport can also serve as traffickers' airstrips. Limiting this spillover is the best that can be achieved. A further problem is that infrastructure represents a fixed investment. USAID can dole out infrastructure and services according to the amount of coca that a community eradicates (this indeed is USAID's current policy); yet it cannot tear down schoolhouses and rip up roads if farmers revert to coca—certainly a possibility given the always-uncertain markets for legal crops.

Second, development specialists as individuals and aid organizations as institutions want to promote development rather than to fight narcotics. Therefore, in coca-growing regions, they do what will best raise legal income, which is not necessarily what will best fight coca cultivation. Specifically, USAID personnel interviewed did not, as a rule, consider important conditioning the provision of USAID-funded services on a community's or a farmer's progress in moving away from coca cultivation. In fact, measures to make such a link often remained a dead letter. Nor has USAID been especially have in promoting local organizations and institutions that have taken on the political power of the coca lobby. To be fair, USAID La Paz does fund and support noncoca farmers' groups and a radio station that publicizes them and alternative development activities; however, neither those groups nor that station take a stand against coca.

Third, even if the farmers currently growing coca switch to legal crops, ample unused land and unemployed labor can begin coca cultivation. Consider the situation in Peru. As many as 2 million hectares of tropical land may be suitable for coca cultivation, located in remote areas where the government has little presence and where settlers can readily appropriate the land. The move in recent years away from the Upper Huallaga to valleys to the east and to the south is a small example of what could occur. The entire coca industry would fit comfortably in one of several Peruvian valleys in which there is now little cultivation. It will be at least another generation before the Peruvian economy and the Peruvian state have established an effective presence in all the remote Amazon regions of the country. And labor is even easier to find than land. The labor going to the coca regions is a small trickle in the flood of people leaving the highlands. According to the 1993 census, 1.71 million Peruvians had moved from one of the country's twenty-five departments to another within the last five years; that is, 8 percent of the national population made what was probably a long-distance move in a five-year period.[54] Of that rush, 717,000 went to Lima and its port, Callao. If all the existing coca farmers (300,000 with their families) were to switch out of the crop, replacing them with a new set of coca farmers would require diverting less than half of the normal five-year flow to Lima—less than one-fifth the normal five-year interdepartment migration.

In other words, until national economic development provides enough good-paying jobs to absorb the underemployed who are now streaming out of the highlands and into the cities, alternative development could just be farmer rotation—some leave coca, others enter. Providing that many jobs is an ambitious target, at least for the next decade.

Fourth, alternative development may well actually be parallel development. That is, farmers may welcome the opportunity to diversify their crop mix and raise their income by adding noncoca crops without abandoning their coca bushes. Farmers are aware of the dangers of monoculture; they want to reduce the risk that they will be financially ruined if the coca is hit by a fungus or if law enforcement activities prevent them from selling their leaves for a time. But the decision to plant legal crops is not necessarily connected to a decision to abandon coca.

The evidence to date suggests that alternative development programs have been successful in making legal crops more attractive in the Chapare zone of Bolivia. The planting of legal crops, which began in the early 1990s as the coca boom faded, has led to a maturing of the new plants and therefore to a substantial increase in the harvest of licit crops. At the same time, prices have risen, in some cases substantially due to two developments. First, the USAID-improved road system has cut transport costs, allowing farmers better access to markets (in La Paz or in Buenos Aires), so that the increased volumes have found ready buyers. Second, the marketing assistance from USAID has helped farmers improve the quality of the produce they sell—for example, packing bananas into boxes that keep them from being crushed and bruised in transit. Thanks to the increased prices and volumes, the value of licit crops in the Chapare went from $9 million in 1992-1993 to $22 million in 1993-1994, while the value of the coca leaf crop dropped due to lower prices. (See Table 9.1.)

However, there is no evidence that the reduced dependence on coca has translated into less coca. In fact, the area planted to coca has grown slightly. In other words, what has occurred to date in the Chapare is parallel development, not alternative.

In Peru's Upper Huallaga, the picture in 1990-1993 was less encouraging. The UNDCP maintains it has had some success in its project zone, which is only a small part of the Upper Huallaga.[55] The area planted to coca in the project zone went from 24,500 hectares in 1986 to 17,042 hectares in 1992 and 7,000 hectares in 1993, but that may have been primarily because of the fungus outbreak. In the early 1990s, 800 families in that zone grouped in several cooperatives abandoned 2,400 hectares of coca to plant 500 hectares of cashew and palm heart. In the Tocache area, 650 families in a cooperative abandoned 1,200 hectares of coca to dedicate themselves to cacao and other legal crops.

TABLE 9.1

BOLIVIA—TROPICAL ZONE OF COCHABAMBA: CROP PRODUCTION

| | Area Planted (ha) | | | Value of output (000 $) | |
	1985/6	1992/3	1993/4	1992/3	1993/4
Coca	27,000	31,600	32,900	89,958	70,313
Licit Crops	27,388	41,334	59,078	9,140	22,444
Citrus	3,000	11,773	18,964	3,971	12,180
Banana	7,075	10,956	13,458	1,142	2,138
Plantain	2,700	3,547	5,362	504	1,023
Cassava	3,400	4,564	5,808	1,131	2,345
Rice	8,500	6,177	7,985	1,472	1,884
Other	2,713	4,317	7,501	920	2,874
TOTAL	54,388	72,934	91,978	99,098	92,757
Coca as % total	50%	43%	36%	91%	76%

Sources: 1993 and 1994 Agricultural Surveys, Government of Bolivia; 1986 from PDAR project; 1992/3-3/4 coca area, U.S. Government data prepared for the 1994 INCSR.

The data from the Upper Huallaga Special Project (PEAH) show that the percent of value added coming from coca was flat from 1990 to 1993 at 73 percent. (See table 9.2.) And that understates the role of coca in local agriculture. Most of the value added from legal crops— $21 million out of the $33 million total in 1993—came from food crops. A good part of that food went to feed those working in the coca industry, either the farmers themselves or the workers in the valley (the processing pit laborers, the transport workers, and the dealers themselves). Most of the food crops are not cost competitive for markets outside of the coca-growing region and its surroundings; that is, if the cocaine industry faded, so too would this food crop production.

As discussed in chapter 5, when the price dropped in 1995, a substantial number of Peruvian coca farmers apparently stopped harvesting coca. It is too early to tell if the 1995 price shock will lead farmers to abandon coca permanently. Preliminary indications are encouraging but the most realistic forecast is that farmers will diversify into other crops instead of relying on coca alone.

In Colombia, the only alternative development project with results to date has been the UNDCP program in southern Cauca. According to UNDCP, more than 3,000 hectares of coca have been eliminated in the project area, amounting to approximately 60 percent of the area's total coca cultivation but only a small proportion of Colombia's total coca area. Only in the late 1990s will it be possible to judge how well the various alternative development projects approved since 1991 are functioning.

TABLE 9.2
PERU—UPPER HUALLAGA VALLEY PEAH PROJECT ZONE CROPS

	Area Planted (ha)			Value of output (000 $)		
	1987	1990	1993	1987	1990	1993
Coca	17,874	34,238	31,880	21,269	108,474	88,770
Legal Crops	49,223	51,062	34,540	24,856	40,369	33,488
Food crops	28,879	34,568	23,228	15,902	29,210	21,351
Plantain	9,075	9,669	10,614	7,148	14,457	10,230
Cassava	5,736	6,898	6,254	3,562	9,109	9,898
Rice	4,788	9,131	1,346	2,759	3,081	888
Maize	8,014	7,858	4,622	2,007	1,982	123
Beans	1,266	1,013	392	426	581	212
Industrial crops	20,344	16,493	11,312	8,954	11,159	12,137
Cacao	7,262	7,770	4,127	2,985	1,391	899
Coffee	4,180	4,186	2,027	1,079	237	579
Palm oil	8,509	4,150	4,614	4,439	8,931	10,258
Papaya			382	226	300	363
Tea	393	387	161	226	300	37
Total	67,097	85,300	66,420	46,125	148,843	122,258
Coca as % total	27%	40%	48%	46%	73%	73%

Source: Government of Peru, Instituto Nacional de Estadísticas e Informatica, *Compendio de Estadísticas de Producción y Consumo de Drogas 1980-93,* with obvious errors corrected.

If we look at economic alternatives to coca on the national level, there is reason for hope from the Bolivian and Peruvian experience, where the recent recovery of the legal economy has been matched by a slowdown in the growth of the cocaine industry. The record of those two countries seems consistent with the theory that when national economic development takes place, illegal activities that thrive in difficult times become less attractive. However, the Colombian experience runs counter to this proposition. As shown earlier, the Colombian economy has done reasonably well in the 1990s—not as well as might have been expected given the country's situation, but still with slightly increasing real per capita income. Yet the country seems to be in the midst of a coca and poppy cultivation boom. Apparently the job opportunities, which are primarily in the west and north of the country, have not been sufficient to attract the residents of isolated and poor eastern and southern Colombia, who have instead turned to illegal crops.

POLICY IMPLICATIONS

There is little evidence that any of the counternarcotics effort in the Andes have to date had much effect on the supply of cocaine in the United States. One could argue that the more active Andean counternarcotics programs implemented in the mid- and late 1980s slowed the growth of the cocaine industry. To be sure, the industry was growing rapidly in the decade before Andean counternarcotics efforts were strengthened, and it has not grown much since. But it is by no means clear that the reason for the change was the Andean counternarcotics effort.

The lack of demonstrated success applies to all phases of the Andean counternarcotics effort—eradication of coca bushes, seizures of precursor chemicals, destruction of labs, interception of planes, and alternative development projects. There is no empirical evidence to suggest that one source country program is more effective than another. Partisans of each approach are likely to continue to argue that their favorite method is the best, but to make their point, they will have to rely on theories, anecdotes, or prejudgments rather than demonstrated success.

That said, one can find reasons for hope with regard to each of the programs, though probably less so for eradication. So far none of the existing programs can be considered a complete failure. In particular, there is no compelling evidence to accept the critics' proposition that efforts in Latin America will have little effect on cocaine price and supply in the United States.

Our suspicion is that the most effective counternarcotics programs for the Andean nations will be ones that are designed and implemented by the governments concerned, rather than by the United States or international aid agencies. The regional governments are better positioned than outside experts to determine what programs will work, especially which ones will command the public support that is so vital for success. And commitment by the local authorities is one of the most vital ingredients for the success of any program: A theoretically ideal program that is not supported by them is less useful than a theoretically flawed program that they are determined to make work.

10

Where Do We Go from Here?

We cannot wipe out drug production in source countries or stop drug exports. The potential supply of drugs is virtually unlimited; trafficking routes and points of entry into the United States are multitudinous; and once destroyed laboratories, drug shipments, planes, money, chemicals, and other trafficking assets can be replaced easily.

Furthermore, the United States has to manage its counternarcotics efforts abroad through sovereign governments. Governments in drug-source countries typically are weak, power is diffused, and instability and lawlessness are rife. Those governments have other concerns, such as generating employment, lowering poverty, or fighting insurgent movements. To the general public in Andean countries, eliminating drug trafficking is a low national priority compared to other problems that affect their daily lives.

What can the United States do in face of these barriers to controlling the Andean cocaine trade? Advocates of more drastic policies point to the fact most of the world's coca production is concentrated in three small areas: Peru's Upper and Central Huallaga Valley, Bolivia's Chapare, and a zone that spills over three departments in Colombia (Guaviare, Caquetá, and Putumayo). This pattern of concentration makes a very tempting target. The opportunities to eliminate a substantial portion of South American coca via a massive aerial spraying program are theoretically quite high. As coca plants take about eighteen months to reach maturity, effective spraying could truly disrupt the market for some time.

But the United States does not exercise sovereignty over these areas, and the political cost of eradication would devolve mostly on the host governments. Consider the downside. Powerful combinations of farmers, traffickers, armed guerrillas, and environmentalists (including those in the United States) oppose spraying. The farmers doubtless would occupy strategic areas such as transportation nodes and oilfields as they have when spraying was tried in the past. They might even seek public sympathy for their cause, displaying deformed fetuses, sick children, or dead animals in front of television cameras and attributing these calamities—rightly or wrongly—to the herbicide. World television networks would pick up the stories. Lawsuits could ensue—financed, of course, by wealthy trafficking interests. Indeed, Andean and U.S. agencies and companies could spend years fighting litigation over the spraying issue, even though the negative environmental effects of spraying are less than those of growing and processing coca. Dispossessed farmers could swell the ranks of guerrilla movements, which, faced with declining drug revenues, would focus efforts on extracting resources from legal economic sectors. Guerrillas would retaliate by shooting down spray aircraft and indeed already have done so in Colombia. Not a very attractive prospect!

Spraying offers certain advantages, however. It could achieve a significant long-term reduction in coca were it implemented on a large scale, sustained over time, and extended to any new areas opened up as the older coca-growing regions are sprayed. As of this writing, Colombia has embarked on a significant aerial eradication effort, claiming to have sprayed 24,000 hectares of coca between January and December 1995. (The area destroyed was only one third of that size according to U.S. estimates.) However, opposition already is beginning to coalesce against the program. Perhaps spraying would be more acceptable politically to Andean governments if they could provide substantial compensation to farmers who lose their drug crops, but financial constraints prohibit that.

Just as massive spraying is so extreme that it would cause a host of problems for the Andean nations, so too legalization is too extreme in the other direction. Many proponents of legalization argue that such a step will take most of the profits out of smuggling and distribution. However, legalization is not a panacea for crime. Look at U.S. history. Prohibition spawned the growth of major criminal enterprises in the United States, but when prohibition was repealed and alcohol again became legal, these criminal enterprises just expanded into new areas—drugs, loan sharking, gambling, and the like.

Similarly, legalization would not mean that all the criminal expertise, trafficking networks, and smuggling routes now devoted to drugs will just fold into the legal economy, with the criminals becoming simple ranchers, businessmen, pilots, chemists, and so on. Their illegal occupations have provided criminals with new lifestyles and expectations. Were drugs to become legalized, they probably would shift their efforts to other, possibly equally illegal areas. The criminal enterprises will perpetuate themselves by producing accomplished kidnappers and assassins, by moving into white-collar crime, or by smuggling other dangerous substances (nerve gas, atomic bomb parts, and fissionable materials). That is why the U.S. government must continue to attack crime and criminal organizations, even while redefining its strategies to focus less on the traditional goal of stopping the flow of illicit drugs.

Another caveat about legalization is that it might not benefit the drug-source countries much if at all. Were drugs to be legalized, the United States probably would emerge as the world's most efficient producer of the newly legal drugs, because it has access to the most advanced plant genetics, agricultural technology, and processing methods. That is, Third World producers would have a difficult time competing with the United States. Colombia, which now has a strong advantage in illegal production and smuggling compared to the other Andean nations, would find that its talents are no longer needed and is especially unlikely to benefit from an international legalization of cocaine.

It is not correct to conclude from these dismal realities of Andean narcotics control policies that the United States should shut down its international programs and put the money into enforcement, treatment, and prevention on the home front. It is inappropriate to demand all or nothing, that is, to tell the counternarcotics officials, "Either entirely eliminate the drug trade or we will cut your funding to zero." International narcotics control policies can have some effect; it just is not as dramatic as we would like. As Harvard professor and ex-Justice Department official Mark Kleiman quipped, "Making drug policy has something in common with taking drugs: both are activities prone to excess. . . . The problem is to replace excess with moderation in a double sense: a policy to encourage moderation in use, and moderation in the making and implementation of policy. This would mean abandoning unreasonable goals. . . ."[1]

We should not evaluate the performance of international cocaine control in the years 1990 to 1995 by asking whether it ended the cocaine trade but instead by asking what change it accomplished. In fact, the cocaine industry has stagnated in the 1990s after a decade of explosive

growth. The change was not due solely to the counternarcotics program, but it did have some effect. For instance, the restoration of the
legal Bolivian economy and the development of legal agriculture in
the Chapare had something to do with the stagnation in coca output
after years of rapid growth: Poor Bolivians were no longer as likely to
migrate to the Chapare, and Chapare farmers were no longer as likely
to concentrate on coca to the neglect of all other crops.

Furthermore, drug control is not just about drugs. U.S. narcotics
assistance programs abroad are extensions of diplomacy. They serve
important foreign policy goals, such as advancing U.S. prestige and
influence and promoting stability, social peace, and economic
growth in countries where the United Sates has ongoing or potential strategic interests. U.S. counternarcotics policies should not
be judged simply the standard of reducing the quantity of illicit
drugs that appear in America's streets—we need other indica-
tors of success.

International counternarcotics programs need to be refocused,
and some programs should be ended. For instance, some U.S. supply-
side actions are self-defeating because to the extent they are effective,
they just cause narcotics prices to rise, which in turn attracts new
actors into the business who are willing to take great risks to achieve
huge profits. Other programs have to be phased out gradually in order to avoid compounding the errors of the past. The U.S. government supports a multitude of Andean police agencies, security forces,
military establishments, judiciaries, academic researchers, media types,
and consultants to continue the failed policies of the past. If Washington suddenly cuts off the funding for all these people, their resentment about their income loss would hurt the United States politically
in these countries. In a way, the United States is stuck with the consequences of past programs.

The programs that should be sustained are those that support
three legitimate and appropriate U.S. goals: to break up trafficking
cartels, to take a stand against high-level corruption, and to encourage
the development of legal economies.

Powerful trafficking aggregates such as the Medellín cartel of
the 1980s or the Cali cartel can inflict enormous damage on governing
institutions, on national economies, and on the international system
generally. The Medellín cartel sponsored a campaign of bombing,
kidnapping, and execution in Colombia in the late 1980s and early
1990s. In the mid-1990s, the Cali cartel is on the road to infiltrating
and corrupting the highest levels of the Colombian government.

Efforts to break up these large power aggregates have been partly successful in the past. Between 1990 and 1993, for example, the Colombian government managed to eliminate virtually all of the top tier and much of the middle-echelon leadership of the Medellín cartel. Some 200 to 250 criminals were exterminated and approximately 40 surrendered under a government leniency program. Unfortunately, this success had little impact on drug control, because the epicenter of the cocaine trade simply shifted to Cali; however, the crackdown wiped out an important narcoterrorist threat to the Colombian state.

While the U.S. government may not be able to control drugs, it may be able to influence the particular configuration of actors in the market—that is, the organizational environment of the drug trade. It may be preferable for the drug traffic to originate from a large number of small producers, each of whom has limited power and influence, than from a small circle of powerful kingpins able and willing to use their economic clout to buy legislators, cabinet ministers and presidents. It might be better to have 1,000 mom-and-pop refining and trafficking operations sending packages of cocaine to the United States via couriers than to have ten very large organizations each with hundreds of millions of dollars in annual revenues, shipping tons of cocaine in containers or DC-9 airplanes, negotiating with governments, issuing communiqués to the press, bankrolling political campaigns, and using violence as a political tool. Conceivably the negotiations option discussed in chapter 4 can help authorities make important tactical successes against the cocaine multinationals. The United States would have to take an active, if unofficial, role in the negotiations process—shaping the agenda of discussions and providing corroborating evidence and proofs—to ensure that a deal actually results in dismantling large trafficking enterprises. Without U.S. participation, a negotiated settlement could become either a comfortable retirement program for drug dealers or a prelude to de facto legalization.

A second legitimate preoccupation of U.S. policy is to take a stand against high-level corruption in countries where the United States has a vital political stake. For instance, Washington demonstrated its abhorrence of flagrantly narcocratic regimes such as those of General Manuel Noriega in Panama and Luis Garcia Meza in Bolivia. In 1991 the United States forced the Bolivian government to cancel three appointments to high government posts because the officials involved had links to the cocaine trade. In Colombia, a

U.S. threat of decertification in 1995 spurred investigations of political corruption as well as the Samper administration's offensive against the Cali cartel leaders. (The U.S. decision to decertify Colombia in 1996, however, could produce a nationalist backlash that undercuts U.S. allies in the drug fight in that country.) Yet no amount of U.S. prodding can substitute for an internalized commitment by Latin American governments themselves to combat the drug trade and its associated social evils. Such a drug-fighting consensus cannot betaken for granted. As mentioned, despite the obvious baneful effects of narcotics businesses in Colombia's society and political system, only 8 percent of Colombians consider drug trafficking as a serious national problem, according to a June 1995 poll commissioned by *El Espectador*.[2]

Finally, the United States should encourage the development of the legal economy in these countries, in part to reduce the relative weight of the narcoeconomy and by implication the drug traffickers' relative political clout. The encouragement of economic development means not only aid but also access to U.S. markets without harassment (such as the trumped-up allegations designed to impede Colombian flower exporters) and help in attracting foreign investment. The prospects for foreign investment improve when the influence of drug dealers and organized crime groups diminishes, because such groups raise the cost of doing business overseas in numerous ways. By the same token, measures that actually damage the legal economy in source countries (such as trade sanctions that might ensue from decertification) can work to the benefit of narcotics traffickers.

A reoriented policy would remove U.S. personnel from the front lines of the drug war, which would minimize their risk of physically dangerous and politically incendiary confrontations with peasants and small-time traffickers—an especially unnerving prospect in guerrilla-torn countries such as Colombia and Peru, but a problem anywhere in Latin America, where suspicions of U.S. alleged hegemony run deep. Not only are Andean governments likely to be more effective than U.S. agents, but also the principal responsibility for combatting narcotics belongs to the Andean governments, not to the United States, and so they should take the lead. If the Andean governments are not committed to combatting narcotics, then nothing the United States can do will make much difference. Contrary to the myth that the Andean governments are indifferent to (or supportive of) the cocaine trade, in fact, these governments generally understand that the drug trade hurts their national interests. The political problems it creates, such as lack of respect for the rule of law, outweigh its often exaggerated economic advantages. To be sure, these governments face many problems, of which narcotics is by no means their top priority. In that context, it is not surprising that the United States wants a more vigorous counternarcotics program than the Andean nations want. The difference in priorities is precisely why the United States has to provide financial and technical aid, to put its thumb on the scale to give a heavier weight to fighting the narcotics trade.

Some U.S. resources now earmarked for crop-spraying and raids on maceration pits and drug laboratories in Latin America might be better spent on developing a more effective antinarcotics presence in the increasingly important but politically troubled ex-Communist states, including the former Soviet Union, China, and Vietnam. While international drug policy may not substantially curtail drug trafficking where it has entrenched itself, supply-side efforts can be reconfigured to promote stability and growth in the victimized countries, strengthen the social fabric, and expand U.S. influence in beneficent ways.

Past failures and general budget constraints require that the United States redefine its priorities. The question is what combination of measures, within the limits of resources that U.S. taxpayers are willing to provide, produces the maximum impact on the political and economic reach of drug dealers as well as on the overall flow drugs. Even if the long-term solution to the drug problem is to reduce domestic demand rather than the chimera of reducing foreign supply, Washington and foreign capitals still can apply their resources internationally to good effect, destabilizing the malevolent drug lords who threaten the stability of Latin American nations.

Appendix

Steps in the Manufacture of Cocaine

Leaf to Paste **(40 percent pure cocaine)**	*Step 1* The coca leaves are placed in a plastic container and soaked in a solution of alkaline material (usually sodium bicarbonate) and water are added to the leaves.
	Step 2 A water immersible solvent (usually kerosene or gasoline) is added to water, solution, and leaves.
	Step 3 Cocaine alkaloids and kerosene separate from water and leaves and are placed in a second container.
	Step 4 Cocaine alkaloids are extracted from the kerosene into a hydrochloride acid solution. Alkaline material (sodium bicarbonate) is added to the remaining solution which causes a precipitate to form. The acid and the water are drained off and the precipitate is filtered and dried to produce coca paste, a chunky, off-white to light brown, putty-like substance.
Paste to Base **(90 percent pure cocaine)**	*Step 5* The coca paste is dissolved in a weak solution of sulfuric acid or hydrochloric acid.
	Step 6 Potassium permanganate is combined with water. This mixture is added to the coca paste and acid solution. Potassium permanganate is used in this step to extract other alkaloids and material that is undesired in the final product.
	Step 7 The solution is filtered through paper and the precipitate is discarded. Ammonia water is added to the filtered solution and another precipitate is formed.
	Step 8 The liquid is drained from the solution and the remaining precipitate is usually dried with heating lamps. The resulting powder is cocaine base.
Base to HCL **(99 percent pure cocaine)**	*Step 9* Acetone or ether is added to dissolve the cocaine base and the solution is filtered to remove undesired material.
	Step 10 Hydrochloric acid diluted in acetone or ether is added to the cocaine solution. The addition of the hydrochloric acid causes the cocaine to precipitate (crystallize) out of the solution as cocaine hydrochloride.
	Step 11 Cocaine HCL is dried under heat lamps, in microwave ovens, or outside with the aid of fans.
CHCL to Crack	*Step 12* Cocaine HCL powder is mixed with water and baking soda to form a thick paste. Paste is heated in a microwave oven or on a stove. Resulting product, crack, is broken into small chunks or "rocks" and placed in clear plastic vials for sale to customers.

Sources: DEA; Gilda Berger, *Crack: The Drug Epidemic* (New York: Franklin Watts, 1987), pp. 56-59.

Notes

Introduction

1. All data on U.S. government drug control spending are from Office of National Drug Control Policy (ONDCP), *National Drug Control Strategy 1995 Budget Summary* (Washington, DC: ONDCP, 1995).

Chapter 1

1. U.S. Department of State, *International Narcotics Control Strategy Report 1996* (Washington, DC: Government Printing Office, Publication 10246, 1996), pp. 22-23.
2. Ibid., p. 20.
3. No estimates of the nonharvested portion are available but some U.S. and Colombian narcotics experts believe that this could be large.
4. U.S. Drug Enforcement Administration, Intelligence Division, *Operation Breakthrough: Coca Cultivation and Cocaine Base Production in Bolivia,* Report No. DEA-94032, (Washington, DC: DEA, July 1994).
5. USAID La Paz, *Bolivia's Coca Sub-Economy* 1994 (La Paz: USAID La Paz, June 1995), Table 4.
6. The INCSR figure for production in 1993 was a range of 770 to 805 tons.
7. More technically, when the demand curve shifts to the left, then the equilibrium price and quantity sold both drop. When the supply curve shifts to the right, then the equilibrium price drops while the quantity sold rises. In the U.S. cocaine market in the 1990s, the price has dropped and the quantity sold has dropped, which more resembles a leftward shift of the demand curve than a rightward shift of the supply curve.
8. Sergio Uribe, "La Coca," Bogotá, June 1995, pp. 6, 11; Cuánto S.A., *Impact of the Coca in the Peruvian Economy 1980-1992* (Lima: Cuánto S.A., September 1993), p. 8.
9. *Statistical Abstract of the United States* (Washington, DC: Government Printing Office, annual) table on "Food Prices—distribution of retail price according to farm value and marketing function" (not present in recent issues). The next figure is from the table on civilian consumer expenditures for farm foods.
10. Thomas Kellerman, "Overall Importance and Impact of the Coca Subsector with Regards to the Economies of the Andean Countries of Bolivia, Colombia, and Peru," in U.S. Department of State, Bureau of Intelligence and Research and the Central Intelligence Agency, *Economics of the Narcotics Industry Conference Report* (Washington, DC: State Department and CIA, 1994).
11. Elena Alvarez, "The Political Economy of Coca Production in Bolivia and Peru" (ms.), Center for Policy Research, State University of New York at Albany, July 1993;

and Cuánto S.A., *Impact of the Coca in the Peruvian Economy 1980-1992*. The latter report says cocaine industry employment supported 750,000 people in 155,000 families.

12. USAID Lima, *Project Paper: Alternative Development Project* (Lima: USAID Lima, 1995), p. 29.

13. USAID La Paz, *Bolivia's Coca Sub-Economy* (La Paz: USAID La Paz, September 1992, June 1995). (Two editions of the same study.)

14. Lee interview. La Paz, July 1995.

15. "Interview of Pablo Escobar by El Nuevo Siglo", *El Nuevo Siglo,* September 8, 1992, pp. 13A-17A.

16. National Drug Council, "National Plan for Overcoming the Drug Problem." (Bogotá: NDC, 1994), pp. 11, 59.

17. Sergio Uribe's personal communication, June 1995.

18. "Amarrados a la coca," *El Tiempo,* June 25, 1995, p. 1B.

19. Sidney Zabludoff, "Colombian Narcotics Organizations as Business Enterprises," in U.S. Department of State, Bureau of Research and Intelligence and the Central Intelligence Agency, *Economics of the Narcotics Industry Conference Report* (Washington DC: State Department and CIA, 1994).

20. Olga Sanmartin, "Después de Cali, Qué?" *Revista Diners* (Bogotá: August 1995), p. 15.

21. Sidney Zabludoff, "Colombian Narcotics Organizations."

22. Gilberto Arango Londoño, *Estructura Economica Columbiana* (Bogotá: Colección Profesoras, 1993), p. 93.

23. Dario Betancourt and Martha C. Garcia, *Contrabandistas, Marimberos y Mafiosos* (Bogotá: Tercer Mundo, 1994), p. 98.

24. Francisco Thoumi, "The Economic Impact of Narcotics in Colombia." In Peter Smith, ed., *Drug Policy in the Americas* (Boulder, CO: Westview Press, 1992), p. 62.

25. Francisco Thoumi, "Some Microeconomic Characteristics and Unknowns About the Illegal Drug Industry in Bolivia, Colombia and Peru." Economics of the Narcotics Industry conference report.

26. DANE (Departamiento Administrativo Nacional de Estadisticas), *Colombia Estadistica 1990* (Bogotá: DANE, 1992), p. 422.

27. All data on per capita GNP come from World Bank, *World Tables 1994* (Baltimore: Johns Hopkins University Press, 1994). Constant pesos measure what Colombians' income can buy inside Colombia. Constant dollars measure what Colombians' income can buy on the international (dollar-based) market.

28. Francisco Thoumi, *Economía Política y Narcotráfico* (Bogotá: Tercer Mundo, 1994, p. 260.

29. Clawson interview with Bolivian Planning Minister Samuel Doria Medina, August 26, 1992.

30. David Musto, "Lessons of the First Cocaine Epidemic," *Wall Street Journal,* June 11, 1986, p. A30.

31. Mark Kleiman, *Against Excess: Drug Policy for Results* (New York: Basic Books, 1992), p. 301.

32. James Brooke, "Colombia Becoming an Oil Power in Spite of Itself," *New York Times,* March 20, 1995, p. D2; and Sarita Kendall, "Economic Prospects Closely Linked," *Financial Times,* October 7, 1995, p. 3 of survey on Colombia.

33. Sally Bowen, "Peru's Growth Prospects Prompts Worries," *Financial Times,* June 2, 1995, p. 6; and James Brooke, "Peru: On the Very Fast Track," *New York Times,* January 31, 1995, pp. D1 and D19.

34. Sally Bowen, "Latin America Yields Golden Opportunities," *Financial Times,* February 3, 1995, p. 27; and Kenneth Goulding, "Foreign Mining Companies Pour Money Into Peru," *Financial Times,* March 30, 1995, p. 25.

35. This analysis of Bolivia's growth prospects relies on the articles in the twelve-page supplement on Bolivia in *The Financial Times,* November 9, 1994, as well as on the Economist Intelligence Unit reports.

Chapter 2

1. Miguel García, *Los Barones de la Cocaína* (Mexico City: Planeta, 1991), pp. 59-60.

2. Thoumi, *Economía, Política y Narcotráfico* (Bogotá: Tercer Mundo, 1994), pp. 148-149.

3. Ibid.

4. Maria Duzan, *Death Beat* (New York: Harper-Collins, 1994), p. 198.

5. Anonymous, *Un Narco Se Confiesa y Acusa* (Bogotá: Editorial Colombia Nuestra, 1989), p. 43.

6. Mary Beth Sheridan, "Fed's Big Catch: Man at Center of Cali Cartel." *Miami Herald,* October 5, 1995, p. 24A; "Palomari lo sabia todo," *Cambio-16,* December 11, 1995, p. 15.

7. Bruce Bagley, "Colombia and the War on Drugs," *Foreign Affairs* (Fall 1988), p. 83.

8. Bruce Bullington, "A Smuggler's Paradise: Cocaine Trafficking Through the Bahamas." In Alfred McCoy and Alan Block, eds., *War on Drugs Studies in the Failure of U.S. Drug Policy* (Boulder, CO: Westview Press, 1992), pp. 224-225; Phil Reeves, "Guns for Antígua," *The Independent,* December 6, 1990, p. 8; Tim Weiner, "Colombian Drug Dealer Implicates Haitian Police Chief," *New York Times,* April 22, 1994, p. 7.

9. Rensselaer Lee, *The White Labyrinth: Cocaine and Political Power* (New Brunswick, NJ: Transaction Publishers, 1989), p. 180.

10. Editorial José Marti, *Fin de la Conéxion Cubana* (Bogotá: Editorial Retina, 1989), pp. 23-35. This is a collection of Cuban press articles and documents about the Arnaldo Ochoa Sánchez corruption affair.

11. Ibid.

12. "Confesiones desde el Calabozo," *Semana,* August 25, 1992.

13. Luis M. Cañon, *El Patrón: Vida y Muerte de Pablo Escobar* (Bogotá: Planeta, 1994), p. 232; *Fin de la Conéxion Cubana,* pp. 96-97.

14. Ivan Ivanov, *Mezhdunarodnaya Contrabanda Narkotikov v Byvshei SSSR* (Moscow: Feliks, February 1995), p. 12.

15. Carlos Enrique Bayo, "Arranca la guerra sucia de información," *Cambio-16,* October 9, 1995, p. 13.

16. Peter A. Lupsha, "Transnational Narco-Corruption and Narco-Investment: A Focus on Mexico." *Transnational Organized Crime,* no. 1 (Spring 1995), p. 93.

17. Luis Cañon, personal communication, January 1995.

18. García, *Los Barones de la Cocaína,* p. 58.

19. Ibid., p. 135.

20. Cañon, Luis M., *El Patrón: Vida y Muerte de Pablo Escobar* (Bogotá: Planeta, 1994), pp. 20, 129.
21. Ibid., pp. 21-22.
22. "En La Mitad del Camino," *Medellín Cívico*, March 1994, p. 3.
23. Rensselaer Lee, *The White Labyrinth: Cocaine and Political Power*, p. 136.
24. Ibid., p. 139.
25. Ivan Roberto Duque, "Tenemos derecho a ejercer nuestro dominio politico," *Semana*, August 15, 1989, p. 30; Garcia, *Los Barones dela Cocaína*, p. 104.
26. Betancourt and Garcia, *Contrabandistas, Marimberos y Mafiosos*, p. 298.
27. Rensselaer Lee, "The Cocaine Dilemma in South America." In Donald Mabry, ed., *The Latin American Narcotics Trade and U.S. National Security* (Westport, CT: Greenwood Press, 1989), pp. 69-70.
28. Cañon, *El Patrón*, pp. 233-234.
29. Michael Isikoff, "2 Colombians Held in Missile Scheme," *Washington Post*, May 8, 1990, p. A1.
30. Ken Dermota, "A Hit Man At 11," *Washington Times*, June 11, 1991, p. A1.
31. "Basque Terrorist Group Directed Car Bomb Attack," Hamburg, DPA 1859 GMT, December 8, 1989.
32. Garcia, *Los Barones de la Cocaína*, p. 383.
33. "Un Año Después," *Semana*, November 29, 1994, p. 42.
34. Peter Lupsha, "Nets of Affiliation in the Political Economy of Drug Trafficking and Transnational Crime," in U.S. Department of State, Bureau of Intelligence and Research and the Central Intelligence Agency, *Economics of the Narcotics Industry Conference Report* (Washington DC: State Department and CIA, 1994).
35. Lee interview with Luis Cañon, Bogotá, January 1995.
36. Lupsha, "Nets of Affiliation."
37. Lee interview with Luis Cañon, January 1995.
38. Duzan, *Death Beat*, pp. 137-138.
39. Betancourt and Garcia, *Contrabandistas, Marimberos y Mafiosos*, pp. 180; Alvaro Camacho Guizado and Alvaro Guzman Barney, *Colombia: Ciudad y Violencia* (Bogotá: Foro Nacional, 1990), p. 192.
40. "Possible Cali Cartel–FARC Feud Investigated," *El Espectador*, November 21, 1992, p. 11B.
41. "El Alacran de Venadillo," *El Tiempo*, June 20, 1995, p. 14A.
42. "Wave of Murders in Cali Investigated," *El Tiempo*, August 15, 1994, p. A10.
43. "Police Link Officials to Cali Cartel," *Miami Herald*, April 12, 1995, p. 16A.
44. "Signe en limbo el narcoproyecto," *El Tiempo*, October 14, 1994, p. 6A.
45. Douglas Farah, "Colombia's Culpables," *Washington Post*, August 23, 1995, p. A28.
46. U.S. State Department, "Statement on Certification: Colombia" (Washington DC: State Department, March, 1, 1996).

Chapter 3

1. Dr. Lee performed much of the research for this chapter while under contract to the Police Executive Research Forum in 1993-1994.
2. Phil Williams, "Transnational Criminal Organizations: Strategic Alliances," *The Washington Quarterly*, vol. 18, no. 1 (Winter 1995), p. 57.

3. Lee interview with Greg Passic, DEA Headquarters, Pentagon City, October 18, 1993.

4. Passic interview and author telephone interview with DEA, Rome, October 19, 1994.

5. Carlos Gosch, "Zapatos Calientes," *La Prensa,* March 29, 1994, p. 13.

6. "Droga: Il nuova impero del male. Una guerra globale e planetaria," conference proceedings, Rome, March 12, 1992, p. 4.

7. *Request from Italy Pursuant to the Treaty Between the United States and the Italian Republic in Criminal Matters in the Matter of Aponte et. al.,* Hearings, U.S. District Court, Washington, D.C., July 16, 1992 through July 27, 1992, pp. 49, 378, 385-390. (Hereafter: *Request from Italy.*)

8. Ibid., pp. 385-386; Attorney's Office at the Law Court of Palermo, *Request for Extradition to Italy of Giancarlo Formichi-Moglia,* N48G5/91 N.C., p. 9. (Hereafter: *Extradition Request.*)

9. Alan Cowell, "Italy Finds Break in Mafia's Crimes," *New York Times,* October 4, 1992, p. 7.

10. Lee interviews with DEA officials, Rome, October 18, 20, and 28, 1993; Chief Prosecutor's Office, Palermo, October 2 , 1993; DEA Pentagon City, October 14, 1994. Knowledgeable observers cite the Sicilian mafia's unwillingness to transfer cocaine funds through the Italian banking system as a reason for repatriation delays.

11. Lee interview with DEA officials, Rome, October 18, 1993. (Hereafter: DEA interview.)

12. Lee interview with Alessandro Pansa of the Servizio Centrale Operativo, Rome, October 28, 1993 (Hereafter: Pansa interview); and Maurizio Martinelli, "Bettein Martens. Bella i Pentita," *Il Tempo,* October 28, 1992, p. 6.

13. "Una per una. Ecco le 15 Societa Sequestrate," *L' Unita,* September 29, 1992; Enrico Fierro, "Colpo al Cuore della Coca Connection," *L' Unita,* September 29, 1992; and author interviews with DEA, Rome, October 18 and October 28, 1993.

14. Martinelli, "Bettein Martens. Bello i Pentita."

15. Ibid.; and DEA interview.

16. See, for example, Massimo Martinelli "Colpo al Cuore del Narcotraffico," *Il Messagero,* September 29, 1992, p. 2; and Aldo De Luca, "Coca: Il Grande Sbarco in Europa," *Il Messagero,* September 29, 1992, p. 3.

17. DEA interview; and Giuseppe D'Avanzo, "Alla Corde in re della Droga," *La Republica,* September 29, 1992, p. 6.

18. DEA, "Summary of Pickups from Bettein Martens," Ms., September 1992; and DEA interview.

19. D'Avanzo, "Alla Corde in re della Droga;" author telephone interview with Claire Sterling, November 7, 1993; author interviews with DEA officials in Washington, D.C., November 22-24, 1993. (Hereafter: Washington interviews.)

20. Washington interviews.

21. *Request from Italy,* pp. 284-324. (Testimony of Joseph Cuffaro, an associate of John Galatolo's).

22. Lee interview with Nitto Palma and Piero Grasso, Direzione Nazionale Anti-Mafia. Rome, October 19, 1993 (hereafter: Palma and Grasso interview); DEA interview; Robert Graham, "A Message from the Mafia," *Financial Times,* July 7, 1992, p. 2; Alison Jamieson, "Mafia and Institutional Power in Italy," *International Relations* (London: April 1994), pp. 18-19; and "Itinerario de la caida de un capo," *El Tiempo,* March 9, 1993, p. 12B.

23. Jamieson, "Mafia and Institutional Power," p. 23.

24. Pansa interview.

25. Lee interview with DEA officials, Rome, October 20, 1993.

26. Lee interviews with DEA officials, Rome, October 18, 20, and 28, 1993; Paolo Soldini, *L'Unita*, April 21, 1992, p. 7; Colombian National Police, *Anti-Narcotics Police Activities Balance 1992*, p. 15; and "Catturati i Cuntrera. Boss del Riciclaggio," *Avanti*, September 13, 1993, p. 5.

27. DEA interview; and Lee interview with Giusto Schiacchitano (former Palermo magistrate) at the Foreign Ministry, Rome, October 18, 1993.

28. Pansa interview; Lee interview with Italian police representative at the Italian Embassy, Bogotá, Colombia, November 13, 1993 (Hereafter: Italian interview, Bogotá); and "Caen 4 Colombianos Acusados de Narcotráfico," *El Tiempo*, April 11, 1993, p. 72.

29. Pansa interview and DEA interview.

30. Lee interview with U.S. narcotics experts in Bogotá, November 9, 1993.

31. *Request from Italy*, pp. 1031-1033.

32. Ibid., p. 199.

33. U.S. Department of State, *International Narcotics Control Strategy Report 1996* (Washington, DC: Government Printing Office, March 1996), p. 108.

34. Edgar Torres, "Heroína, Otro pasa de la mafia Colombiana," *El Tiempo*, October 18, 1992, pp. 1A, 3A.

35. Ernesto Savona, "Money Laundering vs. Italian Legislation," paper prepared for the issue on cross-border crime of the European Journal on Criminal Policy and Research, June 1993, pp. 7-8.

36. Lee interview with DEA officials in Rome, October 20, 1993; and "A State Within a State," *Economist* (April 29, 1993), pp. 21-22.

37. Lee interview with Giancarlo Casselli and other Palermo prosecutors, Palermo, October 27, 1993. (Hereafter: Casselli interview.)

38. Lee interview with Salvatore Guglielmino, the Servizio Centrale Operativo, Rome, October 22, 1993; and *Extradition Request*, pp. 6-10.

39. See, for example, Luca D'Alessandro, "Casi Abbiamo Sconfitto il rei del Narcos." *Il Tempo*, September 30, 1993, p. 7.

40. D'Avanzo, "Alla Corde in re de la Droga"; and Martinelli, "Colpo al Cuore del Narcotráfico."

41. Ibid.; and Palma and Grasso interview.

42. Casselli interview; and Lee interview with Pietro Soggiu of the Comitato por Servizi Anti-Droga in Rome, October 18, 1993.

43. DEA interview.

44. Italian interview, Bogotá.

45. Washington interviews.

46. Claire Sterling, *Thieves' World* (New York: Simon and Schuster, 1994), pp. 134-135.

47. See the excellent discussion in Phil Williams, "Transnational Criminal Organizations and Strategic Alliances," *The Washington Quarterly* (Fall 1992), pp. 31-32.

48. R. W. Lee and Scott MacDonald, "Drugs in the East," *Foreign Policy*, no. 90 (Spring 1993), p. 100.

49. Ivan Ivanov, *Mezbdonarodnaya Kontrabanda Narkotikov v Byushei SSSR*. (Moscow: Feliks, February 1995), p. 40.

Chapter 4

1. "No soy tan ingenuo," *Semana*, October 18, 1994, pp. 26-27.
2. Ivan Noguera "No habra uno nuevo narcoguerra: Botero," *El Tiempo*, September 2, 1994, p. 1A.
3. "De Grieff Letter to Kerry," *El Tiempo*, April 13, 1994, pp. 1A, 3A.
4. "Colombia's Other Gangsters," *Economist* (March 25, 1995), p. 3.
5. "ELN Leader Vows to Contain Political Violence," *Voz*, September 27, 1990, p. 3.
6. Douglas Farah, "New Focus: Political Violence," *Washington Post*, January 15, 1996, p. A22.
7. Douglas Farah, "Pardons for Drug Lords Proposed in Colombia," *Washington Post*, March 24, 1991, p. A24.
8. Telephone interviews in July 1991 with officials of the Colombian Embassy in Washington, D.C.; Farah, "Pardons for Drug Lords"; "Quintín Lamé Rebels Sign Peace Agreement" (in Spanish), Bogotá Inravision, Television Cadena. 1736 GMT, May 31, 1991; and James Brooke, "With Buyouts for Rebels, Colombia Buys Peace," *New York Times*, July 1, 1994, p. A4.
9. Sidney Zabludoff, "Colombian Narcotics Organizations as Business Enterprises," in U.S. Department of State Bureau of Intelligence and Research and the Central Intelligence Agency, *Economics of the Narcotics Industry Conference Report* (Washington D.C.: State Department and CIA, 1994).
10. "La bomba del diálogo," *Semana*, October 10, 1989, p. 25.
11. Gilberto Rodriguez Orejuela, unpublished letter to President Cesar Gaviria, January 20, 1994.
12. David van Biema, "Sweet, Sweet Surrender," *Time*, November 7, 1994, p. 42.
13. "Letter to Juan Lozano," *El Tiempo*, November 7, 1994, p. A6.
14. David van Biema, "Sweet, Sweet Surrender."
15. Mary Cooper, *The Business of Drugs* (Washington DC: Congressional Quarterly, 1990), p. 18; and "Problems with Seized Property Outlined," *El Espectador*, February 16, 1991, p. 11A.
16. U.S. Drug Enforcement Administration (DEA), *U.S. Drug Threat Assessment: 1993* (Washington DC: DEA, September 1993), p. 4; U.S. Agency for International Development (USAID), *Coca Prices: April 1988-March 1991* (La Paz: USAID, 1991); and United Nations Development Program (UNDP), *Peru: Prices of Coca and Other Crops* (Tingo Maria: UNDP, April 1991).
17. "El enemigo de Escobar," *Semana*, April 16, 1991, pp. 14-22.
18. "La gran encuesta," *Semana*, January 8, 1991, p. 29; "Sobre amnistía a los narcos," *Semana*, January 8, 1991, p. 13; Carlos Arrieta et al., *Narcotráfico en Colombia: Dimensiones Políticas, Economicas, Juridicas, e Internacionales* (Bogotá: Tercer Mundo, 1990), p. 358.
19. "Problems with seized drug property outlined," *El Espectador*, February 16, 1991, p. 11A; U.S. House of Representatives, Committee on Government Operations, *Stopping the Flood of Cocaine with Operation Snowcap: Is It Working?* (Washington, DC: Government Printing Office, 1990), p. 79.
20. "Communique Announces Extraditables Disbandment," *El Tiempo*, July 4, 1991, pp. 1, 14A.

21. For an earlier discussion of Colombia's negotiations with the Medellín cartel see R. W. Lee, "Colombia's Cocaine Syndicates," in Alfred McCoy and Alan Block, eds., *War on Drugs: Studies in the Failure of U.S. Narcotics Policy* (Boulder, CO: Westview Press, 1992), pp. 111-120.

22. "Texto de la Propuesta de Narcotraficantes," *El Tiempo,* July 7, 1984, pp. 1A, 11C.

23. "Political Parties Reject Dialogue," *El Tiempo,* July 6, 1984, p. 8A.

24. "Diálogo: Que ha pasado," *Semana,* October 17, 1989, pp. 27-30; "No habra diálogo con los narcotraficantes," *El Siglo,* July 20, 1984, p. 1.

25. Bruce Bagley, "Colombia and the War Against Drugs," *Foreign Affairs,* vol. 67, no. 1 (Fall 1988), pp. 82-83.

26. "La bomba del diálogo," p. 26.

27. Ibid., pp. 28-29.

28. Jorge Tellez Mendoza and Juan Alvaro Castellanos Diaz, *Los Hilos de Poder* (Bogotá: Planeta, 1992), p. 212.

29. U.S. House of Representatives, *Stopping the Flood of Cocaine,* pp. 73-74.

30. "Letter to Juan Lozano," *El Tiempo,* November 7, 1994, p. A6.

31. Cañon, *El Patrón,* p. 187.

32. Mendoza and Castellanos, *Los Hilos de Poder,* pp. 213-215.

33. Miguel Garcia, *Los Barones de la Cocaína* (Mexico City: Planeta, 1991), p. 328.

34. Ibid., p. 332.

35. Foreign Broadcast Information Service, "Text of Communiqué Issued by the Extraditables," *Daily Report: Latin America,* January 18, 1990. From Bogotá Inravision, Cadena 1, January 17, 1990. For a discussion of the Notables' role, see: "¿Cumplirá Pablo Escobar?" *Semana,* January 23, 1990, pp. 22-27.

36. Mendoza and Castellanos, *Los Hilos de Poder,* pp. 70-71.

37. Garcia, *Los Barones de la Cocaína,* pp. 337-338.

38. Ibid., p. 343.

39. "Donde esto el piloto," *Semana.* April 3, 1990, pp. 25-26.

40. Cañon, *El Patrón,* p. 224.

41. "Gaviria no quiere asumir compromisos," *Semana.* April 17, 1990, p. 31; Duzan, *Death Beat,* p. 261; and Cañon, *El Patrón,* p. 224.

42. Lee interview with Rodrigo Lloreda Caicedo, Bogotá, February 22, 1991; "Cual es su propuesto de solucionar al problema del narcotráfico," *El Tiempo,* May 23, 1990, p. 3A; and Lloreda's Views on Narcoterrorism, Debt," *El Tiempo* March 7, 1990, pp. 1A, 8A.

43. Foreign Broadcasting Information Service, "Gaviria Gives News Conference on Drug Decree," *Daily Report: Latin America,* September 10, 1990, from Bogotá Radio Cadena Nacional, O136 GMAT, September 10, 1990.

44. "Memorandum," *El Tiempo,* November 23, 1990, p. 8A. On the Notables, see: "Sigue la espera," *Semana,* November 6, 1990, p. 38.

45. "Communicado de Los Extraditables," *El Tiempo,* November 24, 1990, p. 8A.

46. Cited in "Diálogo: Que ha pasado," p. 28.

47. Ibid., p. 26.

48. Twig Mowatt, "Colombian Kingpins May Surrender: Hundreds in Cartel Offer Deal." *USA Today,* November 26, 1990, p. 4A; Henry Goethels, "Medellín Cartel Offer Poses Dilemma, *The Times of the Americas,* December 12, 1990, p. 14.

49. Cecelia Rodriguez, "Colombians Forced to Bargain with the Devil," *Wall Street Journal,* February 1, 1991, p. A11.

50. Douglas Farah, "Sweet Surrender in Colombia," *Washington Post,* June 10, 1991, p. A1; "El mundo al reves," *Semana,* November 29, 1994, p. 48; and Cañon, *El Patrón,* p. 301.

51. James Brooks, "Drug Baron's Prison Has Every Comfort: Even Mom and TV," *New York Times,* June 22, 1991, p. 1; Garcia, *Los Barones de la Cocaína,* p. 450.

52. "La fórmula Gaviria," *Semana,* July 25, 1991, pp. 35-42.

53. "Mi sometimiento no dependa de la extradición: Escobar," *El Tiempo,* June 20, 1991, p. 11A.

54. Bogotá Inravision Television, Cadena 1, August 3, 1992.

55. Cañon, *El Patrón,* pp. 25, 326.

56. Ibid., p. 40.

57. Ibid., p. 372.

58. Bogotá Inravision Television, Cadena 1, January 18, 1993.

59. Bogotá Inravision Television, Cadena 1, February 16, 1993.

60. Bogotá Inravision Television, Cadena 4, October 12, 1994; Garcia, *Los Barones de la Cocaína,* p. 268.

61. "Reformas al codigo de procedimiento penal," *Legislación Economica* (Bogotá: Republica de Colombia, December 15, 1993), pp. 776-777; Ministerio de Justicia. "Decreto numero 264 de 1993." Bogotá, February 5, 1993; and María Teresa Herrán, *El Fiscal. La Dualidad del Imagen* (Bogotá: Tercer Mundo, 1994), p. 90.

62. "Cartels Send Letters to Congress Offering Surrender," *El Tiempo,* December 17, 1993, p. 7; "¿Se entrega Gilberto Rodriguez?" *Semana,* November 1, 1993, pp. 38-43.

63. Rodriguez, unpublished letter.

64. "De Grieff y el cartel de Cali," *La Prensa,* October 11, 1994, p. 12.

65. "De Grieff Letter to Gaviria," *El Tiempo,* April 6, 1994, pp. 1A, 8A.

66. "War Secrets," *Semana,* March 15, 1994, pp. 32-34.

67. "No soy tan ingenuo," *Semana,* October 18, 1994, pp. 26-27.

68. "Arranco lo entrega," *Semana,* February 15, 1994, pp. 30-33.

69. Quoted in Herrán, *El Fiscal,* p. 275.

70. "Arrieta Calls on De Grieff to Stop Making Isolated Decisions," *El Tiempo,* April 9, 1994, p. 5A.

71. Douglas Farah, "U.S. Teamwork with Colombia Against Drugs Becoming Unstuck," *Washington Post,* June 12, 1994, p. A29.

72. John Kerry, "Law Enforcement a Kingpin Could Love," *Washington Post,* April 6, 1994, p. A19.

73. Lee interview with Gustavo de Grieff, June 14, 1994.

74. David Arizmendi, telephone interview with Colombian Attorney General Carlos Arrieta, Bogotá Emisorias Caracol, April 8, 1994; and Herrán, *El Fiscal,* p. 81.

75. "De Grieff Defends Surrender Policy," *El Tiempo,* August 3, 1994, pp. 1A, 8A; Herrán, *El Fiscal,* p. 268; and "De Grieff Letter to Kerry."

76. David van Biema, "Sweet, Sweet Surrender,"

77. 104th Congress, first session. Bill S. 681, "To Provide for the Imposition of Sanctions Against Colombia with Respect to Illegal Drugs and Drug Trafficking," April 5, 1995, pp. 2-3.

78. Tatiana Paola Escarraga, "El Confesor," *Cambio 16,* June 26, 1995, pp. 18-20.

79. "Y cayo la tentación," *El Tiempo,* June 25, 1995, p. 3A.

80. Ken Dermota, "Defense Minister Resigns in Colombia," *Washington Times,* August 3, 1995, p. A17.

81. "Soy narco pero decente," *Cambio 16,* November 21, 1994, pp. 14-19.
82. "La paz del país es mi reto histórico," *El Tiempo,* August 8, 1990, p. 8A.
83. "Letter to Juan Lozano."
84. "Texto de la Propuesta de Narcotraficantes."
85. Rensselaer Lee, "Making the Most of Colombia's Drug Negotiations," *Orbis,* vol. 35, no. 2 (Spring 1991), pp. 247-248.

Chapter 5

1. Sergio Uribe and Sara Mestre estimate those three departments have 65,500 hectares of coca out of a national total of 80,800. "El Desarrollo Alternativo en Colombia," paper prepared for United Nations Drug Control Program (UNDCP), November 1994. A fourth department, Putumayo, with 2,400 hectares of coca, has also been a center of coca-producing activity.

2. Elena Alvarez, "Coca Production in Peru," in Peter Smith, ed., *Drug Policy in the Americas* (Boulder, CO: Westview Press, 1992), p. 76.

3. Alberto Rivera, *Diagnostico Socio-economico de la Población del Chapare* (Cochabamba: PDAR, 1990); and James Jones, *Farmer Perspectives on the Economics and Sociology of Coca Production in the Chapare* (Binghamton, NY: Institute for Development Anthropology, Working Paper 77, January 1991).

4. Jones, *Farmer Perspectives.*

5. Clawson interview with Luis Osihuelo, president of Unapega, December 1994.

6. Rivera, *Diagnostico Socio-economico.*

7. The discussion of coca in Peru draws heavily on USAID Peru, *Project Paper: Alternative Development Project* (Lima: USAID, 1995); and Tito Hernández, "El Enfoque Competitivo en el Marco del Control de Cultivos Ilícitos, Estrategías y Logros del Program UNDCP-OSP/PNUD en las Regiones del Huallaga, Pachitea y Ucuyali" (Lima: UNDCP, October 1994).

8. USAID Peru, *Project Paper,* p 29.

9. National Narcotics Intelligence Consumers Committee (NNICC), *The NNICC Report 1993* (Washington, DC: DEA, August 1994), p. 16.

10. For a scholarly account of the limited role coca has played in Andean life and the vigorous opposition to it in the Andes, see Joseph Gagliano, *Coca Prohibition in Peru: The Historical Debates* (Tucson: University of Arizona Press, 1994). For the contrary view, see the classic work in praise of coca, W. Golden Mortimer, *History of Coca: The Divine Plant of the Incas* (San Francisco: And/Or Press, 1974) (originally published 1901), or the more recent apologia by Andrew Weil, "The New Politics of Coca," *The New Yorker,* May 15, 1995.

11. The 1961 Single Convention on Narcotics Drugs banned all uses of coca, including for chewing and tea, except when the alkaloids are removed, as in Coca-Cola. The World Health Organization (WHO) is empowered by the convention to modify its prohibitions if a product is shown to have nutritional or therapeutic value, but it has not done so with respect to any coca product. (Letter of WHO director general Nakajima to the Peruvian minister of health, March 20, 1992). Therefore, all countries belonging to the 1961 convention have committed themselves to making coca and all its products illegal; in practice, however, many countries have not done so.

12. Baldomero Caceres Santa Maria, "La Empresa Nacional de la Coca y el Narcotráfico," paper distributed by government of Peru, Minister of Interior Executive Office for the Control of Drugs, 1993. According to Caceres, the 17,862 hectares registered as legal under law 22095 of 1978 are largely in Cuzco Department (41 percent) in southern Peru and in Huanuco and San Martin departments surrounding the Upper Huallaga Valley (36 percent). However, USAID/Peru, in its *Project Paper*, states that there are 12,000 legal hectares in Cuzco Department, while agreeing with Caceres that there are that about 18,000 legal hectares in all; USAID also says the registrations for legal coca in the Huallaga were cancelled in the early 1980s. ENACO buys 240 kilograms per hectare, when the U.S. government estimated the average yield in 1994 was 1,520.

13. Clawson interview with Sherman Hinson, U.S. Embassy, Lima, February 23, 1996.

14. U.S. DEA Intelligence Division, *Operation Breakthrough: Coca Cultivation and Cocaine Base Production in Bolivia*, (Washington, DC: DEA, July 1994), p. 8.

15. Uribe and Mestre, "El Desarrollo Alternativo en Colombia," pp. 14 and 24.

16. Fernando Rospigliosi and Jimmy Torres, "Huallaga ila guerra oculta," *Caretas*, July 1, 1993, p. 38. Many articles appeared on this in the Peruvian press; for example, Liz Mineo, "Palma pampa: nuevo centro del narcotráfico," *Expreso*, August 25, 1993, p. A14 and Liz Mineo, "Narcotráfico se desplaza," *Expreso*, September 5, 1993, p. A14.

17. Clawson interviews with officials of UNDCP, USAID, the Ministry of Agriculture, the antinarcotics police (DINANDRO), and the CORAH Upper Huallaga antinarcotics agency, November 1994.

18. Clawson interviews with Merrit Broady, USAID, Lima, and Tito Hernández, technical director of the UNDCP Peru project in the Huallaga, February 1996.

19. Eduardo Bedoya Garland, "Intensification and Degradation in the Agricultural Systems of the Peruvian Upper Jungle: The Upper Huallaga Case." In Peter Little and Michael Horowitz, eds. *Lands at Risk in the Third World* (Boulder, CO: Westview Press, 1987).

20. Kenneth Eubanks, "Cochabamba Regional Development Project: Analysis and Recommendations," report for USAID, August 1991, pp. 7, 11.

21. Jones, *Farmer Perspectives*, p. 61.

22. Iban de Rementeria, *Sustitucion de Cultivos de Coca: Acciones y Estrategia* (Lima: Comision Andina de Juristas, 1989), p. 15; author interview with Marion Ford, USAID, Cochabamba.

23. The average for 1987, 1990, and 1993 data for the PEAH project area, as given in Institute Nacional de Estadísticas de Informática, *Peru: Compendio de Estadisticas de Producción y Consumo de Drogas 1980-93* (Lima: Direccíon Nacional de Estadísticas Básicas, February 1994).

24. Lawrence Jay Speer, "Legal, illegal firms share Peru jungle," *Washington Times,* July 13, 1993, p. A12.

25. "The Guerrillas' Big Business," *Semana,* July 7, 1992, pp. 26-32.

26. Bruce Bagley, "Sustainability of Coca Eradication and Crop Substitution," photocopy, February 1993, p 3.

27. Liz Mineo, "While Policies Fail, Coca Prospers," Foreign Broadcast Information Service–Latin America, January 12, 1993, p. 53 (translated from *Expreso,* December 25, 1992, p. A12).

28. Clawson interviews with pineapple farmers in the Chapare, December 1994.

29. Clawson interview with Jorge Gutierrez Andrade, Regional Alternative Development Project (PDAR), Cochabamba.

30. *NNICC Report 1993,* p. 18.

31. World Bank, *Peru: Agricultural Policies for Economic Efficiency* (Washington, DC: World Bank, 1992), p. 69.

32. The economics of processing in the early 1990s are discussed in R.W. Lee and Patrick Clawson, *Crop Substitution in the Andes* (Washington, DC; Office of National Drug Control Policy, 1993), pp. 38-41. Data relating to 1994 are found in USAID, *Bolivia's Coca Sub-Economy 1994,* tables 9 and 10.

33. U.S. Department of State, *International Narcotics Strategy Report (INCSR) 1996* (Washington, DC: Government Printing Office, Publication 10246, 1996), p. 102. Similar sentiments were cited by Tito Hernández, UNDP-Lima, Clawson interview, February 20, 1996.

34. The higher estimate is from Tito Hernández, "El Enfoque Competitivo," p. 18. The lower estimate is from Eric Rosenquist, U.S. Department of Agriculture, "Narcotics and Agricultural Economics," in U.S. Department of State, Bureau of Intelligence and Research and the Central Intelligence Agency, *Economics of the Narcotics Industry Conference Report* (Washington DC: State Department and CIA, 1994).

35. Rosenquist, describes the fungus. The quote about the effect on legal crops is from "Uchiza Agoniza," *Caretas,* July 8, 1993, pp. 46-49.

36. Hernández, "El Enfoque Competitivo," p. 18.

37. Don Podesta, "Tenacity in Peru's Coca Zone: A Bridge Bypassing Traffickers," *Washington Post,* September 1, 1993, pp. A25 and A27; and author interview with Merritt Broady, USAID, Lima, November 1994.

38. U.S. Agency for International Development (USAID), Krishna Kumar, team leader, *A Review of AID's Narcotic Control Development Assistance Program* (Washington, DC: USAID, 1986), pp 38-39.

39. Lee interview with Jukka Pietkainen, UNDCP advisor, Pepayan, February 1993.

40. USAID, *Andean Counter-Drug Initiative: Annual Report 1992* (Washington, DC: USAID, 1993), p. 3.

41. USAID, Kumar, *A Review,* p. E-4.

42. Jones, *Farmer Perspectives,* pp. 1-12, has scathing comments about the quality of the personnel involved on both the U.S. and the Bolivian side. See also Don Botwick, Joseph Dorsey, and James Jones, *Evaluation of the Chapare Regional Development Project* (Washington, DC: USAID, 1990), which is critical of the project's design and execution.

43. USAID, *Andean Counter-Drug Initiative,* p. 9; and, for the next data, "Bolivia Alternative Development Programs," prepared for CORDEP by DAI, February 1995.

44. The next two paragraphs are based on extensive Clawson discussions with USAID personnel in La Paz (including those based in Cochabamba), November 1994, and interviews with farmers in the Chapare, December 1994. Harry Peacock of USAID was responsible for the Chapare interviews, for which we are very grateful.

45. Clawson interviews in the Chapare, December 1994. Inflation over the two years was less than 20 percent.

46. The milk plant was functioning at a level well below design in late 1994. Its history is recounted in Leida Rijnhout and Joep Oomen, *"Mala Leche": Una historia amarga de desarrollo en el Chapare* (La Paz: CEDOIN, 1994).

47. Information on UNDCP activities in Peru from Clawson interviews with Heinrich Pichler, UNDCP director in Lima, and Tito Hernández, December 1994.

48. The information on other donors comes from USAID Peru; *Project Paper,* pp. 33-34; U.S. Department of State, INCSR 1996, p. 101; and Clawson interview with Merritt Broady.

49. USAID, "Alternative Development Project—Peru," photocopy, April 1995.

50. Uribe and Mestre, "El Desarrollo Alternativo."

51. Quotes from the San Antonio summit from Michael Isikoff, "Bush, Latin Leaders Agree to Stepped-up Drug Fight," *Washington Post,* February 28, 1992, p. A2, and Joseph Treaster, "On Days of Drug Summit, U.S. Seems Concerned," *New York Times,* February 29, 1992, p. 41.

Chapter 6

1. Peter Lupsha, "Narco-Investment in Domestic Economies. Mexico: An Example of Narco Democracy?" in U.S. Department of State, Bureau of Intelligence and Research and the Central Intelligence Agency, *Economics of the Narcotics Industry Conference Report* (Washington DC. State Department and CIA, 1994), p. 2; and Peter Lupsha, personal communication, June 6, 1995.

2. See, for example, Fernando Cortes. *Rodriguez Gacha: El Mejicano* (Bogotá: Intermedio, 1993),p. 13 and Ciro Krauthausen and Luis Fernando Sarmiento, *Cocaína y Co.* (Bogotá: Tercer Mundo, 1991), p. 81.

3. "Report Says Valle Drug Lords Have Consolidated Power; Financed Political Leaders," *El Tiempo,* May 23, 1994, pp. 1, 11A.

4. "Por que no cae Escobar," *Semana,* October 19, 1993, pp. 44-47.

5. Jorge Teller Mendoza and Juan Alvaro Castellanos Diaz, *Los Hilos de Poder,* (Bogotá: Planeta, 1992) p. 182.

6. Maria Duzan, *Death Beat* (New York: Harper-Collins, 1994), p. 138.

7. "El Golpe,"*Semana,* April 25, 1995, p. 39.

8. Carlos Enrique Bayo, "Arranca la guerra sucia de información," *Cambio-16,* October 9, 1995, p. 13.

9. Marc Chernik, "Colombia's Fault Lines," *Current History,* Vol. 95, No. 598 (February 1996), pp. 76-77. "More Compromising Tapes Revealed," *El Siglo,* August 10, 1995, p. 14.

10. Steven Gutkin, "DEA Agent Attacks Colombia as a Narcodemocracy," *Washington Post,* October 1, 1994, pp. A1, A18.

11. "La Indigatoria de Santiago Medina," *El Tiempo,* August 3, 1995, pp. 8A, 9A.

12. "Pallomari lo sabia todo," *Cambio-16,* December 11, 1995, pp. 12-13.

13. "Samper on Accusations Committee Decision," Panama City Telemetro Television, 2325 GMT, December 15, 1995.

14. "Lo que dijo Botero. Lo que contestó el President," *Cromos,* January 29, 1996, p. 25.

15. "Samper fue el la idea de acudir a los narcos," *El Tiempo,* January 27, 1996, p. 3A.

16. Enrique Santos Calderón, "Debe irse (contraescape)," *El Tiempo,* January 25, 1996, p. 2A.

17. "Descenso Peligroso," *Semana,* January 30, 1996, pp. 50-51.

18. Mexico City, NOTIMEX 0449 GMT, January 12, 1996.

19. Christopher Wren, "Clinton Declares that Colombia Has Failed to Curb Drug Trade," *New York Times*, March 2, 1996, p. 5; José de Cordoba and Carla Anne Robbins, "U.S. Rebuke Puts Colombia's Samper in the Hot Seat." *The Wall Street Journal*, March 4, 1996, p. A11.

20. "En La Mira de Lehder," *Semana*, November 26, 1991, p. 35.

21. "El diario oculto de Alberto Giraldo," *El Tiempo*, June 4, 1995, p. 24A.

22. "El Show de Helms," *Semana*, April 4, 1995, p. 42.

23. On ACDEGAM see Carlos Medina Gallego, *Autodefensas, Paramilitares y Narcotráfico en Colombia* (Bogotá: Editorial Documentos Periodisticos, 1990) pp. 219-293.

24. Letter of Gilberto Rodriguez to President Cesar Gaviria. Lee interview with Gustavo de Grieff, Bogota, June 14, 1994.

Chapter 7

1. Rensselaer Lee, "Why The United States Cannot Stop South American Cocaine," *Orbis* (Fall, 1988), p. 509.

2. "Narcoguerilla," *Semana*, September 27, 1994, p. 28; Gordon McCormick, *The Shining Path and the Future of Peru*. (Santa Monica, CA: RAND, March 1990), p. 22.

3. Miller Rubio, "National Police Report Examines Drug Trade," *El Tiempo*, December 19, 1994, p. 27A.

4. Michael Brown and Eduardo Fernandez, *War of Shadows: The Struggle for Utopia in the Peruvian Amazon* (Berkeley, CA: University of California Press, 1991), p. 203; José Gonzáles, "Guerrillas and Coca in the Upper Huallaga Valley," in David Scott Palmer, ed., *Shining Path of Peru*, 2nd ed. (New York: St. Martin's Press, 1994), p. 139; Simon Strong, *Shining Path* (New York:Times Books, 1992), pp. 114-115.

5. Displayed at a news conference of the Counterterrorism Directorate (DINCOTE); see also "Policía confirma conexí narcotráfico-terror," *El Comercio*, January 28, 1994, p. A17.

6. "MRTA Reportedly Protecting Foreign, Domestic Drug Firms," *Expreso*, May 18, 1994, p. A11.

7. Carlos Aponte, "Coca Leaders Reportedly Paid $200 Million to Shining Path Leader," Foreign Braodcast Information Service–Latin America (FBIS-LAT), May 18, 1994, p. 45 (translated from *Expreso*, May 6, 1994, p. A6). The next sentence relies on Enrique Obando, "Narcotráfico y terror: esas viejos conocidos," *Expreso*, November 20, 1994, p. A2.

8. Peter Lupsha, "Nets of Affiliation in the Political Economy of Drug Trafficking and Transnational Crime," in U.S. Department of State, Bureau of Intelligence and Research and the Central Intelligence Agency, *Economics of the Narcotics Industry Conference Report* (Washington DC: State Department and CIA, 1994).

9. "Con sofisticados equipos terroristas orientan a avionetas de narcotraficantes," *El Comercio*, June 29, 1991, p. A12; and McCormick, *Shining Path and the Future of Peru*, p. 22.

10. USAID, "The Upper Huallaga Valley" (Lima: USAID, 1991), p. 3; and Jim Laity, "The Coca Economy in the Upper Huallaga" (Lima: USAID, 1989), p. 15.

11. "Campesinos desertan de Sendero," *La Republica*, October 30, 1989, p. 10.

12. Authors' interviews with General Arciniega, April 1991; text of his July 13, 1990 speech, "Las nuevas amenazas y sus respuestas en el caso de la subversion y el narcotráfico"; and *Sí*, September 30, 1990.

13. Authors' interview at the Institute of Liberty and Democracy, October 1991.
14. Rosario Mayorga, "Army Involvement in Drug Trafficking Viewed," *La Republica*, November 27, 1994, pp. 23-25.
15. Clawson interview with Merrit Broady, USAID Lima, February 23, 1995.
16. Miguel Gutiérrez, "El negocio que se fue al carajo," *La Republica*, February 11, 1996, pp. 8-13.
17. Lee interview with former M-19 guerrilla, January 1995; Alfredo Rangel Suarez, "Glifosato para la paz," *El Tiempo*, February 15, 1995, p. 3A.
18. "Narcoguerrilla," *Semana*, September 27, 1994, p. 27.
19. Dario Betancourt and Martha Garcia, *Contrabandistas, Marimberos y Mafiosos*, (Bogotá: Tercer Mundo, 1994), pp. 124-125.
20. Douglas Farah, "Cartel Enforcer Linked to Massacre," *Washington Post*, May 6, 1990, p. A2.
21. Cited in Carlos Medina Gallego, *Autodefensas, Paramilitares y Narcotráfico En Colombia*, (Bogotá: Editorial Documentos Periodisticos, 1990), p. 143.
22. Ibid., p. 173.
23. Miguel Garcia, *Los Barones de la Cocaína* (Mexico City: Planeta, 1991), p. 104.
24. Maria Duzan, *Death Beat* (New York: Harper-Collins, 1994), p. 118.
25. Ibid., pp. 98, 118.
26. Gallego, *Autodefensas, Paramilitares y Narcotráfico En Colombia*, p. 223.
27. Garcia, *Los Barones de la Cocaína*, p. 141.
28. "Morena se Destapa," *Semana*, August 15, 1989, p. 22-23.
29. Ivan Roberto Duque, "Tenemos derecho a ejercer nuestro dominio politico," Semana, August 15, 1989, p. 30; ibid., p. 30.
30. Duzan, *Death Beat*, p 117.
31. Gallega, *Autodefensas, Paramilitares y Narcotráfico En Colombia*, p. 365.
32. "Una Cura en Infierno," *Semana*, October 11, 1994, pp. 40-41.
33. Duzan, *Death Beat*, p 105.
34. "Cuestion de Negocios," *Semana*, June 20, 1995, p. 39.

Chapter 8

1. James Brooke, "Drug Baron's Jailing Heartens Colombia," *New York Times*, June 21, 1991, p. A8.
2. Francisco Thoumi, "The Economic Impact of Narcotics in Colombia," in Peter Smith, ed., *Drug Policy in the Americas* (Boulder, CO: Westview Press, 1992), pp. 68-70.
3. Douglas Farah, "Raiding the World's Cocaine Capital," *Washington Post*, June 10, 1995, p. A14. The information about Peru and Bolivia come from U.S. Department of State, International *Narcotics Control Strategy Report (INCSR)* (Washington DC: Government Printing Office Publication, 1995).
4. Paul Haven, "Death Squads, Armed Groups Kill with Impurity in Medellín," *Washington Times*, May 21, 1995, p. A9.
5. U.S. Department of State, *Narcotics: The Environmental Consequences*, pamphlet (transparently the product of the CIA), 1992.
6. Buenaventura Marcelo, "Victims of the Drug Trade: Peru's Jungle Rivers," in Congressional Research Service, *Cocaine Production, Eradication, and the Environment:*

Policy, Impact, and Options (Washington, DC: Government Printing Office, 1990), pp. 143-148.

7. Marc Dourougeanni, "The Environmental Impact of Coca Cultivation and Cocaine Production in the Peruvian Amazon Basin," in ibid., p. 85. The next two sentences draw on an author interview with Peruvian Agricultural Minster Enrique Rossl Link, April 1991. The rest of the paragraph draws on U.S. Department of State, *Narcotics: The Environmental Consequences.*

8. Remarks of Marc Dourougeanni in Congressional Research Service, *Cocaine Production, Eradication, and the Environment: Policy, Impact, and Options* (Washington DC: Government Printing Office, 1990), p. 5.

9. Marc Dourougeanni, "Impactos Ambientales del Cultivo de la Coca," in Frederico León and Ramiro Castro de la Mata, eds., *Pasta Basica de Cocaína* (Lima: CEDRO, 1989), and U.S. Department of State, *Narcotics: The Environmental Consequences.*

10. Remarks of Joseph Antognini in Congressional Research Service, *Cocaine Production, Eradication, and the Environment; Policy, Impact, and Options* (Washington, DC: U.S. Government Printing Office, 1990), pp. 4-12. The Greenpeace document is in the same source, pp. 149-157.

11. National Drug Council, "National Plans for Overcoming the Drug Problem" (Bogotá: NDC, 1994), pp. 18-19.

12. DINAPRE, *La prevalencia del uso indebido de drogas en Bolivia* (La Paz: Proinco, 1993, pp. 306-307. Lee interview at the Centro de Información y Educacion para la Prevencion del Abuso de Drogas (CEDRO), Lima, July 1995.

13. Francisco Thoumi, *Economía, Política y Narcotráfico* (Bogotá: Tercer Mundo, 1994), p. 206.

14. Jacqueline Guevara Gil, "Narcotráfico Falsea La Economía," *El Tiempo,* October 9, 1995, p. 1B.

15. Ciro Krauthausen and Luis Fernando Sarmiento, *Cocaína & Co.* (Bogotá: Tercer Mundo Editores, 1991), p. 90, citing *El Espectador,* July 17, 1990.

16. "Cocaine Seen Harming Economy of Colombia," *New York Times,* February 19, 1991, p. D2.

17. Susana Vásquez Loayza, "¿El narcotráfico quiere quebrar a la minería?," *Expreso,* April 1, 1991, p. 23. Sotomarino also described overvaluation as "90 percent of the mines' problem." The study cited in the next sentence is by Javier Escobal and Jaime Saaverda, "Las variaciones del tiempo de cambio real y el ingreso agricola," *Debate Agrario,* Number 9.

18. Müller y Asociados, "La Economía de la coca en Bolivia: ?Plaga o Salvación?," in *Evaluacíon Economica 1991* [in italics] (La Paz: Müller y Asociados, 1992), p. 114.

19. David Asman, "Growing Pains Strike Chile's Maturing Free Market," *Wall Street Journal,* August 2, 1991, p. A9.

20. Clawson interview, August 1992. The next sentence is from Lee interview, October 1992.

21. Lee interview with Joseph Finnin at the U.S.-Colombian Trade Council. Bogotá, June 1995; Michelle Celarier, "Finance in the Narco State," *Global Finance,* May 1995, p. 38.

22. Clawson interview, La Paz, August 1992.

23. Mario de Franco and Ricardo Godoy, "The Economic Consequences of Cocaine Production in Bolivia," Harvard Institute for International Development, Harvard University, June 1990, pp. 20-21.

24. To be fair, it must be acknowledged that some parts of the cocaine industry are less import-intensive than others. In particular, the production of coca leaf has extensive linkages with the rest of the economy; it uses many domestically produced inputs, such as simple agricultural implements and simple chemicals.

25. Cited in U.S. Information Agency (USIA), *Consequences of the Illegal Drug Trade. The Negative Economic, Political and Social Effects of Cocaine in Latin America* (Washington, DC: USIA, 1992), p. 21.

26. U.S. Department of State, INCSR 1992, p. 429.

27. Rejoinder by Colombian Finance Ministry to the 1994 DEA report, *Colombian Economic Reform: The Impact of Drug Money Laundering on the Colombian Economy,* distributed by the Colombian Embassy in Washington, 1995.

28. Franco and Godoy, "Economic Consequences of Cocaine Production," p. 20.

29. Thoumi, *Economía, Política y Narcotráfico,* p. 260.

30. Sources: Colombian Chamber of Construction, FENALCO, and the Colombian-American Chamber of Commerce.

Chapter 9

1. C. Peter Rydell and Susan S. Everingham, *Controlling Cocaine: Supply versus Demand Programs* (Santa Monica, CA: RAND Drug Policy Research Center, 1994), p. xiii.

2. William Bennett and John Walters, "Why Aren't We Attacking the Supply of Drugs?" *Washington Times,* February 9, 1995, p. A19.

3. All data on treatment and those needing treatment from ONDCP, *National Drug Control Strategy 1995 Budget Summary* (Washington DC: ONDCP, 1995).

4. Richard Moran, "Treatment on Demand: The Mythology," *Washington Post,* April 19, 1994, p. A15.

5. Jonathan Caulkins, "Evaluating the Effectiveness of Interdiction and Source Country Control," in U.S. Department of State, Bureau of Intelligence and Research and the Central Intelligence Agency, *Economics of the Narcotics Industry Conference Report* (Washington DC: State Department and CIA, 1994); for the tobacco and alcohol studies, see William Manning et al., *The Costs of Poor Health Habits* (Cambridge: Harvard University Press, 1991).

6. Kevin Jack Riley, *Snow Job? The Efficacy of Source Country Cocaine Policies* (Santa Monica, CA: RAND, 1993.

7. The range for 1992 cocaine prices on Colombia's north coast was $1,200 to $2,650 per kilogram, according to DEA, *The Illicit Drug Situation in Colombia* (Washington DC: DEA, 1991), p. 34. The range for retail prices in the United States for 100 percent pure cocaine was $130,000 to $163,000 per kilogram, according to ONDCP, *National Drug Control Strategy 1995* (Washington DC: The White House, 1995), p. 146.

8. For instance, the RAND model assumes that the retail price of cocaine in the United States equals the Andean price plus a markup; see Michael Kennedy, Peter Reuter, and Kevin Jack Riley, *A Simple Economic Model of Cocaine Production* (Santa Monica, CA: RAND, 1994), p. 19. The authors assume that the additive model is completely accurate; they reject (p. 20) the possibility that there may be a multiplicative element in the price. This assumption is a major reason that they conclude (p. 39) that cocaine supply control strategies will have little effect. A similar assumption is made by Riley in *Snow Job?* p. 123.

9. David Boyum, "Reflections on Economic Theory and Drug Enforcement," Ph.D. diss., Harvard University, 1992. The term "additive theory" is from Jonathan Caulkin, "The Distribution and Consumption of Illicit Drugs: Some Mathematical Models and Their Policy Implications," Ph.D. diss., Massachusetts Institute of Technology, 1990.

10. Caulkins, "Evaluating the Effectiveness of Interdiction and Source Country Control."

11. Mark Kleiman, *Against Excess: Drug Policy for Results* (New York: Basic Books, 1992), p. 121.

12. U.S. Government Accounting Office, *Drug Control: U.S. Supported Efforts in Colombia and Bolivia* (Washington DC: U.S. Government Accounting Office, November 1988), pp. 28-29.

13. Charles S. Helling, "Panama Coca Eradication—1993," report prepared by USDA, February 6, 1994, page 4.

14. U.S. State Department, *International Narcotics Control Strategy Report (INCSR) 1996* (Washington, DC: Government Printing Office, 1996), p. 4.

15. On the beginnings of this program, see Kumar et al., appendix D.

16. According to the Peruvian government in INE, Peru: *Compendio de Estadísticas de Produción y Consumo Drogas 1980-1993* (Lima: INE, 1994) p. 44, coca production in the two valley departments (San Martin and Huanaco) went from 45,000 in 1982 to 117,500 hectares in 1989. In a study for USAID (*Impact of the Coca in the Peruvian Economy 1980-92*), the Peruvian firm Cuánto estimated that the coca area in San Martin and Huanaco went from 65,000 hectares in 1982 to 92,000 in 1989.

17. UNDCP, in *Desarrollo Alternativo del Valle del Río Apurímac-Ene* (Project AD/PER/95/939) (Lima: UNDCP, 1995) estimates that the coca there went from 15,000 hectares in 1988 to 32,500 in 1993-1994.

18. The history of eradication efforts is detailed in Hernández, pp. 6-7. Data on eradication are from Government of Peru, *Compendio 1980-93*.

19. The developments in counterterrorism and counternarcotics from 1988 to 1990 are recounted in José Gonzales, "Guerrillas and Coca in the Huallaga Valley," in Palmer, ed., *Shining Path of Peru*, pp. 127-137.

20. James Brooke, "Peru's Leader Proposes a Market to Fight Coca," *New York Times*, October 28, 1990, p. 12.

21. Alberto Fujimori, "The Fujimori Initiative: A Policy for the Control of Drugs and Alternative Development," speech given October 26, 1990. The speech drew heavily on the ideas of Hernando de Soto.

22. U.S. State Department, INCSR 1996, pp.99, 104, and 105.

23. Information on Colombian eradication is from *El Tiempo*, March 9, 1995, and James Brooke, "U.S. Copters are a Target in Colombia," *New York Times*, March 27, 1995, p. A7.

24. U.S. State Department, INCSR 1996, pp. 83 and 88.

25. Quoted in James Brooke, "U.S. Copters Are a Target in Colombia."

26. "Fumigation Denouncements Continue," *Drug Trafficking Update*, March 13, 1995, p. 3.

27. USAID La Paz, *Bolivia's Coca Sub-Economy 1994* (La Paz: USAID La Paz, June 1995). This estimate is consistent with what is implied by the INCSR data, which show that the area under coca cultivation has increased despite the eradications.

28. On the general significance of syndicates in the Chapare, see James Jones, *Farmer Perspectives on the Economics and Sociology of Coca Production in the Chapare* (Binghamton, NY: Institute for Development Anthropology, Working Paper 77, January 1991), pp. 45-48. On the organizational structure and strengths of each of the five

syndicates, see Alberto Rivera, *Diagnostico Socio-economico de la Población del Chapare* (Cochabamba: PDAR, 1990), Annex 2. A 1992 PDAR study showed claimed membership as follows: *Federación Especial de Trabajadores Campesinos del Trópico de Cochabamba* (FETCTC), 20,409; *Federación de Colonizadores de Carrasco Tropical* (FECCT), 9,798; *FYTYZ*, 3,863; *Federación Unica de Centrales Unidas* (FUCU), 2,088; *Federación Especial de Colonizadores de Chimoré*, (FECCH) [which later became *Federación Especial de Trabajadores Campesinos de Chimoré*, FETCH], 1,035.

29. See Corporación Regional para el Desarollo de Cochabamba (CORDECO), *Resumen Ejecutivo—Plan Maestro del Tropico de Cochabamba* (Cochabamba: CORDECO, June 1994), pp. 15 and 21.

30. While stating that "Bolivia, consistent with the values and principles of its people, reaffirms its firm decision to fulfill its moral responsibility by adamantly fighting trafficking and addiction," the statement also said, "We must submit a request for international cooperation to verify the characteristics and nature of coca. Thus, based on these ideas, we can begin an international decriminalization campaign" (*Presencia,* September 17, 1994, p. A7).

31. President Sanchez de Lozada, quoted in *Financial Times,* November 11, 1994. In a November 4 television interview, he explained the Zero Option while at the same time adding that he was personally in favor of decriminalizing drugs, though the Bolivian government could never propose this because of the international reaction that would follow. The next sentence in the text is drawn from *Presencia,* November 15, 1994, p 6.

32. "Vice President on Forceful Eradication of Coca," Foreign Broadcast Information Service–Latin America (FBIS-LAT), March 31, 1995, p. 33, translated from *El Mundo,* March 20, 1995, p. A15.

33. U.S. State Department, INCSR 1996, pp. 66-72. On the actions in Isiboro Secure Park, see "Convulsíon social, misíon complida, y medio ambiate a el Chapare," *Narcotráfico al día,* July 10, 1995, pp. 4-5.

34. Delfin Arias Vargas, "Social Defense Secretary on Bolivia's Antidrug Plans," Foreign Broadcast Information Service–Latin America (FBIS-LAT), January 23, 1996, p. 43, as translated from *Presencia,* January 1, 1996, p. 5.

35. Clifford Krauss, "Colombia Arrests Raise Prices in New York City," *New York Times,* September 15, 1995, p. 1.

36. Kennedy, Reuter, and Riley, *A Simple Economic Model of Cocaine Production,* p. 35.

37. Bureau for International Narcotics and Law Enforcement Affairs (INL), "Drug Strategies: A Review of U.S. International Drug Control Policy," ms., November 15, 1994; and data on the national drug control budget by function, *National Drug Control Strategy Budget Summary* (Washington, DC: ONDCP, 1995), p. 235.

38. "Estados Unidos abondara el campo de batalla," *Expreso,* September 19, 1993. The next sentence is drawn from author interview with Tito Hernández, December 1994, p. 2.

39. "Radar norteamericano: ¿arma poco efectiva?," *Expreso,* May 9, 1993, p. A13; Fernando Rospigliosi and Jimmy Torres, "Huallaga: La guerra oculta,"; *Caretas,* July 1, 1993, pp. 28-31 and 88; "Air Force Resources Lacking Against Traffickers," Foreign Broadcast Information Service–Latin America (FBIS-LAT), June 29, 1994, p. 37 (translated from *Expreso,* June 20, 1994, p. A8).

40. James Brooke, "U.S. Halts Flights in Andean Drug War Despite Protests," *New York Times,* June 4, 1994, pp. 1 and 4.

41. Barton Gellman, "Feud Hurts Bid to Stop Drug Flow," *Washington Post,* May 29, 1994, pp. A1 and A14.

42. Steven Greenhouse, "U.S. to Resume Spy Flights to Help Latin Drug Efforts," *New York Times,* June 24, 1994, p. 1. The next quote is from an editorial, "Drug Unintelligence," *Wall Street Journal,* July 22, 1994, p. A10.

43. U.S. State Department, INCSR 1996, pp. 101-102; Clawson interview with Sherman Hinson, U.S. Embassy Lima, February 23, 1996.

44. Jones, p. 60.

45. U.S. State Department, INCSR 1995, p. 68 and U.S. State Department, INCSR 1996, p. 66.

46. U.S. State Department, INCSR 1995, p. 46.

47. U.S. State Department, INCSR 1996, pp. 101 and 22.

48. The numbers were 3,105 arrested for consumption and 1,817 for trafficking in 1993, compared to 1,446 and 2,968 respectively in the first quarter of 1995.

49. This paragraph is based on author interviews with DINANDRO personnel, November 1994.

50. Clawson interview with Sherman Hinson, U.S. Embassy Lima, February 23, 1996; Orlando Farias, "Project to Focus on Colombian Border," Foreign Broadcasting Information Service–Latin America (FBIS-LAT), December 13, 1995, pp. 34-35, as translated from *Jornal do Brasil,* December 10, 1995, p. 4; and U.S. State Department, INCSR 1996, p. 99.

51. James Brooke, "Brazil's Amazon Basin Becomes Cocaine Highway," *New York Times,* April 14, 1993, p. 14.

52. Gabriel Escobar, "Casting Radar Net Over Amazon Proves Touchy," *Washington Post,* December 4, 1995, p. A3; and Paul Constance, "Radar Firms Vie for Amazon System," *Aviation Week and Space Technology,* February 28, 1994, p. 62.

53. Leandro Fortes, "DEA Agents Reportedly Operating 'Illegally,'" Foreign Broadcasting Information Service–Latin America (FBIS-LAT), December 13, 1995, p. 31, as translated from *Jornal do Brasil,* December 9, 1995, p. 2.

54. Richard Webb and Graciela Fernández Baca de Valdez, *Peru en Numeros 1994* (Lima: Cuánto, 1994) p. 195.

55. Clawson interview with Hernández; and UNDCP, *Consolidation of Alternative Development in the Huallaga,* (Project AD/PER/93/759) (Lima: UNDCP, 1993).

Chapter 10

1. Mark Kleiman, *Against Excess: Drug Policy for Results* (New York: Basic Books,1992), p. 388. The comment about moderation in use appears to refer primarily to drugs like alcohol and tobacco.

2. "Ande propone comisíon evaluadore sobre dineros del narcotráfico," *El Espectador,* June 28, 1995, p. 10A.

Selected Bibliography

Books

Arango Londoño, Gilberto. *Estructura Economía Colombiana*. Bogotá: Coleccion Profesores, 1993.

Arango Jaramillo, Mario. *Impacto del Narcotràfico en Antioquia*. Medellín: J.M. Arango, 1988.

Arrieta, Carlos, et al. *Narcotràfico n Colombia*. Bogotá: Universidad de los Andes, December 1990.

Bagley, Bruce, and William Walker, eds. *Drug Trafficking in the Ame* Felipe Mansilla, H.C., and Carlos Toranzo Roca. *Economía Informal y Narcotràfico*. La Paz: ILDIS, 1991.

Gagliano, Joseph. *Coca Prohibition in Peru: The Historical Debates*. Tucson, AZ: University of Arizona Press, 1994.

Gallego, Carlos Medina. *Autodefensas, Paramilitares y Narcotràfico en Colombia*. Bogotá: Editorial Documentos Periodisticos, 1994.

García, Miguel. *Los Barones de la Cocaína*. Mexico City: Planeta, 1991.

Godson, Roy, and William Olson. *International Organized Crime: Emerging Threat to U.S. Security*. Washington, DC: National Strategy Information Center, 1993.

Guizado, Alvaro Camacho, and Alvaro Guzman Barney. *Colombia: Ciudad y Violencia*. Bogotá: Foro Nacional, 1990.

Herran, Maria Teresa. *El Fiscal: La Dualidad de la Imagen*. Bogotá: Tercer Mundo, 1994.

Kleiman, Mark. *Against Excess: Drug Policy for Results*. New York: Basic Books, 1992.

Krauthausen, Ciro, and Luis Fernando Sarmiento. *Cocaína & Co*. Bogotá: Tercer Mundo, 1991.

Lee, Rensselaer. *The White Labyrinth: Cocaine and Political Power*. New Brunswick, NJ: Transaction Publishers, 1989.

Mabry, Donald, ed. *The Latin American Narcotics Trade and U.S. National Security*. Westport, CT: Greenwood, 1989.

Malamud-Goti, Jaime. *Smoke and Mirrors: The Paradox of the Drug Wars*. Boulder, CO: Westview Press, 1992.

Manwaring, Max, ed. *Gray Area Phenomena. Confronting the New World Disorder*. Boulder, CO: Westview Press, 1993.

McCoy, Alfred, and Alan A. Block. *War on Drugs. Studies in the Failure of U.S. Narcotics Policy*. Boulder, CO: Westview Press, 1992.

McCormick, Gordon. *The Shining Path and The Future of Peru*. Santa Monica, CA: The Rand Corporation, March 1990.

Mendoza, Jorge Tellez, and Juan Alvaro Castellero Diaz. *Los Hilos de Poder*. Bogotá: Planeta, 1992.

Mermelstein, Max. *The Man Who Made It Snow.* New York: Simon and Schuster, 1990.

Ministerio de Prevision Social y Salud Publica. *La Prevalencia del uso Indebido de Drogas en Bolivia,* La Paz: DINAPRE, 1993.

Morales, Edmundo. *Cocaine: White Gold Rush in Peru.* Tucson, AZ: University of Arizona Press, 1989.

Mortimer, W. Golden. *The History of Coca: "The Divine Plant" of the Incas.* San Francisco: And/or Press, 1974, originally published, 1901.

Palmer, David Scott, ed. *Shining Path of Peru,* 2nd ed. New York: St. Martin's Press, 1994.

Perl, Raphael, ed. *Drugs and Foreign Policy: A Critical Review.* Boulder, CO: Westview Press, 1994.

Smith, Peter, ed. *Drug Policy in the Americas.* Boulder, CO: Westview Press, 1992.

Sterling, Claire. *Thieves' World,* New York: Simon and Schuster, 1994.

Sterling, Claire. *Octopus, The Long Reach of the Sicilian Mafia.* New York: W.W. Norton, 1990.

Tarazona-Sevillano, Gabriela. *Sendero Luminoso and the Threat of Narcoterrorism.* New York: Praeger, 1990.

Thoumi, Francisco. *Economía, Política y Narcotràfico.* Bogotá: Tercer Mundo, 1994.

Articles and Reports

Abt Associates (William Rhodes, team leader). *What America's Users Spend on Illegal Drugs, 1988-93.* Washington, DC: ONDCP, Spring 1995.

Alvarez, Elena. "The Political Economy of Coca Production in Bolivia and Peru: Economic Importance and Political Implications." Center for Policy Research, State University of New York at Albany, July, 1993.

Asociación Peruana de Estudios e Investigación Para la Paz. *Cocaína: Problemas y Soluciones Andinos.* Lima: Asociación Peruana de Estudios e Investigación Para la Paz, 1990.

Bagley, Bruce. "Colombia and the War on Drugs." *Foreign Affairs,* vol. 67, no. 1 (Fall 1988): pp. 70-92.

Botwick, Don, Joseph Dorsey, and James Jones. *Evaluation of the Chapare Regional Development Project.* La Paz: USAID/Bolivia, November 1990.

Brown, Loyd. *Results of the 1994 Agricultural Survey of the Tropical Zone of the Department of Cochabamba, Bolivia.* Bethesda, MD: Development Alternatives International, 1994.

Centro Amazónica de Antropología y Aplicación Práctica (CAAAP). *Violencia y Narcotràfico en la Amazona.* Lima: CAAP, May 1992.

Centro de Documentación e Información—Bolivia (CEDIB). *Coca-Cronología: Bolivia 1986-1992.* Cochabamba: CEDIB, 1992.

Centro para el Estudio de las Relaciones Internacionales y el Desarrollo (CERID). *El Impacto del Capital Financiero del Narcotràfico en el Desarrollo de America Latina.* La Paz: CERID, 1991.

Centro Peruano de Estudios Internacionales (CEPEI). *El Convenio Contra el Narcotráfico Entre el Perú y los Estados Unidos: Un Debate de Interes Nacional.* Lima: CEPEI, 1991.

————. *Crop Substitution in the Andes.* Washington, DC: ONDCP, December 1993.

Chernik, Marc, "Colombia's Fault Lines." *Current History,* vol. 95 no. 598, February 1996, pp. 76-81.

"Colombia's Drug Business: The Wages of Prohibition," *Economist,* December 24, 1994–January 6, 1995, pp. 21-24.

Comisión Andina de Juristas. *Drogas y control penal en los Andes.* Lima: Comisión Andina de Juristas, 1994.

Congressional Research Service. *Cocaine Production, Eradication and the Environment: Policy, Impact and Options.* Washington, D.C.: U.S. Government Printing Office. August 1990.

Corporación Regional para el Desarrollo de Cochabamba (CORDECO). *Plan Maestro del Tropico de Cochabamba.* Cochabamba: CORDECO, June 1994.

Cuánto S.A. *Impact of the [sic] Coca on the Peruvian Economy 1980-92.* Lima: Cuánto S.A. September 1993.

Cuellar, Fidel Boada. "Incidencia del Cultivo de Coca en la Economica Colombiana y Comparacion con los Casos de Peru y Bolivia." Bogotá: Institute Inter-Americano de Cooperacion para la Agricultura, November 1991.

de Franco, Mario, and Robert Godoy. "The Economic Consequences of Cocaine in Bolivia: Historical, Local and Macroeconomic Perspectives." Cambridge: Harvard University, 1991.

Dombey-Moore, Bonnie, Susan Resetar, and Michael Childress. *A System Description of the Cocaine Trade.* Santa Monica, CA: RAND, 1994.

Editorial José Marti. *Fin de la Conexion Cubana.* Bogotá: Ediciones Plus, 1989.

Everingham, Susan, and C. Peter Rydell. *Modeling the Demand for Cocaine.* Santa Monica, CA: RAND, 1994.

Garcia-Sayán, Diego, ed. *Coca, Cocaína, y Narcotráfico.* Lima: Comisión Andina de Juristas, 1989.

————. *Narcotráfico: Realidades y Alternativas.* Lima: Comisión Andina de Juristas, 1990.

Gómez Restrepo, Hernando José, and Mauricio Santa Maria Salamanca. "La Economica Subterranea En Colombia." Bogotá, N.D. 1994.

Hernández, Tito. "El Enfoque Competitivo en el Marco del Control de Cultivos Ilícitos: Estrategías y Logros del Program UNDCP-OSP/PNUD en las Regiones del Huallaga, Pachitea y Ucuyali." Lima: UNDCP, October 1994.

Instituto Nacional de Estadística e Informátivo. *Peru: Compendio de Estadísticas de Producción y Consumo de Drogas.* Lima: Direccíon Nacional de Estadísticas Básicas, February 1994.

Ivanov, Ivan. *Mezhdunarodnaya Contrabanda Narkotika v Byvshei SSSR.* Moscow: Feliks, February 1995.

Jones, James. "Farmer Perspectives on the Economics and Sociology of Coca Production in the Chapare." Binghamton, NY: Institute for Development Anthropology Working Paper 77, January 1991.

Kalmanovitz, Solomon. *Analisis Macroeconomica del Narcotràfico en la Economica Colombiana*. Bogotá: Centro de Investigación y Educación Popular, December 1992.

Kennedy, Michael, Peter Reuter, and Kevin Jack Riley. *A Simple Economic Model of Cocaine Production*. Santa Monica, CA: RAND, 1994.

Lee, Rensselaer. "Making the Most of Colombia's Drug Negotiations." *Orbis*, vol. 35, no. 2, Spring 1991, pp. 235-252.

Lee, Rensselaer. "Global Reach: The Threat of International Drug Trafficking." *Current History*, vol. 94, no. 592 (May 1995): pp. 207-211.

León, Federico, and Ramiro Castro de la Mata. *Pasta Basica de Cocaína: Un Estudio Multdisciplinario*. Lima: Centro de Información y Educación para la Prevención del Abuso de Drogas, 1989.

MacDonald, Scott, and Bruce Zagaris, eds. *International Handbook on Drug Control*. Westport, CT: Greenwood Press, 1992.

Ministry of Finance, Colombia. "Comments on the DEA Document Entitled, 'Colombian Economic Reform: The Impact on Money Laundering Within the Colombian Economy.'" Washington, DC: Colombian Embassy, November 1994.

Müller y Asociados. *Estadisticas Economicos 1991*. La Paz: Müller y Asociados. August 1991.

————. "La Economía de la coca en Bolivia: ¿Plaga o Salvación?" In *Evaluación Economica 1991*. La Paz: Müller y Asociados, 1992.

National Drug Council (CNE). "National Plan for Overcoming the Drug Problem." Bogotá: CNE, 1994.

National Narcotics Intelligence Consumers Committee (NNICC). *The NNICC Report 1993*. Washington, DC: DEA, August 1994.

Office of National Drug Control Policy. *National Drug Control Strategy*. Washington, DC: The White House, 1995 and previous years.

————. *National Drug Control Strategy 1995 Budget Summary*. Washington, DC: ONDCP, 1995.

————. *What America's Users Spend on Illegal Drugs*. Washington, DC: ONDCP, June 1991.

Orozco, Ivan Abed. "Los Dialogas con el Narcotràficos. Historia de La Triumformicon Fallida de un Delincuente Common en un Delincuente Politico." *Analisis Politico*, no. 11 (September-December 1990): pp. 28-68.

Perl, Raphael. "United States Foreign Narcopolicy: Shifting Focus to International Crime." *Transnational Organized Crime*, vol. 1, no. 1 (Spring 1995): pp. 35-46.

Peru, Government of. *Plan Nacional de Prevención y Control de Drogas 1994-2000*. Lima: Government of Peru, October 1994.

Rasnake, Roger, and Michael Painter. "Rural Development and Crop Substitution in Bolivia: USAID and the Chapare Regional Development Project." Institute for Development Anthropology, October 1989.

Rijnhout, Leida, and Joep Oomen. *"Mala leche": Una Historia amarga de Desarrollo en el Chapare*. La Paz: Centro de Documentación e Información, 1994.

Riley, Kevin Jack. *Snow Job? The Efficacy of Source Country Cocaine Policies*. Santa Monica, CA: RAND, 1993.

Rivera, Alberto. *Diagnostico Socio-Economico de la Población del Chapare*. Cochabamba: Programa de Desarrollo Alternativo Regional, 1990.

Rydell, C. Peter, and Susan Everingham. *Controlling Cocaine: Supply versus Demand Programs*. Santa Monica, CA: RAND Drug Policy Research Center, 1994.

Schober, Susan, and Charles Schade, eds. *The Epidemiology of Cocaine Use and Abuse*. Alcohol, Drug Abuse, and Mental Health Administration Research Monograph 110. Washington, DC: Government Printing Office, 1991.

Sístema Educativo Antidrogaddicion y de Movilizacion Social (SEAMOS). *Los Effectos de La Interdicción en los Organismos Nacionales de Seguridad y en la Institucionalidad del Estado Boliviano*. La Paz: SEAMOS, 1991.

————. *La Economía de la Coca en Bolivia*. La Paz: SEAMOS, 1992.

————. *Problemas Juridico Legales Asociados a la Aplicación de la Ley 1008*. La Paz: SEAMOS, 1991.

United Nations Drug Control Programme (UNDCP). "Bolivia 1994-1995." N.D.

————. *Desarrollo Alternativo del Valle del Río Apurímac-Ene*. Project Document for Project AD/PER/95/939. Lima: UNDCP, 1995.

————. *Peru: Programa y Actividades*. Lima: UNDCP, 1994.

USAID (U.S. Agency for International Development). *Bolivia: Project Paper, Cochabamba Regional Development*. Washington, DC: USAID, 1991.

————. (Krishna Kumar, team leader). *A Review of AID's Narcotics Control Development Assistance Program*. Washington, DC: USAID, March 1986.

USAID La Paz. *Bolivia's Cocaine Sub-Economy 1994*. La Paz: USAID La Paz, May 1995 (also 1993 and 1994 editions).

USAID Lima. *Project Paper: Alternative Development Project*. Lima: USAID Lima, 1995.

U.S. Department of Justice, National Drug Intelligence Center (NDIC). *Strategic Organizational Drug Intelligence Symposium*. Johnstown: NDIC, 1995.

U.S. Department of State, Bureau of Intelligence and Research and Central Intelligence Agency. *Economics of the Narcotics Industry Conference Report*. Washington, DC: State Department and CIA, 1994.

U.S. Department of State, Bureau of Narcotics and International Law Enforcement. "Drug Strategies: A Review of U.S. International Drug Control Policy." *Ms.*, November 15, 1994

U.S. Department of State. *International Narcotics Control Strategy Report*. Washington, DC: Government Printing Office, Publication 10246, 1996 (and previous years).

U.S. Drug Enforcement Administration (DEA), Intelligence Division. *Colombian Economic Reform. The Impact of Drug Money Laundering Within the Colombian Economy*. Washington, DC: DEA, September 1994.

————. *Operation Breakthrough: Coca Cultivation and Cocaine Base Production in Bolivia*. Report no. DEA-94032. Washington, DC: DEA, July 1994.

————. "Coca Cultivation and Cocaine Processing. An Overview." Washington, DC: DEA, September 1993.

————. *Illegal Drug Price/Purity Report United States: January 1990–December 1993*. Washington, DC: DEA, April 1994.

U.S. General Accounting Office (GAO). *Drug Control: U.S. International Narcotics Control Activities*. Washington, DC: GAO, March 1988.

————. *Drug Control: U.S. Supported Efforts in Colombia and Bolivia*. Washington, DC: GAO, November 1988.

U.S. Information Agency. *Consequences of the Illegal Drug Trade. The Negative Economic, Political and Social Effects of Cocaine on Latin Commerce*. Washington, DC, 1992

Uribe, Sergio. "El Desarrollo Alternativo en Colombia." Bogotá: November 1994.

Webb, Richard, and Graciela Fernández Baca de Valdez. Peru en Numeros 1994. Lima: Cuánto S.A., 1994.

Weil, Andrew. "The New Politics of Coca." *The New Yorker*. May 15, 1995.

Williams, Phil. "Transnational Criminal Organizations: Strategic Alliances." *The Washington Quarterly*. Vol. 18, no. 1 (Winter 1995): pp. 57-72.

World Bank. *Peru: Agricultural Policies for Economic Efficiency*. Washington, DC: World Bank, September 1992.

————. *Bolivia: Agricultural Sector Review*. Washington, DC: World Bank, April 1992.

————. "Bolivia: Updating Economic Memorandum." Washington, DC: World Bank, October 8, 1992.

Index